Long River Winding

Life, Love, and Death
Along the Connecticut

The Connecticut River

CANADA

NORTHEAST
KINGDOM

Colebrook

GREAT
NORTH
WOODS

ME

Burlington

St. Johnsbury

Danville

VT

White River
Junction

Hanover

Cornish

Cavendish

Townshend

Brookline

Newfane

Brattleboro

NY

NH

Northfield

Deerfield

Watertown

MASSACHUSETTS
BAY

Amherst

Northampton

Hadley

Holyoke

Chicopee

Stockbridge

Springfield

Hampden

MA

Thompsonville
(in Enfield)

Sandwich

Hartford

Wethersfield

Glastonbury

RI

East Haddam

CT

Essex

Lyme

Old Saybrook

The 410-mile Connecticut River and its watershed.

Long River Winding

Life, Love, and Death
Along the Connecticut

Jim Bissland

Berkshire House Publishers
Lee, Massachusetts

Library of Congress Cataloging-in-Publication Information

Bissland, Jim.
Long river winding : life, love, and death along the Connecticut / Jim Bissland.
    p. cm.
Includes bibliographical references and index.
  ISBN 1-58157-060-0 (pbk.)
1. Connecticut River—Description and travel. 2. Connecticut River Valley—Description and travel. 3. Connecticut River Valley—Social life and customs. I. Title.

F12.C7 B56 2003
974—dc21

                    2002153408

ISBN 1-58157-060-0

Editor: Sarah Novak.
Book design and typesetting: Jane McWhorter, Blue Sky Productions.
Cover design: Sheila Smallwood.
Index: Diane Brenner.

Berkshire House books are available at substantial discounts for bulk purchases by corporations and other organizations for promotions and premiums. Special personalized editions can also be produced in large quantities. For more information, contact:

Berkshire House Publishers
480 Pleasant St., Suite 5, Lee, MA 01238
800-321-8526
www.berkshirehouse.com
info@berkshirehouse.com

Manufactured in the United States of America
10 9 8 7 6 5 4 3 2 1

On the cover: View from Mount Holyoke (*detail*) *Thomas Chambers, 1845, courtesy of the Fruitlands Museums, Harvard, Massachusetts. A folk artist, Chambers exaggerated the peaks and idealized the Connecticut River Valley landscape below, limning neat white buildings and near-perfect trees. Chambers was only one of many artists and writers to be charmed by the view from the mountain in Hadley, Massachusetts. A century later, Sylvia Plath remarked of the vista, "All's peace and discipline down there."*

Dedicated to the memory of
James Hope Bissland, Jr.
Elsie Christie
They were my parents

Guy Henry Bemis
Marion Alice Knapp
They were my parents, too

Their rivers flow on

CONTENTS

This book is a journey, a long one, for we'll be making two trips at the same time, you and I. One will be up the Connecticut River Valley, from the river's mouth on Long Island Sound, northward more than four hundred miles through the heart of New England to the Canadian border. The other will be a trip through time. We'll meet people from past and present and learn their stories—stories about the things that matter most, for these are stories of life, love, and death.

TIME, THE RIVER, AND US

> There is no end.
> There is no beginning.
> There is only the infinite passion of life.
> — Federico Fellini

Call me a Connecticut River Yankee. Whenever it is Deep Mud Season in my soul; whenever I start listening to telemarketers and tuning in to Martha for company; whenever the pursuit of loneliness finds me bowling alone; whenever I am ungrounded, disconnected, and uninspired, then I account it high time to drive off the spleen by going somewhere. I am not Herman Melville's Ishmael, so I don't go to the sea. Instead, I follow the river.

The Connecticut River. I once asked a man whose daily work involves the river what gender it was. After visibly struggling with the PC-ness of the whole thing, he finally admitted, under vigorous prodding, that it seemed like a woman to him—nurturing, graceful (and also rather curvy). I'd call it a Grace Kelly among rivers. Moving at a stately pace and wrapped in an elegant green gown, the Connecticut is an American princess—beautiful, proud and yet demure, and usually very gentle.

She rises near the Canadian border in the Great North Woods of New Hampshire, with only moose and woodsmen to witness her birth. Then she flows south for four hundred and ten miles, presents a pretty face to the sea at Old Saybrook, and, then, nodding politely to the ladies who lunch, pours into Long Island Sound to blend smoothly with the elegant waters of the Connecticut Gold Coast. On her journey to the ocean she keeps New Hampshire and Vermont from bumping into each other, draws the mental and geographic boundary between Bostonopolis and western Massachusetts, and divides wealthy Connecticut into eastern and western halves ("Rich" and "Richer").

It's a lot to do, but she doesn't do it alone, for this river of water and silt and shad is only one of two streams flowing through the valley. The other is a concourse of people, an endlessly moving strand of human lives, blended from many sources, stretching backward for millennia and forward forever, turning this way and that, always changing and always the same. Two streams, endlessly flowing: I grew up beside one and am part of the other. Even though I left the valley a few years ago, I keep coming back, looking for the connections that tell me who I am and who I was before I was born, and for hints of what may become of me. Travel up and down the valley in that mood and you begin to see the people who aren't there as well as the ones who are. They call from the shadows, they tug at your sleeve, and they say, *Remember us.* Because, if you live long enough and think about it, you begin to understand this: *the dead have not really died until we stop telling their stories.*

So we and the dead need each other. When I understood that, I began collecting stories from the valley, stories of the living and the dead, all part of the same endless stream. A lady with golden hair who rode her horse near the seashore. A man who saved words. The Mark Twain burglar, said to be a very bad man. The girl who never came home. A myth dressed in white. The stranger who was Captain Thunderbolt. God-like Daniel and Black Dan. A hairy guy of the woods named Big Al and those who cherish him. And more, always more stories, because stories beget stories. The best stories connect me and ground me and energize me and make me want to tell them. Some of them are in this book.

These are stories of the famous, the infamous, and some of the rest of us who have passed this way. Stories of triumph and defeat, of courage and deception, of wisdom and silliness and things in between, of saints and scoundrels and secrets and mysteries. The things we care about, the things that make us human. The old verities and truths of the heart, as Faulkner called them, the only stories worth remembering and the only things worth writing about.

And so, mostly, these are stories of love and of death.

Long River Winding

Life, Love, and Death
Along the Connecticut

LOOKING UP THE DEAD

The evening of June 29, 1881, in East Haddam was "perfect," according to the *Connecticut Valley Advertiser*. A crescent moon rose in a starry sky over the river town that night, and the air was balmy. In a part of East Haddam called the Upper Landing, the Maplewood Music Seminary blazed with light, for this was graduation time. Earlier in the evening the night boat from Hartford had passed nearby, hugging the curves of the Connecticut River's eastern shore, foam from its paddlewheels sparkling in the evening light. As the boat chugged south toward Goodspeed's Landing a mile downriver, its engine, fading, had sounded like the beating of a human heart.

Drifting over the surface of the water and vanishing like the phosphorescence from the paddlewheels was the music of Maplewood's students. They were playing their final concert under the direction of Principal Dwight S. Babcock, whom the students called "Prof." Babcock was a flamboyant, longhaired taskmaster and the graduation concert seemed to go on forever in the flickering gaslight of Maplewood Hall. Finally, however, Prof laid down his baton and the formal ceremony drew to a close before its audience of ladies in snowy dresses and gentlemen in boiled shirts.

And then my grandmother danced.

Agnes Spencer (right) and Nora Potter, Commencement 1881

She swept across the parquet floor in a gown she adored, swirling and spinning, soaring on the wings of young promise, while the orchestra sweated in the warm summer night and played the school's traditional dance fare of waltzes, quadrilles, galops, and lanciers. Agnes Isabel Spencer was twenty years old, the daughter of Roswell Doane Spencer, an up-and-coming storekeeper at the Upper Landing. Not a classic beauty, Agnes had a shy, elfin quality that attracted young men nonetheless. She was tiny and endowed with huge, dark eyes. They, with her hair styled in ringlets across her forehead, gave her an exotic air. And, with her dark complexion, she had the dusky glow of youth.

Later that night, the dance over, Agnes floated home through the summer night, diploma in hand. She wrote in her diary: *The longed-for evening has come and I graduated. Our dresses were perfectly lovely! I had a lovely basket of flowers. Frank Kendall came and [we] went on the Grand March. . . . Had such a nice time.*

If only the good times would last. Lately it has been fashionable for writers to talk of the arc of a person's life, as if lives were bright stars that rise smoothly from the horizon and curve across the sky before disappearing into the black again. Lives and stars all move relentlessly onward, of course, but the course of a human life is more like a river, twisting and turning, rising and falling, sometimes changing so suddenly it takes your breath away. That's what happened to my grandmother.

Sadly, only six months after graduation its pleasures had faded into distant memory. *The last day of this old year 1881 and a most miserable year it has been,* Agnes told her diary on New Year's Eve. Her miseries began the very day after graduation, when a disappointed suitor confronted her so angrily that she later wrote, *I was afraid.* Even harder was parting with Nora Potter, a fellow graduate who was returning home to upper New York State. In the months before graduation Agnes and Nora had become deeply attached to each other. *I'm so lonely,* Agnes wrote that night, and for the rest of her life she would sadly note Nora's birthday each year in her diary.

Things got worse. A month after graduation, Roswell Doane Spencer uprooted his family, moving them forty miles upriver to Thompsonville, Connecticut, where he had purchased a larger store. For shy, quiet Agnes, who had known life only in bucolic East Haddam, the change to bustling Thompsonville with its huge carpet mills must have been unnerving. There, the clatter of looms and cursing of teamsters filled the air, while in placid East Haddam the loudest sounds came from the whistles of passing steamboats and the ancient bell in St. Stephen's Episcopal Church. The last straw of 1881 was yet another failed romance, this with someone from Hartford named George. Despite George's fervent pleas, she declined to marry him, confiding to her diary, *I shall wait to be asked by a certain person.*

But that mysterious "certain person" never asked, so the years began to fall away like the leaves of autumn. For nearly two decades Agnes would stay at home, doing her parents' housework and slowly turning into a spinster while her mother dreamily read poetry, history, and religion. Agnes was living the hard part of a Cinderella story, for her mother, though not a cruel woman, yearned for a life of the mind and was only too happy to let Agnes scrub the floors. Meanwhile, Agnes's father was preoccupied with building "the biggest store between Hartford and Springfield." There was tragedy, too. A younger brother drowned in the Connecticut River and Agnes and her mother had to sit up all night in the parlor with the recovered body. "Nora dear," far away in New York State, began to fade even further from view as a fatal illness overwhelmed her. And, although Agnes didn't realize it at the time, as the 1800s were drawing a close, so were the Spencer family's finances and its honor.

Then, suddenly, the river took another turn. Just as Agnes's biological clock was winding down, yet another man, a Scottish immigrant, came into her life, this time to woo and win her. He arrived in the nick of time, James Hope Bissland did, for only a few months after he had carried her off the House of Spencer would collapse in a scandal that rocked Thompsonville. (More about this later.) On June 14, 1899, James and Agnes were married. Like a butterfly emerging from its chrysalis, Agnes was transformed overnight from lonely drudge to new bride.

Things would get even better. In 1901, James, age fifty, and Agnes, age forty, claimed a joy unexpected at their ages: they became the parents of a child, the only child they would ever have.

They named the child James Hope Bissland, Jr. He would grow up to be my father.

My Time Machine

One day in 1925 Helen "Elsie" Christie was leaving work at a bank on Main Street in Springfield, Massachusetts, when she spotted a good-looking young man she had once dated but hadn't seen in years. Her mother had forced them to break up because of Elsie's youth, but the young woman hadn't stopped thinking about him. Elsie yoo-hooed and, expertly zigzagging through a street filled with Model T's, ran after the man, who was trying to catch a bus. A year later they were engaged, the ring presented on the grounds of a local mausoleum. ("It was a very pretty spot," according to Elsie.) The man was James H. Bissland, Jr., the child who had been born in 1901 just as my grandmother's biological alarm was starting to sound. Within a few years, James Jr. and Elsie would become my parents.

Sometimes I marvel at the apparent serendipity of it all, not to mention my mother's fleetness of foot or (thinking back to Agnes) my grandmother's hardy reproductive cycle.

It seems as if I am here to tell the tale of lives converging only because of chance encounters and surprising intersections. Not really. Take care with your choices, because actions have consequences, as we used to tell our children while their eyes rolled. My grandfather *chose* to propose to Agnes in 1899 and my mother *decided*, against all decorum, to pursue my father on that day in 1925. Carrying the past inside us, we, too, make our choices, converge with others, then pass along the results—good, bad, and indifferent—to new generations. Not only are we what we eat, so are our grandchildren. And the stream flows on. It's another example of the Butterfly Theory: the large and small decisions made long ago by ancestors we never knew help make us what we are today. And so it shall be for thee.

Agnes was one of those ancestors I never knew, for she died before I was born, but I've seen her many times. Lying in the dark and drifting on the edge of sleep, I sometimes roam through time and space, searching for Connecticut River Valley people whose lives fascinate me, people like Agnes Isabel Spencer and Mark Twain and Emily Dickinson

The James H. Bisslands, Senior and Junior, circa 1905

and the witches of Wethersfield and a fugitive schoolmaster in Vermont. It's not hard to construct a time machine. You do it by immersing yourself in the shards and dust of the past: secondhand memories, old newspapers, faded snapshots, diaries, letters . . . the stuff is everywhere, you just have to look for it. Then, if you walk the ground your ancestors walked and use your imagination very carefully, things come together and you start to make connections. There is a synthesis, a new way of knowing. You begin to hear your lost family and other people, too, the way you hear far-off conversations murmuring on a summer night: *Father's coming home next week . . . Jessie's getting married in the spring . . . Take your hand off my knee . . . William is feeling better now . . . Do you still love me?*

After a few trips in my time machine, capturing the flavor of Agnes's life, I realized something else. It made my journalist's nose twitch: as the pieces fell into place, I could see that my grandmother's life was a *story*, a story worth remembering and worth telling.

Robert Darnton, a *New York Times* reporter turned professor, has pointed out how an atavistic urge drives journalists to keep rediscovering the old tales, the same ones we have been telling ourselves since the beginning of time, so they can dress them in new clothes and tell them all over again. It is a very human thing to do. Telling stories is a way we affirm our connection with each other, our shared humanity. All stories are little dramas in which we are the actors, whether we realize it or not. Now, in the relics of lives gone by, my grandmother's and others', I was finding hints of the kind of stories—little dramas of love and loss, courage and cowardice, humor and pathos—for which I had gone hunting as a newspaperman.

These dramas had unfolded (and unfold still) on a stage of eleven thousand square miles, the Connecticut River Valley and its watershed (the region that drains into the river). More and more, as I traveled the valley, I saw it was not just a place where millions of individuals had lived, acted, and died, creating a giant memorial park. Instead, I could see that it was a stream of interwoven lives, stretching backward and forward through time, very much alive and flowing endlessly. And that is a very different thing from a garden of stone.

It's nice to know that a river like that is there whenever we need it. Sometimes people disappoint us and sometimes we disappoint ourselves. Sometimes the accumulation of bad things happening to good people reaches critical mass. Sometimes the creepy-crawlies come slithering out from under the bed where they've been hiding among the dust bunnies.

When that happens, it helps to climb into the time machine and start looking for stories about all the people who went before us: struggling, stumbling, laughing, loving and sometimes losing love, but always being very human, living out their lives and then passing them on after having put their own mark on them. Looking up the dead, we are reminded of how much we share with them and how it is their stories that connect us. We are not alone. *Remember us.*

I remember: Lady Fenwick's bright golden hair streaming behind her as she rides her horse among the salt marshes of Saybrook in 1641. The Reverend John Williams of Deerfield never giving up hope for his daughter, who was captured by the Indians and then chose to stay with them. Gnarly old Ethan Allen sweeping young Fanny Montresor off her feet in a storybook romance. Emily Dickinson in her white dress, peeping out her second-floor window at the passing scene on Main Street on Amherst . . . and then turning to her desk. Mark Twain gathering his children around him for storytelling time in their riverboat of a house in West Hartford. Elsie Christie, so modest she had refused an invitation to portray "Miss America" in Springfield's Independence Day parade, throwing caution to the winds and hotfooting it down Main Street after James H. Bissland, Jr. To be connected to all this!

And sometimes, when it is very dark, I can hear the music from Maplewood drifting out over the water on that starry night in 1881.

And then my grandmother dances.

CHAPTER ONE

AND THE WOLVES DID HOWL IN ZION

The worst thing about the howling was that it never really stopped. It might pause for a few days but then it would begin again as the cold night swallowed the red dusk along the icy New England coastline. Somewhere, a throaty cry would start low, then soar into the darkening sky with a long, lonely oooooooooo that trailed off to nowhere and everywhere at once. Sometimes it seemed as if the howlers were having a mysterious conversation out in the forest, one sending up a cry over here, another answering from over there, with a background chorus joining in from still other places. Huddled under their quilts in tiny, dirt-floored huts and tents, the settlers of Massachusetts Bay in 1630 could only shiver and pray for the wolves to go away.

The baggage the early settlers of New England brought with them from Europe included a deeply ingrained, even irrational, fear of wolves, one that persists to this day, kept alive by stories like *Little Red Riding Hood*. In Europe in the 1600s, wolves signified evil and had been driven out of many areas. But in New England in the 1600s, Governor John Winthrop wrote, they *came daily about the houses* to prey on livestock.

That is why New England's European settlers described their new land as a *howling wilderness* (an enduring phrase coined by one of the Puritans), but it wasn't just the wolves they were thinking about. There were the Indians, with whom the settlers in the early 1600s had an uneasy relationship. There were also, out there somewhere and probably up to no good, Britain's unfriendly rivals in empire building, the French and the Spanish. And then there was the forest: dark and mysterious, concealing God knows what horrors. To the English settlers, used to open fields and meadows, the brooding, uncharted New England forest, so thick it shut out the sky, was frightening in itself, a mysterious place where strange creatures roamed by night and evil lurked in the shadows.

While we whine about modern life's irritations—parking the SUV, cell-phone dolts, people who don't *RSVP*, and the McMicrosofting of America—

Old Saybrook's Robert Duncan and Dorothy Gifford, direct descendants of Governor Winthrop

we forget how real misery was woven into the very fabric of our ancestors' lives. Day by day, they struggled with disease, hunger, cold, mortality, and loneliness. Dieting was not a problem; just staying alive was.

And yet they *chose* to come here and then, weighing the miseries of a grim New England against the miseries of Merrie Olde England, many of them decided to stay and tough it out day by day so they could build the New Zion, a *City upon a Hill* (as John Winthrop had put it) that would be an inspiration to the rest of the world. They felt an obligation to higher purpose, a call to serve, not just survive, and a sense of community obligation that would make members of today's Me-First Generation giggle. To their shame.

Not that the Puritans were perfect angels, but at least they had a sense of mission that rose above going to church on Sunday and screwing over the stockholders on Monday. It came from post-Elizabethan England, where an inept monarchy and a grind-'em-down Church of England had been

Thomas Hooker's congregation trekking from Massachusetts to Hartford, 1636

trying to repress religious diversity during hard economic times. The Pilgrims of 1620 were the first of the oppressed to come to New England and stay there for these reasons, but their early efforts in the wilderness had only gasped and wheezed. They had clung desperately to the rocky coastline for ten years until a high-minded Puritan and ex-government lawyer named John Winthrop organized a fleet of ships and recruited eight hundred people to re-energize the settlement of New England. From 1630 until 1642, when revolution broke out in England, there was a steady flow of settlers from Old to New England, a social movement that historians today call the Great Migration.

At first, most of the settlers made their homes around Massachusetts Bay. It wasn't long, however, until the Great Migration turned into the Great Reshuffling. Land was the basis of most wealth and security in those days and, as families grew larger and more settlers arrived, some of those living around Boston began to feel a mite crowded. There were other factors, too: in a society so engrossed in religion, disputes in faith sprang up like wildfires in a drought season, splitting congregations. Adventurers with big eyes brought back tempting tales of rich new lands beyond the horizon. Even Indians looking for allies against their native enemies urged the English to resettle inland.

And so, not long after the first settlements on Massachusetts Bay and the coast to the north, English men and women began poking around New England's second great frontier: the Connecticut River Valley. Less than a hundred miles from Massachusetts Bay and connected to it by Indian trails as well as the ocean highway, the southern Connecticut River Valley offered grassy meadows of rich bottomland, the convenience of water transportation, and lots of elbow room. Not to mention breathing space from Governor Winthrop's Puritan elders, who were becoming as overbearing as the Anglican church they had repudiated back in England.

The first true European settlements in the valley arose in 1634 near present-day Hartford, not far from where the Dutch had established a fur-trading outpost. By 1636, settlement was beginning in Springfield, twenty miles north. In the other direction, Saybrook was established at the mouth of the river in 1639. Struggling with disease, bad weather, and occasional Indian raids, the settlers gingerly began to fill in along the southern valley and push north, reaching Deerfield, Massachusetts, in the 1670s. In the 1730s, a string of forts arose in southern New Hampshire and by the 1770s Vermont and the Upper Valley had become the new frontier.

Gradually, the valley blossomed. From Saybrook to Hartford, shipyards sprang up and the ships built here sailed under their Yankee skippers to the West Indies and Europe, bringing back rich cargoes. Fishermen harvested a river that abounded with so much shad that farm laborers refused to work unless their employers promised to limit the number of meals of fish served each week. Vast farms of shade-grown tobacco developed in Connecticut and Massachusetts, making the region a center for cigar production. Sheep farms and then dairy farming filled the Upper Valley, turning Vermont and New Hampshire into New England's wool warehouse and then milk shed. Factories making paper, railroad cars, bicycles, motorcycles, children's games, and, eventually, airplane parts arose; so did office buildings, as Hartford became the insurance capital of the nation and Springfield became the country's biggest source of dictionaries. The valley came to rival the Boston area as a center of education: Dartmouth, Amherst, Smith, Mount Holyoke, and Wesleyan were among the colleges founded here, as were a number of preparatory schools. The bustling region attracted artists, writers, poets, journalists, and reformers whose names would become household words.

So the Indians left the valley, replaced by another, more diverse population. The loons retreated north; trees fell to progress; trails turned into highways.

And the wolves . . . they howled no more in Zion.

CHAPTER TWO

THE FEISTY WOMEN
OF OLD SAYBROOK

Old Saybrook lies on the Connecticut coastline halfway between Boston (105 miles northeast) and New York City (one hundred miles southwest). Set on the west side of the Connecticut River's mouth, the town looks out on both Long Island Sound and the river itself. It's like having the corner lot at a major intersection. An inconvenient sandbar kept Old Saybrook from turning into the stew of shipping and dockyard commerce often found at river entrances, so it became what it is today: a white-clapboarded New England small town steeped in history and wreathed in commuter prosperity. It also is a tony resort for Old Hartford Money. Like a lovely woman in a summer dress, Old Saybrook smiles at the sea and thrusts two arms into the harbor as if it were calling to Old Lyme on the opposite shore.

Working hard to preserve its character, the town prohibits apartment buildings and digs in its heels against category-killer chain retailers. The town's ten thousand people and fifteen square miles are governed by a board of three selectmen (when one is a woman she still is called "selectman"), and each year there is at least one town meeting. Old Saybrook also has a boutiquey main street, more than a hundred homes designated as having historical significance, troops of white collars who commute to New

A lock of Lady Fenwick's golden hair

London, New Haven, Hartford, or New York, and serried ranks of volunteers who spring into action like U.S. Marines whenever they spot an opportunity to make the town an even better place in which to live.

Old Saybrook also has its own golden-haired Madonna, which is why I was drawn to the place, driving down Connecticut 9 at the peak of fall foliage season. Route 9 is a commuter highway connecting the state's center with its shore, and for its last thirty miles it parallels the Connecticut River before the river empties into the sea. Connecticut is a very small state and the nation's fourth most densely populated, but for most of the trip all I could see was a symphony of autumn color spread across a rolling, forested landscape.

I was going to meet Elaine Fogg Staplins. Mrs. Staplins is one of those women for whom the word "lady" was invented, a woman so polite that she asks permission to call you by your first name. Elaine (she said I could call her that) is the charter president of the Saybrook Colony Founders Association, although she herself is not a descendant of a founder. She says her lack of local roots helps her keep her objectivity. For her work on behalf of preserving the town's history, the cupola and weathervane of the handsome new Frank Stevenson Archives building were dedicated in her honor in 1998. Sometimes when she drives by the building with her granddaughter, the girl will say, "Grandma! There's your weathervane!"

I came to meet Mrs. Staplins because she is also the official town historian. I wanted her to help me find Lady Fenwick.

The Lady with the Golden Hair

Old Saybrook and Old Lyme are the gatekeepers of the Connecticut River and natural starting points for explorers, past and present. I chose to start with Old Saybrook because of Lady Fenwick. She first appeared on my radar screen when I happened across a Daughters of the American Revolution chapter named in her honor. Then I learned that a sixty-passenger Connecticut River charter boat was named *The Lady Fenwick* and that maps of Old Saybrook show an area called Fenwick Point. And, in 1998, the Old Saybrook High School band commissioned—and presumably played—music entitled "The Tomb of Lady Fenwick." It puzzled me that a member of the British titled class had achieved iconic status in a New England small town, and I wanted to find out why.

Elaine Staplins took me into the Stevenson Archives and worked the files for documents. Then we went to Old Saybrook's Cypress Cemetery where a curious, dark brown, dome-shaped piece of sandstone marks the resting place of the lady in question. This is the second place where Lady Fenwick has been buried, Elaine explained. Originally, she had been laid to rest nearer the shore, within the seventeenth-century fortress at Saybrook Point. By 1870, however, a rail line threatened the site. Old

Lady Fenwick's gravesite in Old Saybrook

Saybrook's immutable civic pride kicked in and volunteers uncovered the lady's bones six feet beneath the surface. The skeleton was "nearly perfect," a newspaper reported. "The teeth were still sound; the skull unusually large; while the rest of the frame indicated a lady of slender mould, and the hair, still partly in curls, and retaining its bright reddish gold hue, gave support to the traditions of her rare beauty."

To satisfy local curiosity, the remains were placed on display on a dining room table in a Main Street home. Then a memorial service was held in the Congregational Church, bells in the town were tolled, and the bones re-interred in Cypress Cemetery. Lady Fenwick's original seventeenth-century grave marker was moved to the new resting place, where it stands now, surrounded by a fence erected to discourage the souvenir hunters who were chipping away at the stone. But while the remains were on display in 1870, some teenage girls were able to surreptitiously snip off bits of Lady Fenwick's hair. Some of it can be seen today, encased in a small picture frame in the Hart House, a museum owned by the Old Saybrook Historical Society.

With Elaine's help, I put together fragments of information that added up to a very sketchy story, but a love story nonetheless. It began in the early

1600s—the exact year is unknown—when Lady Fenwick was born Alice Apsley. She was the daughter of Sir Edward Apsley, member of a distinguished Puritan family in Sussex. Alice was not only born well, she married well, growing up to become the wife of Sir John Boteler, who was also known as Lord Boteler. (The name has evolved into today's "Butler.") Through her marriage Alice acquired the lifelong honorific of "Lady." Alas, Sir John soon died and Alice was left a young widow, though not a poor one, for she had inherited a fortune.

Considerably north of Alice's native Sussex is Northumberland, which lies on England's border with Scotland, making it a staging area—and battlefield—for England's interminable conflicts with the Scots. The Fenwicks were a large, ancient, and prominent family in this blood-soaked land. One of the family's rising stars in the 1630s was George Fenwick, who had been born in 1603, was a lawyer, and was fully endowed with the Fenwicks' brand of daring.

In 1631 a British nobleman with the double-barreled name of Lord Say and Sele, joined by Lord Brooke and others, obtained a patent to settle the lower part of the Connecticut Valley. In 1635 George Fenwick joined this group, which was hoping to attract settlers to their land in the New World. A veteran military engineer with the fearsome name of Lion Gardiner was hired to design and build the fort and see to security at "Saybrook."

In July 1636 Fenwick crossed the ocean to check on progress at Fort Saybrook. He was not impressed. Gardiner had built a fort, all right, complete with palisades, but only thirty-four people, including wives and children, occupied it. No more than three acres of corn had been planted and the only question seemed to be whether starvation or the hostile Pequods prowling nearby would finish off the fragile enterprise. Instead of throwing up his hands at what he had found, however, Fenwick saw the possibility of what it could become. He returned to England and recruited a party of settlers. Taking his measure, the other patentees appointed him governor of Saybrook. Somehow during all this Fenwick found the time to woo and win the widowed Lady Alice.

It says something about young Alice that she fell in love with this daring dreamer and was willing to join his expedition, giving up all the comforts a wealthy lady could expect in her native land. In spring 1639 Fenwick's little flotilla of two ships left England to sail directly to Connecticut. Aboard were Fenwick and his new wife, now, by courtesy, called Lady Fenwick. Not only did Lady Alice join the expedition, she helped finance it. Clearly, when

Alice Apsley Boteler married George Fenwick, she committed herself, her fortune, and her dreams to a daring adventure in an unknown land.

At Saybrook the Fenwicks moved into the "Great Hall," undoubtedly the best house within the palisade. Still, it was not exactly gracious living. In 1642 George wrote that the miseries of the settlers included moths eating their clothing and bugs their fruit, wood rotting in the palisade and buildings, sickness, and scanty communication with the home folks in England. Some of Saybrook's settlers found this more than they could bear, so they returned to England.

Very little is known about Lady Fenwick's life in these years, but we know that her husband tried to bring touches of English gentility to their wilderness life. He built her a walled garden of roses, daffodils, and poppies, and Governor John Winthrop, Sr., of Massachusetts Bay sent the couple some fruit trees. *We both desire and delight in that primitive employment of dressing a garden and the taste of so good fruits in these parts gives us good encouragement*, George wrote Governor Winthrop. Alice was a lady of spirit, too, making a life for herself in the rude new land. Tall and bright-haired, she was said to be seen riding a horse and practicing with her "shooting gun," which she used for sport. *She grew herbs in her wonderful garden*, George wrote. And she was generous, for she gave several cows to a Reverend Whitfield, whose party settled in what is now Guilford, Connecticut.

While Alice was a gracious spirit presiding over the little community at Saybrook, her husband must have had his hands full keeping the fort repaired and food flowing. He also became a father at least twice. Soon after their arrival in Saybrook, Alice gave birth to Elizabeth and then, on November 4, 1645, to Dorothy. But the second birth had a tragic outcome: although Dorothy survived, Alice died during the birth or shortly afterwards. Romanticists like to say she died of heartbreak after long separation from her homeland, but the complications common to childbirth in those times are a more likely explanation. Lady Alice Apsley Boteler Fenwick was buried on the grounds of the fort and is thought to be the first white woman to be buried in Connecticut.

George probably had already been planning to move back to England. The year before Alice died he had sold Saybrook Colony to the Connecticut Colony. The Hartford group had been more successful in building their colony upriver and Fenwick would have seen the handwriting on the wall for his struggling little community on the shore. The death of Alice must have been the last straw. In 1646 or 1647, George Fenwick took his daughters and sailed to England, having commissioned a monument for his wife's grave.

On the day that Elaine Staplins and I visited Cypress Cemetery, we found that a garland of white hydrangeas had been threaded through the top of the tall iron fence around Lady Fenwick's grave. Although the hydrangeas had yellowed and dried, it still seemed like a proper diadem for a lady. School groups and others come here now to see the burial place of a woman who had died more than three and a half centuries ago. But while Alice was a brave young woman, thousands of others like her summoned the courage to come to New England and make a life in the wilderness. She had died young, far from home, the Saybrook enterprise a seeming failure. Even in Old Saybrook most people know few details of her life. Why is Lady Alice Fenwick viewed with such reverence today?

One explanation is suggested by the work of a professor working only thirty-five miles from Old Saybrook. In his book *American Madonna: Images of the Divine Woman in Literary Culture*, John Gatta of the University of Connecticut says the "grace, spirituality, and prospect of salvation" promised by a fair lady—a Madonna figure—have a powerful attraction. Such Protestant writers as Nathaniel Hawthorne, Harriet Beecher Stowe, and Henry Adams have incorporated variations of the "Divine Woman" in their work. In part, this is an attempt to compensate for a lack of femininity in the American experience, which primarily is told as "manly" history. In the story of Old Saybrook, Lady Fenwick becomes the life-bearer, the nurturer, and the tall, golden-haired symbol of grace in what was, in many ways, a brutal age. She is a vulnerable innocent and yet is somehow transcendent. She is, in effect, the town's Madonna. And she is only the first in Old Saybrook's record of remarkable women.

The Seven Harts and Their Broken Hearts

Let us imagine the scene one day in 1804 in the Captain Elisha Hart home on Old Saybrook's Main Street. A gruff forty-five-year-old sea dog, Captain Hart had been a hard-fighting privateer skipper in the Revolution and was now a world-traveling merchant sea captain. In 1785 he had married the beautiful Janet McCurdy of Lyme, his suit prevailing over that of an infatuated Noah Webster, later of dictionary fame.

In 1787, Janet gave birth to the Harts' first child. Like so many men's men, the captain probably had been hoping for a boy, but the Harts named the child Sarah. The captain was willing to try again. Ann was born in 1790.

Then Mary Ann in 1792. The year 1794 brought Jeannette, while Elizabeth followed in 1796. In 1799 Amelia joined the captain's growing fleet of Hart females.

Elizabeth, one of "The Seven Beautiful Hart Sisters"

Now home between voyages, the captain sat in his kitchen, listening to the squeals and giggles echo through the hall-ways. Some of his girls were old enough to flirt with boys, while the youngest still left dolls on the floor for the captain to trip over. With six broadsides fired so far, each and every one yielding a girl, the captain was obliged to ponder the war cries of other brave sailors who had faced overwhelming odds but pressed on nonetheless: *I have not yet begun to fight. . . . England expects every man to do his duty.* The captain stroked his chin thoughtfully and sighed. His gaze fell upon his wife. She was still a beautiful woman.

Within a year, Harriet Augusta Hart was born.

To his credit, the captain knew when he was licked, so he settled down to cosset his maidenly brood. It was a consolation that the girls were unusually pretty, becoming famed in the region as "The Seven Beautiful Hart Sisters." The well-to-do Harts could afford to pamper their children and doting relatives surrounded them. From his world travels Captain Hart brought his family the latest in fashions and other luxuries, including a piano.

The oldest Hart girl, Sarah, was the first to marry. With her drop-dead good looks, she quickly turned the head of an attractive and well connected young Episcopal clergyman, the Reverend Samuel Fermor Jarvis. They wed in 1811. While the marriage would seem to have been made in heaven, it was more likely forged in hell. Sarah was spirited and adventurous, endowed with a hot temper and a voracious appetite for luxuries. Samuel was humorless, engrossed in his ministry, and as stubborn as Sarah was strong-willed. She was a hoyden; he was a prig. It wasn't long before sparks began to fly.

The marriage couldn't have been helped by the large amounts of sherry that Samuel put down daily, although, heaven knows, he probably needed it. Life with the eldest Hart daughter was full of surprises. During a family sojourn in Italy, Sarah became so intoxicated by the cultural climate that she announced her intent to convert to Catholicism. This brought a hasty return of the family to the United States, where Samuel tried to settle down as rector of Christ Church in Middletown.

The tumult in the household continued to such a degree that he was forced to resign the post in 1839 because of "domestic difficulties." Then Sarah shocked him by announcing her intent to seek a divorce. In those days divorce was rare, possible only through petition to the state legislature. Both Sarah and Samuel had powerful friends and they all hunkered down for a very public battle. It took until 1842 and a change in the state's governors before the divorce was granted.

Ann, the second oldest of the seven Hart sisters, was also the second to marry. Though adventuresome like Sarah, she had a calmer personality. Invited aboard a visiting American warship in Boston harbor, she met its young commander, Captain Isaac Hull, and promptly charmed him with the knowledge of nautical matters she had acquired from her father. Hull was smitten, but then his ship was ordered to sea. On August 20, 1812, Captain Hull, commanding the U.S.S. *Constitution,* sank the British frigate *Guerriere* after a pitched battle. Hull and his ship, which would come to be known as "Old Ironsides," returned to receive a grateful nation's acclaim. Ann was reunited with the young hero, and on January 2, 1813, they were married, Captain Hart telling Captain Hull, "Sir, I am sure you realize that by winning the affections of this remarkable girl you have captured a prize far more challenging and far more valuable than the *Guerriere!*"

Unhappily, the third Hart daughter, Mary Ann, did not fare as well. In her early twenties she fell in love with a local youth just as the War of 1812 was beginning. In 1814 the British decided to attack the Essex shipyards, which had turned into a troublesome nest of Yankee privateers just a few miles upriver from Saybrook. The British forces needed a guide to help pilot their vessels, and for a huge bribe they were able to engage . . . Mary Ann's suitor. The attack, which destroyed many ships, was a hard blow to the American side and the local economy. The traitorous young man pocketed his bribe and fled Saybrook, never to return. Mary Ann, brokenhearted, never married.

The Harts' fourth daughter, Jeannette, had a remarkable near-marital adventure. In 1824 her brother-in-law Isaac Hull, now a commodore, was appointed commander-in-chief of all American naval forces in the Pacific. As commodore, he was permitted to take his wife with him on long voyages, so Ann Hart Hull fitted out the commodore's flagship quarters to accommodate them both.

Ann also made up shipboard quarters for sister Jeannette, and so "the girls," as Hull called them, sailed the ocean blue, serving as official hostesses whenever the fleet dropped anchor. Before sailing off with the Hulls, Jeannette had been courted by a noted New York poet, one Fitz-Greene Halleck, but had refused to make any commitment to him. Given the Hart appetite for adventure, perhaps she hoped the voyage would bring her someone more exciting than a poet. In Lima, Peru, she found him.

Simon Bolivar is a giant in South American history, and is known as El Libertador ("The Liberator"). A talented young general, he led uprisings against Spanish rule on the continent, resulting in the liberation of Colombia (which then included Venezuela and Ecuador), Peru, and Bolivia. For most of the 1820s he was the dictator of both Colombia and Peru. During this time the American fleet visited Peru and Commodore Hull and his party attended a grand reception and ball in Lima. Jeannette Hart was introduced to the Liberator of South America, and as the Hart women were wont to do, she melted the great man (who was a widower) with her beauty and charm. It wasn't long before he proposed marriage.

The gossip channels of the western world buzzed with news of the romance. A Connecticut newspaper gushed in September 1826 that "it is the greatest match . . . ever known in this or that country [Peru]. We hope his excellency will come to the United States and consummate the contract by marriage in Saybrook in the good old republican way." Even the celebrities of the time were titillated.

Alas. Things were not what they seemed. While Bolivar was known to be a grieving widower, Jeannette did not know that he had long comforted himself with a mistress, one Manuelita. The frisky Manuelita happened to be the wife of an elderly and unusually forgiving Englishman who nursed hopes of her return to his affections. Although Bolivar wanted a more fitting woman than Manuelita to become mother of his heirs, he had no intention of giving her up, even after he married Jeannette. Unaware of all this, the dazzled Jeannette must have floated on a cotton-candy cloud of sweet illusions puffed up with Latin hot air.

At this point we must briefly shift our attention to Hart sister number five, Elizabeth. With the patented Hart talent for attracting important men, Elizabeth had married Heman Allen, a nephew of the hero of the Green Mountains, Vermont's Ethan Allen. Heman Allen had served in Congress and then been appointed as minister plenipotentiary to Chile. The young Allens were in Chile when Elizabeth gave birth to a stillborn child. The distraught and still bedridden Elizabeth begged Jeannette to visit her. Jeannette rushed from Lima to Santiago, where she was shocked to learn at her sister's bedside that the Allens dared not bury the child in a Chilean cemetery because Roman Catholic zealots might disinter and desecrate the body of a Protestant. Instead, the child's body had been preserved in a cask of brandy.

Jeannette, good scout that she was, volunteered to take the cask and its unusual contents back to Peru, where it could be placed on one of the commodore's ships for return to the United States. Something about the experience must have coalesced Jeannette's thoughts, because while she was making the trip back to Lima she decided to accept Bolivar's marriage proposal.

Alas again. Bolivar had heard about the cask but somehow came to believe it contained not the body of Jeannette's nephew, but of Jeannette's own illegitimate child! Like a character in an opera bouffe, the mighty Bolivar stormed and raged at a stunned Jeannette, denouncing her as immoral and unfit to marry. He would not listen to her explanations. The tearful Jeannette fled to the commodore's ship. Soon, anchor was weighed and the Hulls, brokenhearted Jeannette, and the brandy cask were on their way back to the United States.

Months later, back in Saybrook, Jeannette received a letter from Bolivar. A series of events had demonstrated to him the truth of her explanation. "It is, I know, too much to expect forgiveness," he wrote. Skillful as always at slinging the old moonshine, he went on: "Had I loved you less madly, I had not been so insane with jealousy, so blinded by it as to believe for a moment what seemed at the time incontrovertible evidence of clay feet of the idol I had set up in my heart. . . . You have been the finest woman in my life, so too, you are the last one. Henceforth I devote myself to no other woman than my Motherland." Jeannette never heard from Bolivar again.

Perhaps Bolivar meant what he said about devoting himself only to his Motherland, but it is hard to tell, for he died within three years after writing Jeannette. On the other hand, she lived more than thirty years after Bolivar's death. She never married, but she did not molder away in Saybrook, either. Instead, she kept traveling the oceans with her brother-in-law and sister, Commodore and Mrs. Hull, serving as a goodwill representative of the United States. Jeannette died in 1861. She never forgot her love affair with Simon Bolivar and, one suspects, never quite got over it. After her death a tinted miniature portrait of Bolivar, on which she had written, "Mr. Bolivar, Liberator S.A. 1824," was found in her sewing basket.

Amelia, the sixth Hart sister, probably attended Miss Pierce's School in Litchfield, Connecticut. A young man attending Tapping Reeve's Law School in the same town recorded in his journal that he had had "a peep at Miss Hart . . . most horribly fashionable in her accoutrements. . . . It is a very pretty thing . . . but I question if this be after all the style in which a young man of understanding should see a young lady without danger to his peace of mind." The Hart beauties were always disturbing young men's peace of mind. Eventually Amelia disturbed the peace of mind of none other than Commodore Joseph Hull, nephew of Commodore Isaac Hull, and they were married in 1834.

Mary Ann Hart, whose perfidious lover had vanished in 1814, died in 1830 at age thirty-eight, never having married. Harriet Augusta Hart, the youngest and "less favored" in looks, died in 1840 at age thirty-six; she, too, never married. Captain Elisha, father of the seven Hart sisters, died in 1842. The captain's coffin was carried out the front door of his Main Street home for burial in Cypress Cemetery. His surviving daughters—probably at the suggestion of Sarah, who had lived in Italy—followed Italian custom by placing a large iron bar across the door to prevent it ever being used again.

By now, none of the five surviving Hart sisters lived in Saybrook, but all returned for a few weeks each summer. Jeannette, distressed by the lack of inscription on Alice Fenwick's grave marker, arranged for "LADY FENWICK" and a date of death to be carved on her monument on its original site. The sisters also contributed to improving Cypress Cemetery, where Lady Fenwick would later be re-interred. So the spirit of Lady Alice Fenwick reached down and touched the Harts.

Kate Hepburn and Other Ladies of Distinction

Maria Louise Sanford was a plain-looking schoolmarm from Saybrook, but oh, how the woman could talk. She would hold audiences in the palm of her hand as she made the words dance—words about education, women's rights, moral values, conservation, love of country. She traveled the country giving speeches, even earning her living as a lecturer for a while.

But most of all, Maria Sanford was a *teacher* and a *nurturer*. Born in Saybrook in 1836, she used her dowry money to pay for college tuition, and then taught school, first in Connecticut, then Pennsylvania. It wasn't long until she was teaching other teachers how to teach. In 1880 the University of Minnesota hired her as its first woman professor. She taught there for twenty-nine years, packing lecture halls as she lectured on topics ranging from rhetoric to art history.

Maria Sanford retired from the University of Minnesota in 1909. She had made such a deep impression that the university's first residence hall was named after her and so was a Minneapolis public school. There is still a Sanford Hall housing students at the University of Minnesota. In 1920, Maria Sanford, age eighty-three, died and was honored with a memorial convocation at which she was called "the best-loved woman of the North Star State." She is remembered still, and not just in Minnesota. In 1958 a life-sized bronze representation of Maria Sanford was installed as one of Minnesota's two statues in the National Statuary Hall in the United States Capitol.

Maria Sanford sometimes lectured about improving the lot of blacks, but back in Saybrook some blacks were doing it for themselves. Peter Lane, grandson of a slave, scraped together the capital, the know-how, and the gumption in 1901 to open the first pharmacy in the nearly all-white town of Old Saybrook. Then his sister-in-law, Anna Louise James, scored a first of her own. In 1908 she was the first black woman licensed as a pharmacist in Connecticut. Anna James joined the Lane pharmacy in Saybrook and in 1921 took it over when Peter decided to move to Hartford. Anna James renamed the business the James Pharmacy and turned it into a local landmark, adding an ice cream parlor. She ran it until 1967.

So Anna James made her mark in Old Saybrook, but another family member was to make her mark in the world. Ann Lane was Anna James's niece and also a licensed pharmacist, but she spent her spare time writing short stories. In the 1930s she moved to New York City, where she married a freelance journalist and resident of Harlem named George Petry. She became deeply involved in Harlem life, took courses at Columbia, and published magazine stories. In 1946 she published *The Street*, a gritty novel of life in the ghetto for a young black woman determined to create a decent life for herself and her son. The book was a hit, selling 1.5 million copies, the largest ever for a black woman novelist. The book was also published in Arabic, German, Dutch, and Swedish.

Because of the book's success, Petry and her husband were able to buy a two-hundred-year-old home in Old Saybrook and move there permanently in 1948, where she continued to write. Other books followed, including novels, short-story collections, and children's books, among them *The Drugstore Cat*. Ann Petry died in a nursing home in 1997, a major figure in black literature.

In 1913 Dr. Thomas Hepburn, a Hartford physician, and his wife, Katharine ("Kit") Martha Houghton, discovered a place for a summer home on the shoreline in the borough of Fenwick. Fenwick is part of Old Saybrook, but has an unusual status: one of only nine boroughs in Connecticut, it contracts for municipal services from Old Saybrook but has its own system of governance, including a chief executive, called the warden, and six burgesses. Located on a low promontory of land called Fenwick Point, Fenwick faces Long Island Sound.

Dr. and Mrs. Hepburn were buying into an exclusive resort dominated by executives from Hartford's giant Aetna insurance company, but they were not typical members of Hartford's privileged classes. Dr. Hepburn was an athletic, red-haired man with a bellowing voice, Southern accented, and he was not shy about using it on behalf of progressive causes. "Kit" Houghton was a rebel by nature, with a voice to match her husband's. For much of her life she used it, too, leading rallies and marches on behalf of women's suffrage, birth control, and other feminist causes. Frequently the Hepburn children were pressed into service, handing out leaflets at rallies while mother's voice boomed from the podium.

Dr. Hepburn had declared himself a specialist in urological surgery, an unheard-of move at the time. Apparently he prospered, for the Hepburns purchased the Fenwick place in addition to their Hartford residence. The shoreline home offered swimming, golf, and tennis, all activities the athletic Hepburns adored, and it was a place to carry on their free-wheeling family discussions while being cooled by the sea breezes. Ever since then, Fenwick has served as a refuge and a place to refresh the soul of the clannish Hepburns. It serves today as the year-round residence of Doctor Tom and Kit's oldest daughter. Her name is Katharine Hepburn.

Katharine Hepburn was born in Hartford May 12, 1907. She was tomboyish, thin and athletic, swam like a fish, and liked to climb trees. She grew up in privilege, was allowed to drive a car at an early age, and drove all over Hartford with no license. Katharine inherited her parents' spirit of outspokenness, freethinking, and aggressiveness, sometimes at a cost of

Katharine Hepburn and Spencer Tracy in Without Love *(1945)*

popularity with other children. Until she was about thirteen she shaved her head every summer. She had no patience for fools. Like her mother, she attended Byrn Mawr, where on her first appearance in a college dining room she was mortified by an overheard remark, "Self-conscious beauty!"

But Kate Hepburn *was* beautiful, with brick-red hair, which she wore long, and she had legs to die for. She was talented, too, quickly rising from college plays to professional theater and then to Hollywood. Katharine never suffered from lack of confidence, either. When only nineteen, she told a dance partner, "I'm going to be the greatest actress in the world." Katharine Hepburn's lofty attitude earned her such nicknames as "Katharine of Arrogance," but she was not far wrong in her prediction. In her film career she costarred with some of the world's greatest actors, John Barrymore, John Wayne, Cary Grant, and Humphrey Bogart among them. She won no fewer than four Oscars and in 1999 was named by the American Film Institute as "the number-one female film star of all time." Such Hepburn films as *The Philadelphia Story, Summertime, Guess Who's Coming to Dinner, The African Queen,* and *On Golden Pond* are counted among Hollywood's classics.

Perhaps the most meaningful film in Katharine Hepburn's life, however, was *Woman of the Year*, which Metro-Goldwyn-Mayer released in 1942. Spencer Tracy and Kate played the leading roles. The story goes that when they met for the first time on a Metro set, Kate—at five feet seven, already tall by Hollywood standards—was wearing platform shoes and she loomed over Tracy, who was five feet nine. "I'm afraid I'm a little tall for you, Mr. Tracy," she said. To which he supposedly replied, "Don't worry, Miss Hepburn, I'll cut you down to my size."

The story sums up the success of what were to be a series of nine Spencer Tracy and Katharine Hepburn films, and make "Tracy and Hepburn" one of Hollywood's most fabled teams. Their personalities produced a winning formula with movie audiences: the seemingly unconquerable female who meets her match in a man for whom she falls. In fact, Tracy and Hepburn's real lives together reflected the formula: they were both vulnerable and they needed each other.

Tracy and Hepburn were together for nearly thirty years, during which they never married. He was Catholic and could not being himself to divorce his wife. In 1967 he died. In respect to his widow, who seemed to have been in denial about the affair, Kate did not attend the funeral. Kate never asked "Spence" to marry her. But they had the equivalent of a marriage.

In her autobiography, Katharine Hepburn called Fenwick "paradise," and it is there that she has retreated for her last years. At this writing she is still there, in a house from which she can see Saybrook Point, where Lady Fenwick lived, died, and lay buried for many years. Hepburn has written of the view from her Fenwick bedroom: "From my bed I see the sun rise. Between the inner and outer lighthouses. Across a field of marsh grass. Birds circling. A family of white egrets. Swans go honking by. Even an occasional osprey. I see the path of the rising sun gradually shift to the south as winter comes creeping in. . . . Time is passing. Yes. Don't waste it."

A Saybrook Fantasy

I have a daydream in which all the remarkable women of Old Saybrook, past and present, join together to address the women and girls of Old Saybrook today. Elaine Staplins would organize the event, of course, and have a large committee of volunteers. It would be held in the largest auditorium in town, so everyone—little girls in jumpers or jeans, businesswomen in tailored suits and waitress's uniforms, stay-at-home moms holding babies on their hips, elder stateswomen in wheelchairs—could attend.

Maria Sanford would warm up the crowd with a stem-winder extolling the values of education, women's rights, and patriotism. Anna James (who would wear a fine hat and insist on being introduced as *Miss* James) would look sternly at the audience and then tell them how NO barriers exist for those women, black or white, who are willing to work hard. No excuses! she'd thunder. Her niece, Ann Petry, would be softer-spoken but she'd say that anything is possible for those willing to use their minds. Reading and writing are the keys, she'd tell the crowd. The Seven Beautiful Hart Sisters would have some cautionary tales to tell about love and marriage, but also some happy ones. Then Katharine Hepburn, in that memorable voice of hers—throaty and aristocratic—would tell a salty story or two about Hollywood, remind them that Spence was the greatest male actor in films *ever*—and urge: *Be yourself! Speak out! Take action! Don't moan! Don't complain! Onward!*

Finally, the most awaited speaker of all: Lady Alice Apsley Boteler Fenwick. Her golden hair shining in the auditorium's lights, the tall young woman would speak softly in accents of her native Sussex. Showing how up to date she is, the first thing she'd tell the crowd is, "Just call me Alice!" She'd admit it took nerve to come to America, that wild frontier of empire, but she'd found a loving home in Old Saybrook. And, she'd say, for as long as schoolchildren crowd around her fence in Cypress Cemetery, she'll live here still.

And then (since this is my fantasy, I can imagine anything I want), the speakers would form a receiving line at the door. The audience of ponytailed little girls, high school youth, pierced and tattooed college students, mothers, checkout clerks in smocks and executives in pinstripes, plus ladies of a certain age, would file slowly past. As the women and girls passed, the speakers would shake their hands and give them hugs, and Lady Alice would murmur a final message in each one's ear. . . .

You go, girl, she'd say.

———————————

Autumn is a fine time to visit Old Saybrook and other towns in the southern Connecticut River Valley. While hordes of leaf-peepers are heading north, you can head south on Route 9 from central Connecticut to the shoreline. In a good foliage season you'll enjoy some lovely scenery, not as hilly as Vermont and New Hampshire, but charming in its own softly rolling way. In Old Saybrook there are plenty of seascapes and old houses to look at, as well as Fort Saybrook Monument Park. The Chamber of Commerce publishes a guide to a walking tour of the town (860-388-3266);

this and other information is also available at www.oldsaybrookct.com. However, the General William Hart House (350 Main St.) is the only historic home open to the public and then only afternoons on Friday through Sunday in summer months. Built in 1767 by an uncle of the Seven Beautiful Hart Sisters, it is well worth seeing: outside, it is geometric perfection, while awaiting you inside are the furnishings of a typical well-to-do colonial settler, including eight corner fireplaces, fine wainscoting, and Staffordshire tiles. Volunteers have recreated historic gardens, too, including a kitchen garden with over a hundred medicinal, culinary, and fragrant herbs.

CHAPTER THREE

TIDEWATER GRIT

Like a giant heart beating ever so slowly, the Atlantic Ocean expands and contracts twice a day, its tides gliding up and down shorelines and the rivers that run to the sea. In Connecticut, the ocean's pulse is felt as far north as Windsor, just above Hartford and more than forty air miles from the coast. It takes more than four hours for high tide to arrive here from Saybrook, losing nearly half its height along the way, but the ocean still whispers its eternal message to land-dwellers: *Come to me.*

The seductive sea holds out the promise of riches and adventure with one hand, while concealing its dangers in another. A direct connection with the ocean has shaped the southern Connecticut River Valley's history and the character of its people. For many years the estuary, from Saybrook to Windsor, was lined with shipyards. From here, sea captains, fishermen, and privateers—"iron men" all—set forth on their dangerous journeys, making leaps into the unknown over and over again.

Mixed with the rich soil and water of the region is an abundance of what our ancestors called "sand"—meaning strength of character, determination, courage. The imagery persists as "grit." You can find it here today.

The Geek

Geek: Noun *(slang)*. . . a person who is single-minded or accomplished
. . . but is felt to be socially inept. . . .

Noah Webster took notes wherever he went: the population of towns he
visited, the meaning and pronunciation of new words he heard, the weather
and the temperature, new ideas in science and agriculture, *everything*. Tall,
thin, jut-jawed, and endowed with a thatch of unruly red hair, he strode
restlessly across the early American landscape, neatly dressed in black,
gimlet-eyed and seldom smiling, and always writing, writing, writing.

It didn't take long to realize whose intellect the outspoken Webster
esteemed the most (his own) and whose were the secondary talents (everyone else's). Allegedly, someone once welcomed the man by saying, "I
congratulate you on your arrival in Philadelphia," to which Webster
replied, "You may congratulate Philadelphia on the occasion." Pompous,
prudish, and proper (and also highly sensitive), Webster drew wisecracks
and insults the way a magnet draws iron filings. He replied with fusillades
of high-caliber words. Called a "dunghill cock of faction" or "sneaky, snakey
[and] fainthearted," Webster would dismiss his hecklers as "macerated
pre-adomites" and "convoluted stomatopods."

No doubt about it, Noah Webster was a *geek*, a word he would have
loved to add to his collection but a label he would have rejected for himself
with an explosion of sarcasm. There was something oddly affecting about
Noah Webster. All that cockiness, all that bravado concealed a shy, clumsy,
and sometimes lonely young man who had almost more intelligence than
he could use. Thank heavens he did use it, for he became one of the most
important, if least appreciated, of this country's founding fathers.

Webster was born in 1758 in the parlor chamber of a four-room
farmhouse that still stands, with additions, at 227 South Main St., West
Hartford. His father mortgaged the farm to send the boy to Yale. In 1778
young Noah graduated near the top of his class and went to work teaching
in the public schools. Then, studying the law in his spare moments, he
passed the Connecticut bar examination less than three years later.

For a geek, Noah paid a remarkable amount of attention to the opposite
sex. Thereby hangs a tale. In 1781 he tried opening his own school in Sharon,
Connecticut. The school was a success from the start, but, stunningly,
Webster abruptly closed it within a few weeks and left town, crushed by a
pair of romantic disasters.

Noah Webster, man of many words

Finally collecting his wits, Webster arrived in Goshen, New York, with only seventy-five cents in his pocket but a brilliant idea. Inspired by America's war for independence, then winding down, he decided to write a thoroughly American schoolbook. The result was the famous "Blue-Backed Speller," America's first bestseller. As new editions poured off the presses, Webster gradually introduced his ideas for Americanized, simplified, and standardized spelling (humor for humour, theater for theatre, traveler for traveller, for example). Fretting over "those odious distinctions of provincial dialects" which worked against a national self-identity, Webster included rules for phonetics. The speller is still in print today, used for home schooling and as a classroom supplement.

Webster also wanted to promote copyright laws that would protect his "Blue-Backed Speller," so the young man set out on a national lecture tour in 1785 and 1786, addressing legislatures and boldly calling on some of the nation's leading men, including George Washington. The one-man campaign got results. Soon, almost every one of the original states passed a copyright law and eventually Congress did, too, causing Webster to be called "the father of American copyright law."

Webster was always busy. He edited a magazine and later a newspaper, wrote books on a wide variety of subjects (including a history of diseases), helped found Amherst College, held various local and state political offices, and fired off volleys of pamphlets and newspaper articles advocating progressive ideas on issues ranging from public education to city planning. But Webster is best known for his dictionary work, in which he set out to challenge England's domination of the field. His first version, which he called his *Compendious* (meaning condensed), appeared in 1806 and then, in 1828, he published his signature work, the unabridged American dictionary.

The labor required to produce it was staggering. He learned several foreign languages, the better to trace word sources. For years he employed a curved desk on which a number of foreign dictionaries were arrayed. Each day he would work his way through the books from right to left, tracing the history of words. All by himself Webster researched and wrote *by hand* seventy thousand definitions of words, with their origins.

Webster's dictionary not only captured the uniqueness of American English (it included such deliciously American words as *skunk, squash,* and *snowshoe*) and eliminated some Anglicisms, it also standardized as American pronunciation a version of the way New Englanders talked in Webster's day. Today, the name *Webster's* is so closely associated with dictionaries that it is sometimes used as a synonym.

Noah Webster was one of our most important, if least known, founding fathers. He understood that the Revolution did not end with the war but was a continuing process of building a sense of the American identity, part of which was the words people used and the way they talked. He was proud to be an American, and he wanted his words to be thoroughly American. Theatrical types should remember that the next time they are tempted to open a "theatre," and so should developers of shopping malls, who seem to think that calling an emporium a "centre" adds class instead of pretense.

Webster's intellect and passions drove him to be a public figure, when he was really a quiet scholar by temperament. That such a sensitive man could sustain himself in the face of the mockery and criticism that plagued him throughout his life can be credited to a cherished wife and family, who gave him a comforting refuge from the world.

Even so, wounds to a young heart can be hard to heal. As an old man, Noah Webster remembered, with striking vividness, certain events from the fall of 1781. He had come to the little town of Sharon a brash Yale graduate of twenty-three, ready to teach school and court the ladies. In his new social circle he met two pretty young women, Rebecca Pardee and nineteen-year-old Juliana Smith. The latter led a literary group and, to impress her, Noah submitted a clumsy fable to the group's literary magazine. Juliana only sneered and called him duller than her family's horse.

Rebuffed by Juliana, Noah turned his attentions to the beautiful Rebecca Pardee and soon proposed marriage. Rebecca couldn't decide between Webster and another suitor. When the Pardee family couldn't settle the matter either, it went to a church council, which humiliated Webster by choosing his rival. He was stunned and fled the town, wandering in a daze for weeks until he drifted into Goshen, New York, with only his speller in mind.

The speller's success brought publication of a companion grammar book in 1784 in which Webster included some fictitious role models for young readers. One was a young woman "whose personal attractions have no rivals, but the sweetness of her temper and the delicacy of her sentiments." Webster named this paragon "Juliana."

Then, in 1787, Webster met a young woman to whom he was immediately attracted. She was short, fine featured, and gay, a striking contrast to the tall, dour Webster. In 1789, at age thirty, Noah married Miss Greenleaf, age twenty-three. She was called Becca but her true name was Rebecca. In 1790 Becca gave birth to the first of the Webster children. In 1793, the Websters had their second child. She was named Frances *Juliana.*

In his old age, Webster clearly remembered the misery of his thwarted romances in Sharon. Biographers have noted, also, the odd coincidence of names in his life: rejected by both a Juliana and a Rebecca, he married another Rebecca, conceived of an idealized Juliana in writing, and, twelve years after his rebuff by Juliana Smith, used her name again in christening one of his children. Perhaps it is all coincidence, with no meaning.

Perhaps. Or did the highly sensitive Noah Webster still smart a half-century later over his rejections by the lovely Misses Smith and Pardee? Did having their names under his own roof remind him daily of his lost loves? Or did he take some measure of satisfaction that his family had come to include both a Rebecca and a Juliana? One way or the other, did Rebecca Pardee and Juliana Smith live on in some corner of Noah Webster's heart until the end of his days?

And did Becca know?

The Smith Grrrls

Zephaniah and Hannah Smith were not your ordinary small-town residents. They weren't in the late 1700s and they wouldn't be today, even though the bumpkinish Glastonbury of their time has turned into a comfortable suburb of Hartford. Zephaniah, who had graduated from Yale, became a minister. Then he got into a quarrel with his congregation, which dismissed him. Disgusted, he turned to storekeeping, studied the law, and became a successful lawyer. Hannah, his wife, was a mathematician, poet, linguist, and astronomer. While her husband practiced law, Hannah ran the farm, raised the children, and translated poetry from the ancient Greek.

There must have been interesting conversations at the Smith dinner table, for Zephaniah and Hannah raised five daughters just as bright and individualistic as they were. Unwilling to couple ordinary first names to plain old Smith, Father and Mother Smith distinguished their daughters, who were born in the years 1787 to 1797, by

Julia and Abby Smith, a sisterhood of courage

naming them Hancy Zephina, Cyrinthia Sacretia, Laurilla Aleroyla, Julia Evalina, and Abby Hadassah.

The Smith girls were notable for more than their names. For example, Hancy invented a device to help blacksmiths shoe cattle. She also built a boat and sailed it on the Connecticut. Cyrinthia was a horticulturist. Laurilla made watercolor sketches of Glastonbury homes. Julia became a classics scholar and made five translations of the Bible in its entirety: two from Hebrew, two from Greek, and one from Latin. For fun, the five sisters liked to compare the vocabulary in the King James version of the Bible with the original Greek and Hebrew.

The Smith sisters had suitors and social lives as girls and young women but, according to their biographer, Kathleen L. Housley of Glastonbury (writing in *The Letter Kills But the Spirit Gives Life,* published in 1993 by the Historical Society of Glastonbury), the family gradually drew into itself, its members forming their own closed society. The sisters' intellectualism probably shut them out of the local marriage market. Nonetheless, they were highly active in charitable work in Glastonbury and they became strong abolitionists. "They were self-sufficient," a neighbor wrote of them. "But nevertheless their lives were fragrant with good deeds. They were ever at the bedside of the sick, and were ministering angels to the poor."

The Smith sisters welcomed black abolitionist leaders to their home. Unlike some abolitionists, the Smiths did not regard blacks as inferiors, but saw them as equals, deserving equal rights. The Smiths took copies of anti-slavery newspapers to the mill tenements in South Glastonbury, circulated petitions and resolutions (visiting almost every house in town), attended anti-slavery meetings and hosted some, and possibly participated in the Underground Railroad (although there is no evidence of this).

Father Zephaniah died in 1836 and Hannah, the mother, in 1850. Her death established a sad pattern: one of the Smith women would die every seven or eight years until all were gone. Laurilla died in 1857, Cyrinthia in 1864, and Hancy in 1871. But with the end of the Civil War and the abolition of slavery, the two remaining Smith sisters, though elderly, became even more active. Their years of struggle against slavery had prepared them to deal with another injustice: the withholding of the vote to women.

In the fall of 1869 the Smith sisters discovered that an inordinate portion of their Glastonbury taxes, which they paid without having the right to vote, was being used to register *men* to vote. Their dander up, Abby and Julia went to Hartford for the first convention of the Connecticut Woman

Suffrage Association. Fired by speeches by the likes of Susan B. Anthony and Elizabeth Cady Stanton, the Smith sisters came home, determined to fight the good fight for women's suffrage.

In 1872 they made another discovery: the town authorities had increased their taxes and those of two widows, but none of the men's. They paid under protest. About this time three other Glastonbury women attempted to register to vote, but were refused. Julia and Abby began attending selectmen's meetings to press their causes. Their advanced ages (Julia was in her early eighties, Abby late seventies), their high social standing, and their reputation for good works got them a courteous reception, but nothing else. At town meeting in 1872 Abby delivered a ringing "no-taxation-without-representation" speech. "From the men of our town we are never safe—they can come in and take our money from us just when they choose," she declared. The sisters launched a campaign in the press, writing letters to the Hartford and Springfield papers pressing their case.

Meanwhile, the Glastonbury tax collector was pressing his. The Smiths had begun refusing to pay their taxes, submitting only the interest. On January 1, 1874, the tax collector seized for auction seven of the Smiths' eight Alderney cows. The cows, sociable creatures who were pets of the sisters, mooed furiously as they were removed to a neighbor's barn; so did the one remaining. The bovines kept up the racket until the auction, at which the Smiths bought back the animals for a low price.

Two elderly ladies standing their ground, their lowing cows, and the mean-spirited tax collector was wonderful material for the press, and the story spread across the land. The sisters furthered their cause by publishing a pamphlet, *Abby Smith and Her Cows*. People sent money to the Smiths for a defense fund, poets composed verse about the episode with the cows, suffrage groups passed resolutions supporting the sisters, prominent people rallied to the sisters' defense, and editorial writers spoke favorably of them.

Thus bolstered, on April 6, 1874, Julia and Abby went to town meeting and asked to be allowed to speak. Refused, they went outside, where Abby mounted a wagon and delivered a prepared speech, followed by some remarks by Julia. Not realizing they were fighting a public relations war and losing, town officials bore down on the Smiths. The tax collector sold some of their best land at auction. The sisters sued, won back their land in local court, lost on the town's appeal, and appealed to a still higher court. In the meantime, town officials returned twice in 1876 to seize Smith cows again.

By now, the sisters were nationally famous and they traveled through-out the country, despite their advanced ages, to address suffrage conventions. Julia was "short and plain in looks, making many little jerks of her head to emphasize her always strong opinions," one contemporary wrote. "Abby was tall and much more dignified in carriage." Abby usually did the public speaking, Julia the writing, but either could deliver a bon mot. Julia told a convention they had two cows, which they had named Taxey and Votey. She added, "It is my opinion that in a very short time, wherever you find Taxey there Votey shall be also."

The sisters won their appeal to the higher court, but it was a technical victory that neither saved them from paying taxes nor got them the vote. Then, in 1878, Abby, the most sociable of the two remaining sisters, died at age eighty-one. Julia, eighty-six, was left alone.

Among the sympathy letters Julia received was one from an elderly lawyer in New Hampshire named Amos Parker. A friendship developed, and less than nine months after Abby's death, Julia married Parker. One wishes her life could have ended in married bliss, but it did not. Old friendships of Julia's broke up under the stress of misunderstandings. Amos Parker, who had appeared sympathetic to Julia's suffrage activities, nonetheless paid the Glastonbury taxes, making it appear that the Smiths' principled stand had been abandoned. Then he sold the Smith house, dispersing its contents at auction. In 1885 Julia died after a bad fall. That the marriage had been less than idyllic is suggested by instructions she left. She asked to be buried in Glastonbury between her sisters, with her maiden name, not her married one, on the stone. You can see it there today, next door to the old town hall where she was denied the right to speak.

The Painter

Certain titans of talk radio, who shall remain nameless here, spit out the word "activist" as if it could burn a hole in their tongue. *Activists*, they seem to think, are softheaded, longhaired, pot-smoking, young pinko-liberal-socialist-commie-loving atheistic troublemakers who ought to leave the country, since they obviously don't love it exactly the way it is. The titans need to remember that troublemakers founded this country.

And they need to meet Polly Murray.

Polly Luckett Murray is a silver-haired lady of a certain age who talks with a soft and measured voice, doesn't enjoy public speaking, and has no taste for politics. She grew up in a genteel family, graduated, with distinc-

Polly Murray, a pioneer against Lyme disease

tion, from Mount Holyoke College, and loves shutting herself up in her studio to paint all day.

She also is someone who has long been a pain in what doctors—especially *certain* doctors—would call the gluteus maximus. For Polly Murray is an activist and it is a good thing for the rest of us that she is: she prodded the health establishment into attacking a medical mystery that it had long ignored. We now know there is a serious illness called Lyme disease and there are ways to treat it. For that we can thank this quiet artist, doll-maker, and antiques dealer, a self-described "private person" who would just as soon be left alone, thank you.

Like many of us, Polly Luckett grew up in awe of doctors. In college she majored in art history, but happened to spend one college summer as an assistant in medical research, picking up some of the lingo and tradecraft. In 1954 she married a happy-go-lucky Harvard grad named Gil Murray and eventually the couple moved from New York to Connecticut.

One day in August 1955, she felt "absolutely dreadful all day" while on the beach at Old Lyme. With flu-like symptoms and a temperature of 105, she was given penicillin, and recovered in about a week. To this day Polly Murray does not know whether that was the beginning of Lyme disease. She does know that it was the start of a series of illnesses that would recur for many years, eventually including every member of her family. The meticulous records she kept document her family's misery:

- Spring, 1956: The Murrays were living in Essex, Connecticut. Polly, pregnant with their first child, "ached all over and felt feverish." Weakness persisted for months afterwards. Alexander, called Sandy, was born in January 1957.
- 1959: The Murrays moved across the Connecticut River to Lyme. David was born there in August and in May 1961 Wendy arrived. During both pregnancies Polly experienced bouts of sore throat, pleurisy, and rashes on her chest, hands, and arms. From 1961 to 1963 Polly suffered recur-

ring headaches, sore throats, and laryngitis. Radiating pain in her legs was diagnosed as "transient nerve-root irritation."

- In 1963, during her fourth and final pregnancy, Polly's left foot became extremely painful. It was diagnosed as synovitis, a kind of inflammation. Later that year a rash appeared on her face and was diagnosed as erysipelas. The rash receded, but Polly felt exhausted for the rest of her pregnancy.
- In 1963 several of the Murray family broke out in rashes and had fevers. From time to time, aching joints, rashes, diarrhea, and welts plagued them.

And so it went over many long years. With the advent of warm weather, various members of the family would suffer a variety of symptoms, such as aching joints, excruciating headaches, chills, cramps, sore throats, rashes, black-and-blue marks, swellings, coughs, diarrhea, nausea, fever, lethargy, irritability, weakness, facial tics, eye twitch, nosebleeds. It was if the family had been singled out to suffer like Job. Antibiotics helped for a while, but the symptoms would always return. Doctors offered different diagnoses: synovitis, childhood depression, vitamin deficiency, hormonal changes, even something called "vascular fragility."

Polly suffered the longest. At one large teaching hospital the best doctors could do was vote, five to two, that she *didn't* have thyroiditis. The lead physician brusquely told her, "You know, Mrs. Murray, sometimes people subconsciously want to be sick." Next, she checked into a special diagnostic center. After three weeks of medical and psychological tests, all the hospital could tell her was that she was depressed as the result of a chronic health problem that could not be diagnosed.

Polly Murray was fed up. "I decided to become my own expert," she later wrote. In the fall of 1971, with the children in school, she began haunting libraries, eventually steeling herself to walk into the Yale University medical library and act as if she belonged there. Learning from her research how to present herself and her family's data, Polly began seeing a rheumatologist to whom she gave detailed documentation of the symptoms, including photographs. Irritated, the doctor snapped, "Mrs. Murray, how can I convince you to stop this anxious search? I personally think you are a case of wounded intellect and you are obsessed with making a case for a disease that exists most likely only in your own mind." He accused her of "chasing doctors." Another doctor called her a "flighty woman." She was advised to find "a good hobby."

But something else was happening: Polly kept meeting people who also had mystery illnesses. She was becoming convinced that the different illnesses occurring in her family, and perhaps others, were connected, that the different symptoms had a common source. Pointing this out 1975, her newest medical specialist responded with sarcasm. "I suppose you think this is some new disease," he told her. "Why, they might even call it Murray's disease."

But other doctors were supportive, even if they couldn't solve the mystery. A friendly one suggested that Polly call the Connecticut State Health Department. On October 16, 1975, she did, telling an epidemiologist in great detail about the symptoms her family and others had suffered. The epidemiologist was polite but noncommittal. Meanwhile, Polly went looking for a new rheumatologist. She went to the Yale School of Medicine and from that point on, things changed. It later turned out that the state health department had discussed her report with someone at Yale. The "someone" was Dr. Allen C. Steere, a researcher who just happened to be at a point where he was open to new research. Not knowing this, Polly brought him her carefully compiled data, not only on her own family, but eight other cases in Lyme and East Haddam, plus reports of thirty-five other possible instances. Gratifyingly, Dr. Steere and his colleagues took her seriously.

Results did not come overnight. It took endless testing, laboratory work, and collecting of field specimens of animals and insects. But in May 1976 the news media reported that researchers had discovered a new disease, called "Lyme arthritis" at the time. Suddenly, Polly found herself being interviewed by the national press. However, researchers were still treating the illness as a minor disease, and so far only aspirin was being prescribed for treatment. And some Lyme residents were complaining about the unwanted publicity, while skeptics were dismissing Lyme as mass hysteria.

Research continued, and Polly kept pressing Dr. Steere. How about a national registry of sufferers? Would antibiotics, such as tetracycline, help if administered long enough? How about support groups? What about an informational brochure?

Eventually it was determined that the disease in the eastern United States was carried by an insect commonly called the deer tick. By 1980, Yale researchers were increasingly persuaded that early administration of antibiotics could alleviate Lyme symptoms and prevent development of arthritis symptoms later. In recognition that it affected more body systems than the joints, the name of the ailment was changed to Lyme disease.

In 1982 Polly and Gil agreed to start leading "separate lives," and a divorce followed. In 1982 and 1983 came reports that researchers were suspecting a spirochete, a spiral-shaped bacterium, as the culprit in Lyme disease. Polly was distributing information brochures in her area. In November 1983, Polly briefly spoke up, "knees shaking," at the first international conference on Lyme disease, hosted by Yale.

Over the next few years, recognition of Lyme disease spread around the world. Meanwhile, Polly stepped up her work on Lyme disease, counseling the many ill people who called her on how to work with their doctors, circulating exhibits, attending conferences, speaking at medical schools, and giving interviews to every kind of media, from book authors to radio hosts. She circulated a petition asking for additional statewide efforts against Lyme disease; this brought some improvements, most importantly, the designating of Lyme as a reportable disease. Polly and others formed a Lyme Disease Awareness Task Force in Connecticut. She spoke to medical schools and testified before Congress, telling it, "This disease can destroy the normal functioning of a family." In 1996 a major publisher issued her book, *The Widening Circle: A Lyme Disease Pioneer Tells Her Story*. She received many awards, including an honorary doctorate from Mount Holyoke, for her pioneering in documenting of Lyme disease and then goading the medical establishment into recognizing it.

But defeating Lyme disease turned out to be more complicated than originally thought. Lyme disease is a trickster, for it manifests itself differently in different people. Symptoms vary, and so does intensity. Sometimes sufferers test negative to blood tests and their Lyme disease symptoms may be diagnosed as psychosomatic. Sometimes the disease has psychological effects, which can further confuse doctors.

Cases of Lyme disease have been reported throughout the country, but about ninety percent occur in just eight East Coast states, from Maryland to Massachusetts. The disease occurs where deer, white-footed mice, and deer ticks all live, typically in forested areas near people. In Connecticut, about one case for every thousand people is reported each year; many more cases are thought to go unreported.

Administered early enough, antibiotics appear to work in about ninety percent of Lyme cases. It's the other ten percent—the cases where symptoms persist or return after initial treatment—where the trouble lies now. Some researchers feel that something else is occurring here—another

illness or perhaps an autoimmune problem resulting from the initial illness. Doctors subscribing to this point of view refuse to treat patients with
more antibiotics. Other doctors believe in long-term antibiotics. Bitter controversy has broken out in the "Lyme community," with chronic sufferers
insisting that long-term antibiotic treatment helps them and they need it,
but insurance companies, some doctors, and certain researchers—including, sadly for Polly, Dr. Steere—arguing against it.

Today, Polly Murray lives quietly in Lyme, Connecticut, keeping to the
sidelines of the controversy, although she supports the concept of long-
term treatment. The deer continue to lurk in the woods nearby, but she
hasn't moved away—as many have suggested—because the home, the
friends, and the region she loves are here. Although she is "bitten" almost
every year, she has learned how to minimize the likelihood of infection and
how to nip the disease in the bud. She also has cleared brush and trees from
her home to keep deer at a distance.

"Doctors and patients need to listen more to each other," she says. "It's
awful when doctors are trained not to treat. But the patients know how
they feel." She was referring to a medical journal article by Dr. Steere which
warned doctors about "overdiagnosing" and "overtreating" for Lyme disease. That "sent the wrong message to doctors nationwide," with tragic results, she says, because it hindered recognition of the disease by doctors
unfamiliar with it.

To those people who feel they may have Lyme disease, but can't get a
doctor to treat them, she says, "I tell them to keep pursuing it." Which is
what *she* did, after all: in the face of humiliation and rejection by the medical establishment, she plunged into the unknown, kept on going, and eventually made a difference. "I did it for my family," she says. Like the sea captains
who used to live here, she did it with grit.

The Things They Heard

Except for the odd commercial strip of BurgerKingMcDonalds
KMartWalMart tickytack, the river country from Portland, Connecticut,
to the shore is straight out of the travel pages: quaint little towns connected
by roads winding through woods, coves crowded with sailboats, and the
sun glittering off the water as well as the Mercedes automobiles driven by
ladies in hats. It's the kind of place where one town, Essex, unblushingly
advertises itself as "The Best Small Town in America" and no one is so rude
as to argue. It's all so perfect that you begin yearning for a touch of the

weird, some reassurance that Mother Nature can be just as quirky and mankind just as strange as everywhere else. Fortunately, the region can provide.

The first settlers of East Haddam had no trouble persuading the Native Americans to sell their land. There was a reason. Being no fools, the Indians were happy to unload Mt. Tom, which they called Machimoodus ("place of noises"), and its environs, because of the strange rumbling sounds it emitted. They believed the mountain was home to the spirit of evil. Some early white settlers also attributed the noises to wicked forces. The loud rumbling sounds, last heard in 1899, were called the "Moodus noises" and became nationally known. Sobersided experts said earthquakes were the source of the noises, but to people who didn't like being jolted out of their beds at night, it didn't much matter. Moodus was just a noisy place.

A distant uncle of mine, Nathan Augustus Mather, lived in this area long ago, but had different sounds in his head. As a youth, Uncle Gus was so talented with the violin that he was invited to join the musical tour of famed Swedish violinist Ole Bull. Gus's parents wouldn't let him go. Disappointment festered in Gus's breast for years and emerged in its own peculiar way long after he was married.

In those days, country folk warmed themselves with stoves and firewood. Gus would organize his firewood for the coming winter in separate piles, labeling each for the one and only month it could be burned. If an allotment of firewood was exhausted partway through a month, the house could get colder than a banker's heart but Gus and his wife would just shiver until the next month. Water could freeze in the washbowls and they might see their breaths in the parlor, but Gus would touch no wood before its time.

So my uncle fiddled in cold isolation and in winter the Mathers didn't get many visitors near the end of a month. Neither did Moodus, and it took a long time for the feeling to wear off that this was one deal where the Indians got the better part of the bargain.

The towns and villages of the southern part of the river include some of my favorite mind-stretching places. In West Hartford, the Noah Webster House at 227 South Main Street offers tours of the lexicographer's birthplace led by costumed guides (860-521-5362; www.ctstateu.edu/noahweb/index.html). In Rocky Hill, Dinosaur State Park preserves one of North America's largest dinosaur track sites. Under its geodesic dome are hundreds of tracks, a life-size diorama, and enough lighting and sound effects to persuade you that strange creatures passed this way only moments before (860-529-8423; www.dinosaurstatepark.org). It's eerie.

Further down the western side of the river, on Route 9, is the little town of Haddam. Here, the "ghost" of Thankful Arnold can take you on a tour of her home, built in 1794, and tell you how three generations of women lived in this house (860-345-2400; www.cttourism.org/detail.cfm?ID=83). A few miles further south is Essex, home of the Connecticut River Museum, a marvelous collection of river valley history housed in the 1879 Steamboat Dock (860-767-8269; www.ctrivermuseum.org). A full-sized replica of Bushnell's *Turtle* and many other things, including steamboat memorabilia, are on display here. Finally, on the river's west side are the attractions of Old Saybrook (see previous chapter).

Over the river on the eastern side, the Florence Griswold Museum, 96 Lyme Street, Old Lyme, is a Georgian mansion that housed an art colony and now is a showcase for American Impressionist art. (860-434-5542; www.flogris.org). Heading north on the east side of the river, East Haddam's Goodspeed Opera House is not to be missed. Broadway-quality musicals are staged in a building erected in 1876 and fully restored with all its gingerbread. Just like the original, the theater floor does not slope, so short people are issued booster seats (860-873-8668; www.goodspeed.org). Further north and near Hartford, the Museum on the Green, 1944 Main Street, Glastonbury, is housed in the old "Town House" (town hall), where the Smith sisters spoke out. Smith artifacts are among the many things exhibited here. All the Smiths are buried in the cemetery next door, united in death as they were in life (Historical Society of Glastonbury; 860-633-6890).

The Underwater Man

Whenever I hear Southerners claiming that the *Hunley*, their Civil War underwater craft, was the first American submarine, I think, "Wrong again." The credit belongs to the *American Turtle*, the invention of a Connecticut farmer's son named David Bushnell. One of those Yankee geniuses who thrived on New England's rocky soil, Bushnell entered Yale at age thirty-one. There, he distinguished himself by triggering an astonishing waterspout in a campus pond, showing doubting Thomases that underwater explosions really were possible.

I scarcely knew who David Bushnell was until I met Dave and Pam Tuttle in Old Saybrook. The Tuttles had purchased the old Captain Richard Sill house in a secluded part of town and were massively restoring it. It turned out to be the very place where, long ago, Bushnell had secretly tested a weapon that he hoped could turn the tide for the colonists in the American Revolution.

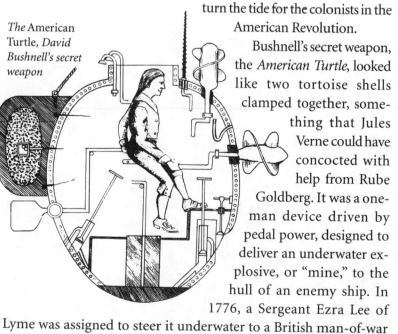

The American Turtle, *David Bushnell's secret weapon*

Bushnell's secret weapon, the *American Turtle*, looked like two tortoise shells clamped together, something that Jules Verne could have concocted with help from Rube Goldberg. It was a one-man device driven by pedal power, designed to deliver an underwater explosive, or "mine," to the hull of an enemy ship. In 1776, a Sergeant Ezra Lee of Lyme was assigned to steer it underwater to a British man-of-war in New York harbor, but he was unable to attach the explosive. A second effort a few days later also failed. Alerted, the British attacked the ship carrying the *Turtle* and sank it. Although the *Turtle* survived, it spent the rest of its days on dry land, where it probably crumbled into dust. (A full-size re-creation of the *Turtle* is on display at the Connecticut River Museum, a jewel of a museum in a jewel of a town, Essex, Connecticut.)

So ended David Bushnell's experiment. He continued to develop ideas for the war, with limited success; after the war, he engaged in other kinds of inventing, again with limited success. Then, in 1787, he disappeared from Connecticut. Apparently, he went south, shed his old name, and became Dr. David Bush, a teacher and doctor of medicine in Georgia, where he died in 1826, unrecognized in his adopted state and mostly forgotten elsewhere. But not entirely. In Iowa City, Iowa, until a few years ago there was a small restaurant that called itself Bushnell's Turtle. Few of that landlocked state's customers understood the reason for the restaurant's curious name, even as they lined up to buy its specialty: submarine sandwiches.

CHAPTER FOUR

THE WITCHES OF WETHERSFIELD

There are several ways to approach Wethersfield, a suburb nestled between Hartford's south side and the Connecticut River, but the best is from Exit 26 on Interstate 91. After the off-ramp and its connector have finished jerking you around, you glide up a quiet street past the Ancient Burying Ground and find yourself in the Eighteenth Century. This is Old Wethersfield.

Feathery trees, some of them exotic species brought back by sea captains, shade the quiet streets. A fine brick church ("Gathered in 1635") sends a white steeple soaring to the sky. And everywhere there are old houses, forming the largest historic preservation district in Connecticut, a rich collection of ancient clapboards, gambrel roofs, and Connecticut River doorways with fluted pilasters and scrolled pediments. In this trove of early American architecture are nearly two hundred buildings constructed before 1850.

Most of the old homes are occupied by the professionals of the Hartford area—the insurance executives, lawyers, and others who punch up the local economy—but the larger town of Wethersfield, which encompasses Old Wethersfield, has neighborhoods with ethnic flavors and blue-collar incomes. And it is big enough to have monotonous miles of franchise-fla-vored strip malls. All this makes Wethersfield (which was Hartford's first trolley suburb) a typical New England bedroom town, the kind of place where most residents go to bed each night to dream of their 401(k)s or muscle cars or perfect weddings.

But those who lie awake and listen closely may hear wolves howling while men moan and women scream. In the dark night of haunted minds, the vines of fox grape form nooses, sheets of blood move beneath the earth, and gravestones dance in the Ancient Burying Ground. In Wethersfield we are on the killing grounds.

Familiarity with the Devil

It was probably a cold winter day in 1650 when they brought Mary Johnson to the hanging tree, and if the terror didn't make her shiver, the bone-chilling cold must have. Poor, alone, and reviled by everyone she knew, the young woman from Wethersfield must have looked up at the noose silhouetted against the leaden sky and searched the faces surrounding her for a hint of kindness.

Finding none, she let her trembling body be guided to the hangman's embrace. After a mind-numbing round of prayers by the horse-faced clergy circling her, she was pushed into eternity, sent to a kinder place than the world she had known. Her hundred pounds or so of weight would have been more than enough to draw the noose tight, snap her neck, and crush her windpipe. Unconsciousness should have come quickly and, if there was any mercy that day, death would have seized her in seconds.

It was, in the minds of the reverend clergy, the perfect finish to a most useful process. Mary Johnson not only had given a full confession but also had been penitent and remorseful, building her last hopes on the mercy of God, so "she died in a frame extremely to the satisfaction of them that were spectators to it." Mary's departure probably was good riddance in their eyes, for she was a no-account, convicted and publicly whipped in 1646 for thiev-ery and now revealed by her own confession to have been that favorite consort of the Devil: a discontented female.

A confessor had coaxed from Mary that she had wished for the Devil "to do this and that" of her chores as a household servant, and so the Devil had carried out the ashes and driven out the hogs for her. But there was worse: she also admitted that she "had murdered a child, and committed unclean-ness both with men and devils." We know no more about the "murder," but a Hartford jury found Mary guilty of "familiarity with the devil" and ordered her hung.

And so the first of Wethersfield's witches was put to death. Before the witchcraft craze had wound down, at least four people from the town were formally prosecuted and three were executed. It is the Connecticut River Valley's sad claim to infamy that, long before

Wethersfield's Buttolph-Williams House, setting for a famous book about fear of "witches"

the Salem hysteria in the 1690s, witches were being executed here. In Connecticut alone, at least forty-two men and women were accused and about a dozen executed, most from the founding towns along the river: Windsor, Wethersfield, and Hartford. Indeed, a Windsor woman, Alice Young, is thought to have been the first person convicted and executed for witchcraft in New England. She was killed in Hartford in 1647, but little else is known about her.

Not long after Mary Johnson's case, a middle-aged married couple from Wethersfield, John and Joan Carrington, were found guilty of having "entertained familiarity with the devil" and were executed in Hartford about 1653. Like Mary, the Carringtons were probably poor, and one of them had already been in trouble with the law. Exactly what else the Carringtons did to provoke the community is not known, but both were convicted of having "entertained familiarity with the devil the great enemy of God and mankind and by his help [each] hast done works above the course of nature for which . . . thou deservest to die."

Rather different from Mary Johnson and the Carringtons was Katherine Harrison, a prosperous widow with, one suspects, an unlovable personality and a knack for getting into trouble. As a young woman, she had been fired from her servant's position for "fortune telling and evil conversation." Later, she married a comfortably established local citizen who was the town crier. Two years after he died in 1666, she was accused by neighbors of a laundry list of misdeeds, including fortunetelling, bewitching bees and cows, and making a neighbor ill. She also had quarrels with her neighbors, over land in one case and alleged slander in another.

When a jury could not come to a verdict on the witchcraft charges, Katherine's furious neighbors accused her a second time, thirty-eight of them signing a petition against her. The magistrates banished her from the colony. Her talent for upsetting her neighbors followed her to Westchester, New York, where once again she was accused of witchcraft, although the charges were dismissed. Later she returned to Wethersfield and is thought to have died a natural death there.

And so it went in the Connecticut River Valley through much of the 1600s, where Satan always seemed to be lurking in the shadows. Moving against "witches" allegedly recruited by the Devil seemed a useful way for dealing with troubling events. Those people considered irritating, eccentric, or defenseless, often elderly women, were the usual suspects. In 1654 Lydia Gilbert of Windsor was indicted (and probably executed) for supposedly causing, by witchcraft, the accidental shooting death of one man by another. In 1662, a woman named Ann Cole accused Rebecca Greensmith in Hartford of causing her various afflictions, such as uncontrollable muttering. The elderly wife of a farmer, Rebecca then "confessed" that the Devil first appeared to her "in the form of a deer or a fawn, skipping about her," and that they had frequent meetings and sexual encounters. When Rebecca's husband attempted to fight back by suing his wife's accuser for slander, he himself was charged with witchcraft. Both were executed.

Throughout the valley and nearby areas, such as New Haven, the threat of witchcraft hung heavy in the air from the 1640s until at least the 1680s. Why?

In the book *Entertaining Satan*, his careful analysis of the phenomenon in early New England, Professor John Demos of Yale University makes an important distinction: witchcraft was no "meandering sideshow, isolated from the larger history" of the region; it was, instead, tightly woven into New England life. There was, first of all, the ignorance, insularity, and Puritan harshness of the times, creating an atmosphere in which repression could grow. But in this atmosphere there occurred "triggers" and "inhibitors," factors which, in sufficient strength, could predispose a community to witchcraft proceedings, or, conversely, inhibit them.

The triggers—which did not necessarily work automatically or immediately—included the stresses of life to which early New Englanders were vulnerable: *harmful events*, such as epidemics, weather disasters, crop failures, Indian raids, fires, and shipwrecks; *signs*, such as earthquakes, eclipses, and other celestial phenomena that played on superstition; and *past community controversies*, which may have been concluded but not without leaving a legacy of bitterness. Inhibitors of witchcraft proceedings include internal controversies still in progress and major external controversies or conflicts, such as an Indian war (because such events drew people together or, at least, engaged them).

Demos' theory not only makes sense but also resonates in our own world: we begin to recognize that, when we are under stress, our urge to demonize enemies, our suspicions about those who are different, and our need to find quick solutions for complex problems all too closely resemble those of our ancestors. The madness of McCarthyism, the unfairness of racial profiling, and the seemingly unwinnable war on drugs, with its ever-burgeoning prison populations, echo the mood on Gallows Hill in Hartford long ago.

Which is why it is heartening to find that Wethersfield today is teaching lessons about tolerance, lessons reminding us that witch hunts were not confined to Puritan New England.

In 1958, Elizabeth George Speare, a Smith College graduate and high school English teacher, published *The Witch of Blackbird Pond*. Her historically accurate novel tells the story of a young girl named Kit Tyler. Kit is an orphan sent from the Caribbean in 1687 to live with her stern aunt and uncle in "cold, bleak" Connecticut Colony. There the lonely girl makes friends with an old Quaker woman, known as the Witch of Blackbird Pond, and comes to be accused of witchcraft herself. Kit comes to understand the dangers of intolerance and misunderstanding. All this takes place, of course, in Wethersfield, where Mrs. Speare herself lived for many years.

Each year hundreds of schoolchildren visit Wethersfield to tour the Buttolph-Williams House, a weather-beaten old structure built in the style of a house that Kit would have known. Many of them have read *The Witch of Blackbird Pond*, as have other schoolchildren and youth across the nation. The Wethersfield Historical Society offers teachers a resource packet that includes an ancient map on which landmarks mentioned in the book are shown.

Highly praised by critics and awarded the prestigious Newbery Medal, *The Witch of Blackbird Pond* has become a classic, valued for the lessons it teaches about the dangers of prejudice, ignorance, and superstition. Wethersfield, where once "witches" were persecuted, has become a place to learn about tolerance.

The Mystery of Silas Deane

There was something about young Silas Deane that could bother a person, something you couldn't put your finger on, but could *feel* nonetheless. Deane was a good-looking young man dressed in the latest fashion, and in the drawing rooms of Wethersfield you could watch him work a crowd with a politician's gift for the right phrase at every turn. But, if you had the ear for it and were listening carefully, something rang false underneath all that bonhomie. Long after you watched Deane move on to yet another gathering and more glad-handing, there remained a nagging suspicion that this man was not quite what he seemed.

Silas Deane, man of mysteries and miseries

Deane had been born in Groton, Connecticut, on Christmas Eve, 1737, and for a while it seemed as if his birth date had foreshadowed a lifetime of glad tidings. His father was only a blacksmith, but Deane managed to attend Yale and become a lawyer. A fast learner, he grew into a charming, well-spoken, and polished young man. No doubt about it, young Silas Deane looked like a comer.

He also had a talent for marrying well. After moving to Wethersfield, in 1763 he wed one of his clients, a prominent local woman named Mehitable Webb. She was a widow five years his senior and owner of a thriving general store in Wethersfield. Joining his wife in business, Deane quickly showed he was no ordinary storekeeper, content to sit beside the cracker barrel. He fancied himself a *merchant* and used his wife's capital to get into the West Indies trade. The Deanes prospered and were able to build a big, new house right beside the Webb house.

After only four years of marriage, however, Mehitable died. Soon, Silas married Elizabeth Saltonstall, granddaughter of a former governor of Connecticut. Deane's second marriage was another step up in his social circle and political connections. The bright, aggressive Deane became more active in Wethersfield social and civic life, winning friends and influencing voters. By 1768 he had been elected to the state legislature, where he quickly achieved prominence and many assignments.

It wasn't long before the Wethersfield attorney moved onto the national stage. In 1774 and 1775 Connecticut legislators made him a delegate to the Continental Congresses meeting in Philadelphia to discuss growing American resentment of Britain. There he worked tirelessly on behalf of the colonists' cause, usually rising at 6 and not retiring until 11 at night after writing long, tender letters to Elizabeth (who herself was destined to die within a few years).

So far, so good.

But as Deane gained prominence, he was demonstrating another attribute: a lifelong ability to attract enemies. This is the first of the mysteries of Silas Deane: the man was charming and intelligent, but there was something about him that could arouse suspicion, even dislike. He was slicker than spit and that made certain people uneasy. And he was patently ambitious, fond of making great plans, bright ideas that made him look like a self-serving schemer, even to his political allies. As you came to know him, you learned he was cocky, short-tempered, and self-righteous—and just a little too grasping. John Adams wrote of Deane to a mutual acquaintance: "You know his ambition—his desire of making a Fortune. . . . You also know his Art and Enterprise. Such Characters are often useful, although always to be carefully watched and contracted. . . ."

Still, in 1776 Deane secured a key assignment on behalf of the rebellious colonists: American representative to France, charged with secretly sounding out the possibilities for an alliance against the British and also with procuring war matériel. It was a crucial job and one that causes him to be referred to sometimes as America's first foreign diplomat. But Deane wasn't as smart as he thought: he made alliances with several gentlemen he trusted but who in reality were British agents. The most intriguing of these was Dr. Edward Bancroft, a scientific type who had once studied with Deane and now was in England to spy for America. Or that was what Deane thought. In reality, Bancroft was a *double* agent, working for the British against the American cause. It was a very tangled web, indeed, into which the talented Mr. Deane was increasingly drawn.

Then, in December 1776, Congress sent Benjamin Franklin and Arthur Lee, of the distinguished Virginia Lees, to join Deane in forming a three-man diplomatic mission. Deane and Franklin seemed to work well together, but Lee, a temperamental, difficult man who trusted no one (and whom

Franklin thought was half crazy), quickly developed an obsessive dislike for Deane. Wired into the power elite back in America, Lee's badmouthing of his fellow agent fell on the receptive ears of the Deane-haters back home.

Late in 1777 Congress recalled Deane, ostensibly for reports but without any other real explanation. He arrived home in July 1778, but what awaited him was not the hearing he expected, but something akin to death by a thousand cuts. Apparently, Congress had heard plenty of rumors, thanks to the whispering campaign of Deane's enemies, and was deeply worried about allegations that he not only had been using insider knowledge to profiteer, but also might even be disloyal to boot. However, Congress lacked the hard evidence for a showdown.

So Deane was allowed to twist slowly in the wind. He was refused hearings, officially told little of what was going on, and yet was ordered to remain close at hand and do nothing. For over two months Congress toyed with Deane. He attempted to strike back by opening a newspaper feud with his enemies, the Lees. Congress continued to fiddle and ignore Deane's entreaties, but finally in April 1779 it "discharged" him from further responsibilities without comment, leaving him on his own to settle accounts left from his work in France.

In 1780 Deane returned to France, but there found that collecting sums due him and clearing his name was far harder than he expected. One hope after another was dashed. Things got even worse. Suspicions arose that Deane had turned against his own country, selling out to the British. The fault for this was partly Deane's own: he shot off his mouth far too often, writing private letters that sounded traitorous and which somehow found their way into print. At the very least, the embittered Deane had become a defeatist. In any case, George Washington, who had previously praised Deane and even dined at his home, declared, "I wish never to hear or see anything more of so infamous a character."

The Revolution ended with America's victory, proving Deane's prognostications wrong. By now he was nearly friendless and almost destitute. He took refuge in Ghent, barely subsisting while he continued to try to collect old debts from Congress and others. Then he moved to London.

In the last decade of his life, Deane was plagued with illness, social snubs, and insults. He continued to think about returning to America, while realizing his unpopularity there would make it most unpleasant. Finally, in 1789, after seven years of exile in England, he decided to go home. By then, Deane was so infamous that Thomas Jefferson wrote James Madison, "Silas

Deane is coming over to finish his days in America, not having one *sou* to subsist on elsewhere. He is a wretched monument of the consequences of a departure from right." In September 1789, having screwed up his courage and cooked up some new moneymaking schemes, the fifty-four-year-old Deane boarded the packet for Boston. But his usual bad luck followed him on board, for he suddenly fell ill and died within four hours. The ship, which had only just departed, returned to England, where Deane was buried—never to return to America, after all. It was widely rumored that he had killed himself.

And therein lies another mystery. During the war, the mysterious Dr. Bancroft, double agent, and Deane, his dupe, had conspired together to secretly profit, in trade, from their insider knowledge. After the war, Bancroft had remained friendly to the lonely Deane. When Deane announced he was returning to America in an effort to vindicate himself and start a new life, Bancroft outfitted him "advice, medicins, and money for his subsistence."

Trouble was, Bancroft had reason to fear that, back in America, Deane might blow the whistle on him while trying to clear his own name. At the very least Deane might blab about their wartime profiteering. Worse, he might even tell about Bancroft's role as a double agent—still officially a secret, though not necessarily from Deane any more. Because Bancroft, a scientist, was a recognized expert on poisons and had outfitted Deane with "medicins," and because Deane had died so suddenly and unexpectedly, suspicions arise. Was Deane's sudden death caused by his unknowingly taking by one of Bancroft's "medicins"? Did Bancroft murder Deane?

Looking into the life of Silas Deane is like looking into a hall of mirrors, lit by candles. Everywhere you look there are flickering images but they fade in and out and sometimes disappear. To this day, historians argue over whether Deane was a patriot or traitor, a shameless profiteer or a sharp businessman no worse than his peers, a suicide or a murder victim. Deane seemed to have been vindicated in 1841, when Congress granted a claim of $37,000 by his descendents and agreed a "gross injustice" had been done the man. But today historians aren't so sure, and neither is anyone else. Edmund Morgan once wrote that "the facts in the case of Silas Deane will probably never be fully known." *So who was the "real" Silas Deane? And how did Wethersfield's most famous citizen die?*

The Burglar's Story

The hero of this story—if "hero" is the right word—is an obscure burglar, long since dead, buried, and probably forgotten. I'm not even sure I have his right name. But I do know this: the man was not only a survivor, but also an example of the human capacity for reform, redemption, and even love. He witnessed man's inhumanity to man in Wethersfield, Connecticut—and he gave testimony.

The story begins in the countryside near Redding, Connecticut, on the dark, still night of September 17-18, 1908. Here Samuel Clemens—"Mark Twain"—had built a large house in Italianate style, called it Stormfield (after a riverboat captain he had known), and announced to the world he was moving "all his earthly possessions" there. That caught our burglar's attention. He liked "earthly possessions" himself.

The state prison at Wethersfield, where spirits of the inmates were broken

America's most famous author was now a widower in his seventies. Among those occupying the Redding house this evening were Clemens, his daughter Clara, a butler, and a secretary. Watching Stormfield from the shadow of some secluded bushes were two men from New York. They were burglars of the old-fashioned type, the kind who carried a black bag for their swag, probably had pug noses and cauliflower ears, and, in my imagination at least, wore soft caps and little black masks. For one of the burglars, this was supposed to be his last job: he wanted enough money to marry his sweetheart, Alice, and then go straight. It all sounds like the plot for another wry crime novel by Donald Westlake—but it was all true.

Finally, it looked as if everyone in Stormfield had retired. The two men entered the house through a kitchen window, inspected the dining room, and found a large, locked sideboard which they lugged out the front door and down the road some five hundred feet, so they could work on it in peace. After emptying it of silverware, they went back to the dining room.

Fortunately for Twain and his earthly possessions, these burglars were cut from the same cloth as The Gang That Couldn't Shoot Straight. On their first tour of the dining room they had removed a large brass bowl from the sideboard and placed it on the floor. On their second tour, they stumbled over the bowl in the dark, causing a noise "as if an earthquake had struck the house."

Soon, a woman in a bathrobe—Twain's secretary—bravely appeared at the head of the stairs and softly called "Hello!" The burglars turned tail and ran. Then Twain's butler appeared and fired several shots (to no effect). The elderly author, momentarily awakened by the shots, imagined a champagne party was under way downstairs and that corks were being popped. He went back to sleep.

The unnerved burglars foolishly decided their best course was not to melt into the darkness but to board an early morning train at nearby Bethel where everyone knew everyone else—except them. It wasn't long before another man on the train, who happened to be a neighbor of Twain's, spotted the suspicious-looking strangers and, when the train pulled into Redding station, he alerted a waiting posse that had armed itself with pitchforks, clubs, and shotguns.

The train resumed its journey with the posse aboard. One of the burglars leaped from the train but was soon captured. The posse fell on the other man, and clubbed him into unconsciousness, though not before his revolver discharged during the struggle to grab it. Unfortunately for the sheriff, a bullet went through his leg.

After everyone's wounds had been dressed, the burglars were taken to a preliminary hearing in the Redding town hall, where they claimed their names were "Henry Williams" (the one with the revolver) and "Charles Hoffman." (One wonders about the names.) Twain, dressed in his famous white suit, accompanied by his daughter Clara and his secretary, appeared at the hearing to deliver a scathing denunciation of his unwelcome visitors. The burglars were returned to jail for a three-month wait until trial. Twain went home and famously posted a notice "To the Next Burglar" in which he announced that only plated ware remained in the house, and that it could be easily found near a basket of kittens. "If you want the basket, put the kittens in the brass thing," Twain asked, closing with the request, "Please close the door when you go away!"

Then, as authors will, Twain set to work capitalizing on his experience. He enjoyed telling audiences that, if those burglars did not reform, they would have no place left to go but Congress. But Twain may have quietly done something else. "Williams" could have received thirty years in prison for wounding the sheriff, but instead his charge was reduced to assault with intent to kill, with a sentence of only four years, in addition to a six-year sentence for burglary. The burglar suspected that Twain had been so impressed by his story—orphaned at fourteen and a hard-lot life—that he had asked that the charges be reduced.

In any case, the burglar who called himself "Williams" arrived at the Connecticut State Prison in Wethersfield on a gloomy day in November 1908. The prison had been here since 1827. Overlooking Wethersfield Cove, the facility was modeled on the Auburn system, which allowed inmates to leave their cells during the day to work in prison shops under contract to outside industries. It also yielded profits for both the state and the industries and, in fact, allowed the Connecticut prison to operate at a net profit. The system appealed to the "pay-as-you-go" values of conservatives, but "Williams" called it "modern slavery."

"Williams" was assigned to a narrow, whitewashed cell on the fifth, or top gallery, of the old brick cellblock, immediately under a leaky roof. The floor was flooded much of the time. Hot in summer, cold in winter, the cell had almost no ventilation and the air was dank and unhealthy. Under the Auburn system, the inmates were prohibited from talking with each other at mealtimes or at work. Violations were punished by solitary confinement in "the cooler," damp, cold, dark cells below ground, where the beds were planks with no bedding and the diet was bread and water.

When Williams arrived, the Wethersfield prison had contracts for the production of cheap shoes and shirts, and over four hundred prisoners labored in the workshops, unpaid, from seven in the morning until noon, and from one until six. The men worked in silence, repeating the same task over and over for years without variation; failure to perform up to expectations was punished with solitary confinement. Now and then an inmate would go mad with the monotony and smash his machine. Some of the machines generated dust and caused lung diseases. But both the state and the contractors made fat profits.

Prison life outside the workshops was no better. Fights were a daily occurrence. Guards carried clubs to subdue the unruly—and used them. Food was coarse, recreation nonexistent, and visitors limited to one a month. One day, "Williams" later recalled, a lifer unable to bear it any longer took a fatal headfirst dive from the cellblock's top gallery—an act common enough, apparently, for inmates to nickname it the "Dutch act." "Williams" later wrote, "Of all the prisons I was in, [Wethersfield] was by far the worst, the most brutal and degrading."

"Williams" made one failed escape attempt, spent a week in the cooler for another offense, and then settled down, working first in the shoe factory and then in making shirts. Prison officials told visitors he was the "Mark Twain burglar, a very bad man," one incapable of reform. But after his release from solitary he began attending chapel regularly, although the attraction was not religion but the kindly attention he got from ministers and other volunteers. He made a number of such friends, and their support made him resolve to give up crime. It was "the human touch"—something he had seldom experienced in his hardscrabble life—that made the difference, he said.

In October 1916 "Williams" was released early for good behavior, having served eight years. He was thirty-five years old, wore a cheap suit and prison brogans, and had four cents in his pocket. He had learned no marketable trade as an inmate and his health and strength had been impaired by prison life. He later wrote, "My most valuable possession was the determination to go straight and stay straight." But he had another possession, an even more surprising one: the works of Mark Twain, of whom he had become a devoted reader.

He walked three miles to Hartford, where he was welcomed by many of the people who had visited the prison. They fed him and found him a room; another ex-convict helped him get a factory job. Later he returned to New York, where he met the great prison reformer Thomas Mott Osborne. Osborne arranged for him to meet a certain woman, the American wife of a Russian pianist, who immediately took an interest in him. She paid for him to take a course in automobile mechanics and then one in welding.

Thanks to the training, "Williams" got a job with an automobile maker in New York and eventually was made head of a department. His shop turned out two hundred ambulances used in World War I, making an important contribution to the war effort. He also became active in the prison reform movement. The most romantic part of the story involved his former sweetheart, Alice. After his arrest he had stopped communicating with her and, never knowing what had happened, she had married another, been divorced, and then had moved to New York. One day "Williams" spotted her at a theater. He explained everything, they resumed their courtship, and were married. So far as I know, they lived happily ever after.

He had one other accomplishment, however. About six years after his release from Wethersfield he wrote a book about his experience that was published by a major New York firm. Entitled *In the Clutch of Circumstance*, by "Anonymous," it not only tells his story but also argues forcefully for prison reform. "A prison should be a place where they make men, not break them," he wrote. In the book, he also gives credit to the many who helped him, including the woman in New York who paid for his technical education. He wrote that what she did for him "was a shining example of the true spirit of forgiveness and friendliness, which could redeem the world."

It was indeed. His benefactor had been in Stormfield the night of the burglary. Her name was Clara Clemens Gabrilowitsch, and she was the daughter of the late Mark Twain.

Death in Wethersfield

"Anonymous" was concerned mostly with the death of the spirit, but there were plenty of other deaths at the state prison in Wethersfield. Inmates lived in dread of tuberculosis, which stalked the damp cellblocks, and the prison cemetery was filled with those who had suffered from the unhealthy living conditions. But there was another way inmates at Wethersfield died: execution.

A gallows house with "a special hanging machine" was used for executions for many years and, later, the electric chair was introduced. By 1937, fifty-five men had been hanged here, and from 1937 through 1960, eighteen were electrocuted. The death chamber had a record day in 1946 when three inmates were electrocuted, one after the other, for having killed a guard during an escape attempt.

In 1963, all of Wethersfield's inmates were moved to a modern prison in Somers and two years later the one-hundred-forty-year-old facility was demolished. Today, the state headquarters of the Department of Motor Vehicles stands on the prison site and the one-time warden's residence nearby, known as the historic Solomon Welles House, is owned by the town and used for meetings, parties, and showers.

So happier sounds have replaced the grim silence that once ruled this part of Wethersfield. From its beginning, however, it seems as if this pretty and prosperous suburb and its people have had to endure more than its share of violent misfortune.

In 1633, an adventurer named John Oldham and three companions from Massachusetts walked to what is now Wethersfield. The next year, Oldham and ten others returned to set up shelters where the cove is today. But by 1636 Oldham was dead, killed on his boat off the Connecticut shore by Indians from Block Island. The murder of a founding father of Wethersfield helped touch off the Pequot War in which things would get even worse for Wethersfield.

One day in April 1637 an estimated two hundred Pequots surprised a number of whites working in a Wethersfield meadow near the river. At least nine whites—six men and three women, or seven men, a woman and a child, depending on the account you read—were killed, as were twenty cattle and a horse. The triumphant Pequots sailed down the Connecticut and, as they passed Fort Saybrook, waved their victims' bloody clothes to taunt the garrison. Their satisfaction was short-lived, for the Pequots themselves were soon brutally attacked and dispersed.

On December 11, 1792, there occurred what one historian called "the saddest day Wethersfield ever knew." (Perhaps he wasn't thinking of the 1637 massacre.)

Early that morning a prominent fifty-two-year-old Wethersfield merchant named William Beadle, using an axe and a knife, moved through the bedrooms of his fine house and killed his thirty-two-year-old wife, Lydia, and then their four children: Ansell, eleven; Elizabeth, nine or ten; Lydia, eight; and Mary, six. He went downstairs, sat down in a Windsor chair, and killed himself, using two pistols. All too common today, mass murders were almost unheard of in Beadle's time, and the news shocked citizens across America and in England.

It turned out that Beadle, who was in such desperate financial straits that he feared he could no longer obtain food, fuel, or clothing for his family, decided killing them was the most merciful thing to do. He had been planning this for three years. The outraged townspeople of Wethersfield buried Beadle in an unmarked grave outside of town and his family in Wethersfield's Ancient Burying Ground. You can see their table stone there today, with its sad story: *Here lie Mrs. Lydia Beadle . . . Ansel, Elizabeth, Lydia & Mary . . . fell by the hands of . . . an infatuated man.*

For a place that has known so much tragedy, it seems appropriate that Wethersfield today has become a place where solace can be found. Located here is the headquarters of an organization with the difficult task of helping those in Connecticut who have had someone close to them murdered. Survivors of Homicide ("SOH"), founded in 1983, is an independent organization funded only by donations and grants. It has about two hundred active members, access to professional counselors, and an office (on Silas Deane Highway, of all places). (Telephone 888-833-4764, toll free.) It calls itself "the organization for people who suffered the murder of a relative or close friend. We help each other cope." Wethersfield has had to do a lot of that.

There are many other, and brighter, sides to the Wethersfield story: for example, the local shipyards and sea captains who tied the town to distant ports from the 1600s through the 1800s. . . . The rich soil and benevolent climate which for almost one hundred years made Wethersfield famous for its Red Onion, shipped to the world in huge quantities. . . . Wallace Nutting, an indefatigable promoter of early Americana through his photography, books, and preservation efforts, who helped save one of the town's most important houses. . . . The Wethersfield Volunteer Fire Department, the oldest in continuous operation in New England.

So Wethersfield not only has an interesting past, but also, thanks to people like Nutting, plenty to see. The Webb-Deane-Stevens Museum, 211 Main Street, features three handsome early American homes side by side: the Joseph Webb House, completed in 1752 (where Mehitable Webb Deane lived, and which Nutting helped preserve); the Silas Deane House, ca. 1766 (built by the merchant-diplomat), and the Isaac Stevens House, completed in 1789. George Washington slept in the Webb House and planned the Yorktown campaign here. The original British wool-flocked wallpaper that Washington viewed is still on the walls of his bedroom. The Society of Colonial Dames in Connecticut owns the houses and also the nearby Buttolph-Williams House, ca. 1720, said to be the setting for *The Witch of Blackbird Pond*. For more information, go to www.webb-deane-stevens.org or call 860-529-0612.

The Wethersfield Historical Society (www.wethhist.org; 860-529-7656) is extremely active in preserving and presenting the town's past. With a professional staff and research library headquartered in the Old Academy Library, 150 Main Street, the society operates a museum (860-529-7161) in the Keeney Memorial Cultural Center at 200 Main Street with both permanent and changing exhibits, all fascinating. The society also manages the Hurlbut-Dunham House, 212 Main Street, and the Cove Warehouse (dating from the late 1600s).

And, of course, the grim old prison has vanished, there have been no mass murders since the Beadles, and the only witches in Wethersfield today can be shooed away with candy bars.

CHAPTER FIVE

HARTFORD'S RIVER OF WORDS

Adriaen Block loved nothing more than a good adventure, but even he knew adventurers have to settle accounts now and then. In the fall of 1613 Block faced some hard accounting. He had sailed a vessel (bravely named the *Tiger*) from Amsterdam to the tiny Dutch trading base at Manhattan, connected with the Indians there, and traded for furs. Then things went terribly wrong. The return trip to Amsterdam had barely gotten under way when the heavily loaded vessel caught fire and everything—ship, furs, and dreams of riches—disappeared before Block's eyes.

With winter setting in, the Dutch captain hunkered down in Manhattan to ponder his options. Of course, he could still find his way home and face up to his disappointed employers, who would probably give him yet another scorching. Block had a better idea. He would combine adventure with redemption by building a small vessel of his own and sailing east into Long Island Sound. There he could chart the New England coastline and search for *new* sources of furs, information that could expand the Dutch trading empire and, not incidentally, the reputation of Adriaen Block, explorer.

So Block and his crew spent the winter building a small boat, which he dubbed the *Onrust,* meaning "restless." The little party set sail to the east in the spring of 1614. After tediously poking along the Connecticut coastline and looking into every cove and inlet, the *Onrust* came to a wide river that was quite shallow at the mouth. Passing over a sandbar and fighting against the current, Captain Block sailed upstream. The tiny vessel passed thick forests that came down to the shoreline and then, after about forty miles, a grassy meadow with cornfields and an Indian settlement which, it was learned later, bore the unmelodious name of Suckiaug.

Block and company went a few miles further until they were stopped by rapids. Then they dined with some of the Indians (who, charmingly, called themselves Podunks), learned that furs abounded in the area, and sailed away contented. They had claimed everything in sight for the Netherlands and named the river the *Voyrest* ("fresh"). Within a few years the Dutch erected a fortified trading post, called the "House of Good Hope," at Suckiaug. However, it wasn't long until English Puritans from the Massachusetts Bay Colony pushed into the region, forcing the Dutch to leave. The resentful Dutch called the intruders *Jankes* (pronounced YAHN-kees), a colloquism for thieves or robbers.

Today, Adriaen Block is remembered by little except Block Island, off the coast of Rhode Island. The river he called the Voyrest is known instead by its Indian name in modern dress, the Connecticut. And Suckiaug and the House of Good Hope have been transformed from an Indian meadow with a Dutch trading post into something bigger. Today, Suckiaug is the capital of Connecticut, the city known as Hartford.

The Sweet Singer of Weltschmerz

When I was a schoolboy stymied by writer's block, my father always had a cure. He'd remind me that we had a long-ago ancestor named Nathan Lanesford Foster *who had actually published a book.* With genes like that, he said, how could I fail?

The ploy worked every time. Our ancestor with the impressive three-barreled name uncorked so many of my writer's blocks that he assumed mythic proportions. And yet I didn't know my father actually owned Nathan Lanesford Foster's sole book until Dad died and a copy turned up among his effects. It didn't take long to figure out why he had never shown it to me.

Entitled *The Last of His Kind*, it is a collection of maudlin poems written in no recognizable meter. It is gut-wrenchingly awful stuff, a merciless landscape of weeping widows of sailors lost at sea, children cut down at an

Lydia Sigourney, the "Sweet Singer of Hartford"

early age by illness or accident (their playthings left where they dropped them), wee babes whose eyes had been closed forever, sole survivors of family lines who were "the last of their kind," and legions of the elderly chewing their cuds while contemplating the Great Beyond. It has the tinkly vacuity of a funeral dirge by Lawrence Welk.

The Last of His Kind had been published in Hartford in the mid-1800s. This was no coincidence. Living in Hartford then was a human gusher of poetic misery and moral instruction named Lydia Huntley Sigourney. Mrs. Sigourney was as famous in her time as Danielle Steele is in ours, and for about the same reason: an ability to churn out an endless stream of pap that is intellectually undemanding but which satisfies a certain hunger. Nathan Lanesford Foster, whose other careers had included the law and schoolteaching to no great effect, was simply trying to duplicate the lady's success. He failed at that, too, but, ultimately, so did Mrs. Sigourney. Today, almost no one remembers "The Sweet Singer of Hartford," as she was fondly called, not even the thousands who travel downtown Hartford's Sigourney Street daily.

Born in Norwich, Connecticut, in 1791, Lydia Huntley was the daughter of a gardener for a well-off widow named Lathrop. Madam Lathrop and Lydia's mother introduced the girl to the Romantic movement in literature. Romantics were especially prone to melancholy, a tendency known by the German term *Weltschmerz*, signifying "a mood of sentimental sadness." The Romantics—Lord Byron, Keats, Shelley, and other pale young men—drew so shamelessly on this that a wag said of one such that he "should not be read, but inhaled through a gas pipe."

Lydia was beside Mrs. Lathrop's deathbed to the very end. Then, thanks to the late widow's connections to Hartford society, that city's distinguished Wadsworth family took in the girl. Tiny and pretty, Lydia caught the eye of old Daniel Wadsworth, who personally edited, then paid for publication in 1815 of Lydia's first book, a collection of schoolroom lessons and other essays titled *Moral Pieces*. The 267-page volume was only one of more than fifty she would publish in the next half century and it contained the ingredients that would become her hallmarks: formulaic morality and cloying sentiment in which death played the leading role.

On her way to teach school each morning, young Lydia found herself passing a recent widower named Charles Sigourney. Mr. Sigourney was thirteen years older than Lydia, a father of three, and less than handsome—his piercing eyes, pointed nose, and thin, tight lips gave him "a peculiar birdlike look," according to one biographer—but right away Lydia saw something that made her heart beat faster: a mournful expression marked by "deep-set and most expressive black eyes [that] spoke unutterable things." Waves of *Weltschmerz* swept over Lydia. In reality, Mr. Sigourney was fussy, unromantic, and fond of geometry, but he was also a prosperous hardware merchant and banker of old New England stock—a good catch, by the standards of the time. And the Wadsworths strongly urged the union.

In June, 1819, Lydia Huntley became Mrs. Sigourney and the next year Mr. Sigourney built the family an elaborate house. To Hartford society, it seemed as if a girl with humble origins had made a splendid marriage—but things were not what they seemed. Not only was he a very dull stick indeed, the prissy Charles thought writing for pay an unsuitable occupation for his wife. For a while, Lydia had to slip work into print without his permission, publishing anonymously and routing proof sheets through confidantes. Then it turned out that Mr. Sigourney was not as wealthy as had been thought nor in a position to withstand business reverses in the early 1830s. The Sigourneys were forced to give up their fine house. Charles swallowed hard and faced the facts: Lydia was going to have to start bringing home the bacon.

That she did. Lydia's *Letters to a Young Lady, By a Young Lady,* first published in 1833, sold amazingly well. An appetite for books and periodicals had arisen in America and Mrs. Sigourney stood ready to feed it. She issued no fewer than six books in 1833 alone: the *Letters* (which contained Mrs. Sigourney's pious moralizing to her own sex), plus an illustrated history of ancient lands, an obituary book, a romance, a report on an association for orphan girls, and a book for children, *How to Be Happy.* ("Being good and obedient" was the key, wrote Mrs. Sigourney. Parents bought the book.)

Almost every year another vaporous book flowed from Mrs. Sigourney's pen and sold to an eager audience. She could write a book in as few as ten days. But it was all hackwork: her moralizing was as tiresome as a dentist's drill and her sentiments were—well, *sentimental.* When it came to imagery, she was a champion recycler: visions of dying children whispering their last thoughts, weeping mothers at the graveside, silver-haired senior citizens facing Eternity with dignity, and flights of angels spiriting away the deceased—all appeared over and over again. The death of little ones especially fired Mrs. Sigourney's powers of doggerel:

> Call thy young children
>   In from their play,
> Cover their faces up,
>   Lead them away;
> Methinks, my enfeebled heart
>   Wilder'd and lone,
> Dreadeth the *going*
>   More than the *gone.*

After plowing through many of her books, one modern scholar said *he* felt "wilder'd and lone," forced to agree that "posterity had judged fairly in denying her claim" to lasting fame. Nonetheless, Lydia Huntley Sigourney was not unimportant. Not only was she was a striking example of a gritty woman succeeding in a chauvinistic age, she also brought both comfort and entertainment to millions, giving voice (as Hallmark cards do now) to those who lacked it. Today, Lydia Huntley Sigourney might only test the gag reflexes of the literati, but she still merits serious attention from those dump pickers of academe, the professors of popular culture.

One of Mrs. Sigourney's favorite forms was the memorial poem. The deaths of friends, acquaintances, or even strangers who had shown noteworthy qualities all set Mrs. Sigourney's pen to work composing valedictories. The certainty with which her sugary tribute followed the passing of any prominent person caused one wit to observe that she had added a new terror to death.

In her last years Mrs. Sigourney's popularity declined, her income dwindled, and death, about which she had written so often, began to stalk her own family. Of her two children, her only son, Andrew, was a strangely precise and taciturn child who became something of an enigma as an adult. In 1850 he died at home of consumption and in his honor his mother published *The Faded Hope*, one of her many lengthy obituary volumes. Four years later, husband Charles Sigourney also died. It had been a marriage with little joy in it. No ray of sunshine to begin with, Charles had soured along with his business prospects, drying up and drifting into a dusty corner of his wife's life.

It is a sad irony that a woman who spent her life writing about matters of the heart enjoyed so little of the romantic. "My own life . . . is little varied by incident, and has no materials for romance," she wrote in her autobiography shortly before her death in 1865. Of all the people she knew, there was only one important person for whom Lydia Huntley Sigourney never composed an obituary tribute: her late husband, Charles Sigourney.

Home Port for Mark Twain

There may be, here and there in North America, people who haven't seen the actor Hal Holbrook in his signature shtick, *Mark Twain Tonight!* but there can't be very many. After all, Holbrook has been taking his one-man production on the road for more than forty years, making it one of the longest-running shows in American history. It opened on Broadway in 1954, CBS presented it as a television special in 1967, and a video version is on the market now. Holbrook's impersonation of Mark Twain on the lecture circuit has been offered more times over more years and been seen by far more people than the original, concocted by a Hartford resident named Samuel Clemens, ever was.

Holbrook is simply the best known and most honored stand-in for the

A jaunty Mark Twain and his family at home in Hartford

famous author, for there is a thriving Mark Twain industry, with impersonators from Maine to California working stages and schoolrooms. That
impersonations of Mark Twain can still attract enthusiastic audiences nearly
a century after his death testifies to the genius of this uniquely American
writer, whose wit seems timeless. (His observation in 1868 that congressmen are "the only distinctly native American criminal class" could have
been uttered yesterday.)

Clemens is an authentic giant—many would say *the* giant—of Ameri-
can literature. His picaresque novel *Huckleberry Finn* is arguably the Great
American Novel, while many of his other works, such as *Tom Sawyer* and
Life on the Mississippi, are still widely read and enjoyed. Often set along the
Mississippi River, many of Twain's books actually were written only a few
miles from the Connecticut River. They were created in the huge house
adorned with balconies, turrets, and chimneys that still stands at 351
Farmington Avenue, a house that Twain biographer Justin Kaplan has called
"part steamboat, part medieval stronghold, and part cuckoo clock." From
1874 to 1891 this was Twain's showpiece, workplace, and family nest. But
in the end the house betrayed him.

Born in Missouri in 1835, young Sam Clemens had knocked around as
a journeyman printer, riverboat pilot, soldier, and prospector before finding a congenial niche as a newspaper correspondent. On a cruise ship to

The Mark Twain House, which helped ruin its owner

the Middle East in 1868 he saw a miniature portrait of a fine-featured young woman carried by her brother, Charles Langdon of Elmira, New York. Some say Clemens fell in love with the picture, and perhaps he did. Later that year he met the young lady in person while her family was visiting New York City. He was enthralled. Olivia Langdon, called "Livy," was twenty-two years old, "sweet and timid and lovely," endowed with angelic calmness (except when it thundered). She had dark eyes and a cameo-shaped face framed with black hair drawn smooth over her forehead.

The day after meeting her for the first time, Clemens called on Livy at a New Year's reception in the city, staying thirteen hours and nearly wearing out his welcome. When the Langdons returned to Elmira, where Livy's father, Jervis Langdon, was a wealthy coal merchant, they invited Clemens to visit them. After scarcely two weeks as a house guest, he proposed to Livy. She refused, so he left Elmira to begin a campaign of moral regeneration that would meet her high standards. He idealized her as "as a visiting *Spirit* from the upper air, *not* a creature of common human clay." Livy allowed him a brief visit a few weeks later, which (he said) he cunningly prolonged by feigning injuries after a fall from a carriage. By November Livy's defenses had crumbled and she was returning his affections. At Thanksgiving she accepted Sam's proposal of marriage, subject to her parents' approval.

Full of Protestant high purpose, the Langdons did not know what to make of the raffish Clemens, by now a well-known humor writer and lecturer, but also a profane man of the world, fond of cigars and hard drink, and ten years older than Livy. It was as if George Carlin appeared on your doorstep, bouquet in hand for your wide-eyed daughter. Mrs. Langdon insisted Clemens furnish a list of references. From carelessness or perversity, Clemens gave her only people who had nothing good to say for him. "Would fill a drunkard's grave" was a typical response. "Haven't you a friend in the world?" the bemused Jervis Langdon said to Clemens, who replied, "Apparently not." Langdon said, "I'll be your friend myself. Take the girl. I know you better than they do."

Samuel Clemens and Olivia Langdon were wed in the Langdon parlor in Elmira on Wednesday, February 2, 1870. Then they went to Buffalo, where Sam was stunned to find that his father-in-law had secretly purchased a fine house as a wedding present. While employed at the *Buffalo Express*, the new bridegroom turned down lecture invitations, saying, "Am just married and don't take an interest in anything out of doors." Within a year, Jervis died and in 1871 Mr. and Mrs. Samuel Clemens moved to Hartford.

Hartford had caught Sam's eye in 1868 on his first visit to meet a prospective publisher for *The Innocents Abroad* (which appeared in 1869 and was a tremendous success). In those days Hartford was a pleasant city of about fifty thousand, made prosperous by its insurance industry. The young family—now including one son, Langdon—moved to a rented house at Nook Farm, an exclusive enclave of the wealthy and prominent on the western edge of the city. Soon, the Clemenses had engaged a prominent New York architect to design the couple's dream house at 351 Farmington Avenue in Nook Farm. In September 1874 they moved into their new home, which had an aging Harriet Beecher Stowe as a next-door neighbor.

The three-story house was immense, with nineteen rooms and five bathrooms and a host of remarkable features, including a fireplace arranged with windows so Clemens could watch snowflakes falling over the fire. In this home the Clemens family life was centered for the next several years, amidst a whirlwind of the author's business and social visitors. "Familiarity breeds contempt and children," Clemens once said, a statement that, for him, was only half true. Little Langdon Clemens died in 1872, but daughter Olivia Susan ("Susy") was born the same year, with daughters Clara ("Bay") arriving in 1874 and Jean in 1880. The Clemens children's awe of their famous, talented father was mixed with a dread of (and later, amusement at) his explosive temper. Daughter Susy wrote, "I never saw a man with so much variety of feeling as papa has." As he was with Livy, Sam was devoted to his children, showering them with presents and entertainment.

"He does tell perfectly delightful stories," Susy wrote of her father. "Clara and I used to sit on each arm of his chair and listen while he told us stories about the pictures on the wall." The children would also bring their father magazine pictures and insist he create a story incorporating, accurately and with imagination, every detail of a picture. If the children judged that the storyteller had made a mistake, they would insist he start all over again. Sometimes Livy would have to rescue her husband from the children by pretending he had a caller.

At 351 Farmington Avenue, Clemens, writing as Mark Twain, wrote or finished a number of his best-known books, including *The Gilded Age* (with Charles Dudley Warner), *The Adventures of Tom Sawyer*, *Life on the Mississippi*, and *The Adventures of Huckleberry Finn*. Clemens would write out his manuscripts by hand, then turned them over to the high-minded Livy to be "expergated," as daughter Susy put it.

By the early 1880s the author had attained the peak of his creative and entrepreneurial success, but in 1885 he made a remark: "Our faces are toward the sunset," he told Livy. It was eerily prescient. He had started a publishing business, successfully issuing Ulysses S. Grant's memoirs, but the company began slip in the late 1880s. Clemens's investments in numerous inventions, such as a typesetter, did more than slip; they failed. The huge house at 351 Farmington Avenue, attractive to an endless stream of guests who had to be expensively entertained, consumed enormous amounts of money.

With expenses outstripping even the famous author's large income, "Mark Twain" went bankrupt. In 1891 the Clemenses were forced to move to Europe in an effort to economize and separate the author from the distractions which were draining his creative energies. "Mark Twain" paid off his debts by 1898, but his powers of authorship continued to decline, burdened by personal tragedy. In 1896, while her family was still in Europe, Susy returned alone to Connecticut, where she contracted meningitis. She spent her last two weeks wandering her own home in a stupor. Finding a dress of her mother's, she kissed it and wept, imagining that Livy had died. Susy died blind and in a coma while her family was rushing to her but still at sea.

So Hartford became "the city of heartbreak" for the Clemens family and they realized they could not live there anymore. Instead, they moved to New York and eventually the Hartford house was sold. Then, in 1902, Livy slipped into her last illness. Ironically, her doctors decided Sam was the chief cause of the nervous states accompanying her symptoms and forbade him entrance to her sickroom. He wrote her playful, loving notes, sometimes using a private code to express his devotion: "Sozodont and sozodont and sal ammoniac synchronously pax vobiscum." On the doctors' advice he took her to Italy, where he was restricted to two short visits a day. The Clemens maid, Katy Leary, said, "He broke the rules pretty often and he'd slip in sometimes . . . just for a glimpse of her. She'd put her arms around his neck the first thing, and he'd hold her soft, and give her one of those tender kisses. . . . It was a great love, I tell you. It was a love that was more than earthly love—it was heavenly."

It was not enough, however, for after seven months in Italy Livy died, on June 4, 1904. As she lay on her deathbed, Sam was "full of remorse for things done and said in the thirty-four years of married life that hurt Livy's heart." He returned to Connecticut, built a house in Redding, and died there on April 21, 1910. Both he and his wife were laid out in the same parlor in Elmira, New York, where they had been married.

In the heyday of "Mark Twain," the author had spoken of the house at 351 Farmington Avenue with a remarkable affection: "To us, our house was not an unsentient matter—it had a heart, and a soul, and eyes to see us with; and approvals, and solicitudes, and deep sympathies; it was of us, and we were in its confidence, and lived in its grace and in the peace of its benediction. We never came home from an absence that its face did not light up and its eloquence welcome—and we could not enter it unmoved."

And yet the house ate Sam Clemens alive, consuming vast amounts of money for its upkeep, remodeling (by Louis Comfort Tiffany's firm), hospitality to myriad numbers of guests, and staffing (six or more servants had to be employed, including, at one time, a wet-nurse who secretly consumed every alcoholic drink and cigar she could find in the house, meaning that Clara Clemens was raised on milk punch). The house was not the only threat to the Clemens economy, but somehow it was the most insidious, draining resources while seeming to offer comfort.

The Mark Twain whom Samuel Clemens created was an enormously complicated man, full of wit and ambition and pride and ideas, both bizarre and wonderful, and so was the house. Its many rooms, lavish decoration, ingenious features, and remarkable decorations, balconies, chimneys, veranda, and windows, all were created in the image of one man and reflected the way he thought.

Today the house is a popular museum, host around the year to school-children, awestruck tourists, and Twain scholars. It is grandiose, playful, Byzantine, both welcoming and a little intimidating, humorous and sad, just like its creator. When you visit 351 Farmington Avenue in Hartford that you are not just visiting a famous house. You are looking at the mind of Mark Twain.

The Two Lives of a Poet

In no way did Wallace Stevens sound, behave, or look like a poet. Instead, he looked like a burly detective in plainclothes with an expression hinting he'd just as soon punch you out as take you in. In fact, Stevens once did get into a punching match that could have earned him a footnote in American literary history all by itself. But Stevens is more than a footnote:

A most unhappy couple: Wallace and Elsie Stevens

he can be called one of the five or six "big deals" of modern American poetry (along with Ezra Pound, T.S. Eliot, William Carlos Williams, Robert Frost, and perhaps e.e. cummings).

Stevens, who won a Pulitzer Prize, two National Book Awards, and a fistful of honorary degrees, has been called Hartford's "most renowned twentieth-century artist," even though he has never achieved the mass appeal of a Frost. Influenced by Surrealist, Cubist, and Abstract painters, his playful, elaborate poetry with its "aggressive, art-for-art's sakishness" (as one reviewer put it) provokes endless analysis and debate by scholars, but on one thing most observers agree: Wallace Stevens was not a nice guy.

Which explains why a group of enthusiasts, formed after his death in 1955, call themselves "The Hartford Friends and Enemies of Wallace Stevens." Each fall the Friends and Enemies sponsors a birthday bash in the great man's honor. Champagne, hors d'oeuvres, and a birthday cake are served and a distinguished man or woman of letters gives a little speech. Stevens, who could be aggressively antisocial, probably would have boycotted the whole thing.

This curious man is a fascinating example of how two different people can live in one body. Stevens was a poet by night, portraying himself as something of an aesthete and a dandy, a man incredibly sensitive to the world around him, one who described it with sensuous words woven into elaborate poetic structures. From 9 a.m. to 4:30 p.m. he was something else entirely. His day job was as a hardheaded lawyer and insurance company vice president. If Stevens were alive today, I can imagine him working for an HMO, defending the company's bottom line against the chronically ill.

Most of Stevens's fellow workers didn't like him. He was aloof, brusque, sometimes deliberately rude, and intimidating in physical size (a husky six-foot-three). "He was not a beloved figure, to put it mildly," one company official told a Connecticut writer searching for traces of Stevens. (Few such traces remain. A company vice president occupying what had been Stevens's office was surprised to learn that it had been the poet's.) Another company official, who had worked with Stevens, was quoted as saying, "I was one of the few in the company who could stand him, and I wanted to knock his block off half the time."

Stevens was born in 1879 in Reading, Pennsylvania, son of a lawyer and a former schoolteacher. He attended, but did not graduate from, Harvard, where he wrote prose and poetry for student publications. Then he moved to New York City where he worked briefly as a reporter before going to law school. Stevens was admitted to the New York bar in 1904. In 1909 he married Elsie Kachel, also from Reading and "the prettiest girl in town." After a series of lackluster law jobs he joined the home staff of the Hartford Accident and Indemnity Company and moved to Connecticut in 1916.

By 1934 Stevens was a vice president of the company, heading the department that settled claims against the performance, or surety, bonds the company sold to guarantee satisfactory completion of projects such as construction jobs. Each day he plowed through a pile of case folders with a stack of law books at his side. It was tough work, an associate recalled: "To be a successful surety-claims attorney you have to be highly practical, realistic; you have to watch a dollar because you [can] throw away money handling surety claims like nobody's business." Stevens was "pretty successful," the associate recalled, and was recognized for many years as "the dean of surety-claims men in the whole country."

Through all this Wallace continued to write poetry. He composed "The Little June Book," a collection of handwritten poems for Elsie before they were married, and in 1914 published eight poems in a little magazine, his first work to see print since college. In 1923 his first volume of poetry, *Harmonium*, was issued to little notice. Gradually, however, he began to attract attention. By his death in 1955 he had published a number of books of poetry and received, among other awards, the Bollingen Prize in Poetry, two National Book Awards, a Pulitzer, and honorary degrees from Bard, Harvard, Mount Holyoke, Columbia, and Yale.

Stevens, who called himself "the hermit of poetry," rarely invited anyone to his home and had little contact with other writers. Asked if he would meet with a prominent intellectual, Archibald MacLeish, he refused, saying "Tell him when he gets a reputation, I'll be glad to see him." He turned other writers away with a blunt, "No." Particularly as a younger man, however, Stevens did not entirely forego social contact, especially if it involved rowdy drinking. On one such occasion he was at a cocktail party in the Florida Keys when he spoke badly of Ernest Hemingway, who was in the Keys at the time. Stevens left the party boasting he could flatten Hemingway with one blow, but soon encountered the novelist himself, and punches were exchanged. Hemingway knocked down Stevens several times, while Stevens was able to land only one blow on Papa's jaw, breaking his own hand in the process.

Stevens liked to say he kept his insurance work and his poetry separate, but they bordered each other and sometimes overlapped. Stevens preferred to walk two miles each way to and from work every day, using the time to compose poetry in his head, occasionally jotting down notes which he would ask his secretary to type. Sometimes he would ask an assistant to look up a word for him in a library dictionary. On lunch hours and weekends Stevens, who never learned to drive, took other long walks, perhaps venturing to the Connecticut River, which he called "The River of Rivers in Connecticut":

> There is a great river this side of Stygia
> Before one comes to the first black cataracts
> And trees that lack the intelligence of trees.
> . . . .
>
> Space-filled, reflecting the seasons, the folk-lore
> Of each of the senses; call it, again and again,
> The river that flows nowhere, like a sea.

Stevens is often described as one of the most important twentieth-century poets, but also one of the most difficult to understand. Perhaps that explains why his poetry seems to be more popular with scholars than the public, and why even the critics did not initially greet his work with enthusiasm. In a review of *Harmonium*, written after a second edition appeared in 1931, *New York Times* poetry critic Percy Hutchinson called Stevens's work "remarkable" for its rhythms and tonality, but ultimately just a clever "stunt" that "cannot endure," arguing, "From one end of the book to the other there is not an idea that can vitally affect the mind, there is not a word that can arouse emotion. The volume is a glittering edifice of icicles. Brilliant as the moon, the book is equally dead. . . . Wallace Stevens is a martyr to a lost cause."

Time and other critics have long since proven Hutchinson wrong, but somehow the image of the icicle remains. For a man so sensitive to the world that he courted it with poetry, he was remarkably tone-deaf, even obdurate in his personal life and especially his marriage. Ivan Daugherty, a bond lawyer who called himself an "intimate" of Stevens (but not a friend, for "Stevens had no friends," he said) told of a troubling incident. Stevens came into the office one day, told of a fight in which his wife had thrown something at him, and said, "I just don't understand women. What should I do?" Daugherty advised him to send Elsie roses, throw his arms around her, and tell her he loved her. "What the hell for?" replied Stevens, finally saying, "All right, I'll do it." Later Stevens reported, "Gee, I don't understand that, but it worked." Daugherty was dismayed that this "tremendously sensitive man" could be so insensitive to his wife.

Elsie Kachel Stevens was a pretty but high-strung woman, not intellectual and not sure of herself in social situations. She made clear that she didn't like her husband's poetry, preferring Longfellow and short stories in ladies' magazines. The romance of Wallace and Elsie's youth faded away and the marriage became what one biographer called "an unloving emptiness that not even the eventual birth of a child could revive." Born in 1924, the Stevens's only child, Holly Bright, could not have had a happy childhood, for as an adult her earliest memory was of wanting to run away from home. She remembered her mother flitting through their huge and sumptuous house at 118 Waverly Terrace, Hartford, nervously raising and lowering window shades. Elsie was as solitary and inhospitable as her husband. "I never saw the inside of that house," one of Stevens's fellow workers remarked.

Toward the end of his life, Wallace and Elsie Stevens were living in separate areas of the house, not even speaking to each other. Dreading retirement, Stevens continued working at the insurance business into his seventies. By then, he was reaching the peak of his literary fame: in 1954 Alfred A. Knopf published *The Collected Poems of Wallace Stevens* and Harvard University offered him a year's appointment (which he turned down). Early in 1955 he received the National Book Award in Poetry for the second time, the Pulitzer Prize, and two honorary doctorates. And then he was diagnosed with stomach cancer.

Surgery at St. Francis Hospital in Hartford in April 1955 revealed the cancer could not be removed, although he could be made more comfortable. After brief intervals at home, during which he attempted to go to the office despite his weakness, he went back to St. Francis Hospital for his last days.

There an acquaintance was amazed find him "completely cherubic. He was a jolly Santa Claus to the nurses.... [I]t was a transformation.... [H]e was a changed person—this time for the better.... [I]nstead of being a sad or strained time, it was light and tripping and gay. . . . I came back [to the insurance company's office] and told Wilson Jainsen. He said, 'Unless they told me he had a heart attack, I never would have known he had a heart.'"

Unbeknownst to his wife and almost everyone else, Wallace had converted to Catholicism on his deathbed, the chaplain at the Roman Catholic hospital having visited him a number of times at his request. Stevens told the chaplain of "a certain emptiness" in his life and asked many questions, particularly about the Catholic view of Hell. Perhaps the priest told him that Hell was a place without love. Finally, Stevens consented to be baptized, saying; "Now I am in the fold."

Stevens died three months to the day after he received the Pulitzer Prize. He had spent an entire lifetime creating glittering icicles of poetry and he died having no close friends at work or in the city. He had not traveled in writers' circles and knew hardly any other writers by their first names. He did not get along with his parents or his siblings. He didn't have a happy marriage or even a spouse who was impressed by his poetry. His relationship with his daughter was strained for most of his life. Despite his prominence in business and literature his funeral was sparsely attended, with few of his fellow workers bothering to come.

"He said if he got well, we would talk a lot more and if not—he would see me in heaven," the priest later wrote. Wallace Stevens died on August 2, 1955, seemingly content and "a changed person."

Perhaps he had seen enough of Hell.

Insurance Capital of the World

In 1868, Mark Twain cast a keen visitor's eye on the city of Hartford, and found it good. "Of all the beautiful towns it has been my fortune to see this is the chief. . . . You do not know what beauty is if you have not been here." He should see it now.

Twain's nineteenth-century Hartford was a literary capital, populated by publishers and authors. Conveniently located halfway between Boston and New York City, Hartford's prosperity graced it with amenities. It had long traditions of both independence and literary interests, too. One of Hartford's founders was Rev. Thomas Hooker, who led an entire congregation there overland in 1636 to escape the stern Puritan oligarchy of the Massachusetts Bay Colony. Later, the Connecticut Colony, which had enjoyed a more liberal charter than its sisters, showed its defiance of a presumptive governor, Sir Edmund Andros, by hiding its charter in an old oak tree. The Charter Oak became an icon for the colony and the state. And after the Revolution the "Hartford Wits," a circle of the intelligentsia, made Hartford something of an intellectual hotbed for the new nation.

Well into the twentieth century Hartford was admired as shining city upon a hill, its downtown offering a glittering array of stores (capped by the glamorous G. Fox & Co.). Its powerful radio station, WTIC, "the voice of the Travelers Insurance Company," beamed its signal throughout southern New England. I remember my mother speaking of Hartford with awe, as if it were the mecca for power shoppers. But in the second half of the century the city went into free-fall, thanks to some of the usual suspects: the lure of the suburbs, white flight, industrial exodus, mismanaged government, gutless politicians (a term Mark Twain would call a redundancy), and radical individualism at the expense of community-mindedness.

Hartford is the southern anchor of the Three Sad Cities of central New England, Springfield and Holyoke, both in Massachusetts, being the other two. In what is, per capita, one of the wealthiest states in the nation, Hartford is one of the poorest cities. City population has been falling for decades. Standardized test scores in its schools have long ranked among the lowest in the state, while its crime rate is among the highest. Its police department was given a failing grade by an outside evaluator. The downtown retail area is a ghost of its former self, G. Fox and all the other fine stores are gone, and crime haunts many neighborhoods. From time to time, law enforcement announces a "crackdown," meaning, apparently, a rush of arrests that should have been made before. (What do police do in between crackdowns? Rest? Knit? Plan the next crackdown?)

Meanwhile, the city still boasts that it is the "Insurance Capital of the Nation." And sure enough, the shining towers and temples of the insurance industry shelter the executives and actuaries who make book on the nation's mortality and morbidity during the day, then flee to the suburbs at night, leaving the city's streets to the pushers and shooters. That's life in Suckiaug.

Could even Lydia Sigourney keep up with all the obituaries that have to be written here? Would Mark Twain storm and rage at the politicians and other leaders who have failed this city? And would Wallace Stevens, the self-styled "poet of the earth" who saw *things* so much more vividly than the rest of us, look at the stained city of Hartford and say, once again:

> Is the spot on the floor, there, wine or blood
> And whichever it may be, is it mine?

The Rough Guide to New England, a kind of smart-mouthed travel advisor, calls Hartford "an unattractive and largely dull city." It's true that the place has been decaying for years, but it still has some wonderful attractions. Sigourney Street is not one of them. The most prominent reminder of Lydia Huntley Sigourney in Hartford, it runs from Capitol Avenue to Albany Avenue. Ask any hundred people walking the street who it's named for and fewer than one will know. On the other hand, most will know about the Mark Twain House, a National Historic Landmark. It is one of the city's major attractions and open all year (860-247-0998; www.MarkTwainHouse.org). The Harriet Beecher Stowe house next door is also open to the public. The Wallace Stevens house at 118 Waverley Terrace isn't open but a map that traces his daily two-mile walk from home to office at the Hartford Insurance Group, 690 Asylum Avenue, is on the Web at www.wesleyan.edu/wstevens/Wallywalk.html. For more about the poet himself, go to www.wesleyan.edu/wstevens. Though not a monument to our writers, the Wadsworth Atheneum (600 Main Street) is the nation's oldest public art museum (founded in 1842), and one of the best, with works from Rubens to Renoir. Fine examples of early American furniture are here, too (860-278-2670; www.wadsworthatheneum.org).

The People of Cautanowit

Throughout New England, thousands of human remains lie in shallow graves, laid out in a northeast-southwest line, the head to the southwest, the face to where the sun rises in the east. The heads are to the southwest because that's where the great house of the god Cautanowit was thought to be, far away, and it was there that deserving Algonquin Indians went to dwell after they died. Liars, thieves, and other miscreants did not go there, but were condemned to wander forever.

Those of us who think that history began in the Connecticut River Valley when the Puritans arrived should think again. At most, we Europeans can trace back our ancestry in these parts less than four hundred years and a dozen or so generations. But other people have been here for ten or twelve thousand years. Historians confuse us by calling the time before Europeans arrived "prehistory," as if everything that happened before them isn't history.

But of course there is history here and it is written on the New England landscape and life in a thousand ways. There are all those Indian generations mingled with the New England soil. Pipes, pots, spear and arrow points, and many other artifacts lie buried, too, although a few have been found and put in museums, where we can read them as messages from the past. So are baked beans, succotash, baked clams, and popcorn, foods the Indians gave us. Some of our modern highways follow the old Indian trails and farmers still work the fields and meadows where Indians grew corn and beans for centuries.

Most visible of all are the place names, such as that of the river itself, "Connecticut," the Indian term for "long tidal river." As you travel up the valley, you pass Mohegan. Occum. Poquonock. Agawam. Chicopee. Ascutney. Coos. All places where people lived before we arrived.

The first people here were the Paleo-Indians, small groups of hunters who roamed continually, using spears to hunt caribou and mammoth on the sparse, cold tundra left by the retreating glacier about twelve thousand years ago. As New England warmed and forests developed to shelter deer, rabbit, beaver, and turkey, the Archaic Period began, in which hunter-gatherers settled down in seasonal camps. About three thousand years ago the still more sedentary Woodland Period began, in which crops of corn, beans, and squash were raised and stored in semi-permanent camps.

Although the first Indian contacts with Europeans were generally friendly, they gradually soured and turned into a series of wars, with white settlers and Indians living in terror of each other. Indians repeatedly attacked white settlements, killing and taking captives; whites retaliated with a vengeance.

There is plenty of guilt and blame to go around, but, in my opinion, what really happened here is not as simple as the old racist hokum about the civilized Europeans having to tame the savages or the modern guilt trip about murderous whites brutalizing the noble children of nature. In reality, the arrival of the Europeans was only the latest reiteration of the old, grim story of one group of people in search of a better life pushing out another, and not always being nice about it. It's not a pretty picture, but it's history.

To some extent, we can redeem our own sins by how we treat the weak and the vulnerable among us today. We can honor the Indians by remembering their stories and adopting some of their reverence for nature. And, for the hundreds of generations of native peoples who passed by here for thousands of years, we can wish them safe journeys to the southwest and the House of Cautanowit.

Settlers viewed the Indians and their rituals as savage

CHAPTER SIX

SCANDAL, SORROW, AND CRACKER CRUMBS

From Springfield, Massachusetts, to Hartford, Connecticut, the river runs as straight and true as it does anywhere. Having wormed its way south through the Pioneer Valley to Springfield, it wiggles once and takes off for Hartford, turning only slightly as it sprints over the Enfield Rapids as though it were rushing to get through the in-betweenness of the two cities. Sometimes I feel that way myself.

I have deep roots here and still the region bothers me. It's not the fault of its pretty little towns, like Suffield, or the well-groomed, richly historical suburbs—Longmeadow, just south of Springfield, and Windsor, just north of Hartford. Those are handsome places, the kind where the doctors like to live. Nor am I bothered by the low-flying jetliners sliding down their glide paths to Bradley Field ("Hartford-Springfield" in airline lingo), ejecting their dazed, starved, and compacted passengers at central New England's major airport, right here in Windsor Locks.

What bothers me—with a fascination that keeps bringing me back—are certain stories of my ancestors and others and what they did here and what happened to them. There are stories of death and disgrace and loss in this place. Thankfully, there are stories of love and redemption as well, but they are all, the good and the bad, part of me.

The View from Mr. Parsons's Window

From his newspaper office in Thompsonville, a village in Enfield, Connecticut, Frederick P. Parsons had the perfect spot to keep tabs on things. Down around the corner from Mr. Parsons's *Thompsonville Press*, a weekly paper appearing each Thursday, was the mill town's principal hostelry, the Thompsonville Hotel. The clattering looms of the gigantic Hartford Carpet Company were just beyond the hotel, and then, farther west along Main Street and almost to the Connecticut River, was the train station where most of the town's visitors arrived and departed, north to Springfield or south to Hartford. Even without leaving his chair, Parsons could hear the chatter of gossip from William Mulligan's fine new furniture store, sniff the odors wafting from Maurice Sullivan's bakery, and cast an eye over the businesses across the street. One of these, in a small wooden building the size of a convenience store, was the R.D. and R.E. Spencer Banking Company.

So editor Parsons didn't have to go far to find news, most of it of the small-bore variety, although there was the occasional fatal collision between train and horse or the odd murder attempted by a thwarted lover. But

Annie and Rob Spencer: an anniversary with mixed memories

perhaps the most painful story Parsons had to report was the Thompsonville banking scandal of 1900, for it involved people he had known for a long time. Over a period of several months the *Press* documented the disgrace of two of the town's most prominent citizens: Roswell Doane Spencer, sixty-two, a well-known businessman, and his son, Robert Emmet Spencer, thirty-five, banker, town clerk and treasurer, and judge of probate. These people matter to me, too: Roswell D. Spencer was my great grandfather and his son, Robert E. Spencer, was my great uncle. My dad called him "Uncle Rob."

Roswell D. Spencer had moved upriver from East Haddam to Thompsonville in 1881 and bought a local general-merchandise emporium called "The North Store." He built it into the biggest and busiest general store in town in nine furious years of living by that old maxim, "Early to bed and early to rise, work like hell and advertise." Roswell D. Spencer was a hard-working, churchgoing citizen, the kind others trusted enough to pick for important town committees.

Son Robert was a little different. As a teenager he upset his parents by impulsively running away, later writing from Georgia that he and a companion were on what the *Press* called a "a boys' freak." On Rob's return, father put him to work in the North Store, hoping to turn him into a productive citizen. Then, in 1887, the elder Spencer opened the "R.D. and R.E. Spencer Banking Company" in a small building a few blocks from the North Store. Robert, only twenty-two, was appointed the bank's cashier— in effect, its manager—but it was the elder Spencer's name over the door that attracted the customers.

The Spencer bank's assets grew steadily as local merchants, fraternal societies, and carpet mill workers deposited their money, trusting Roswell D. Spencer to keep their money safe, for there was no such thing as government deposit insurance. Then, in 1889, the elder Spencer sold the North Store, forced to retire for reasons of health. The *Press* said the elder Spencer would devote time to the bank now and observed sagely, "Mr. Spencer has shown to the public in his life among them that he is a business man of honor." In reality, Roswell's health apparently left him no energy for the bank and young Rob was left to run it on his own. That was a mistake.

More than a decade passed quietly, the Spencer bank under Rob's direction confidently advertising its services every week in the *Press*. As a youngster Rob Spencer may have been a rascal, the kind of boy who loved to torment his older sister, Agnes, but as an adult he must have been the kind of sociable fellow that small-town folks enjoyed chatting with while doing their banking. In 1891 he married James Hope Bissland's sister Annie Bissland in Thompsonville, taking her out west on a long combined honeymoon and business trip, looking at investment opportunities for the bank. The young banker vaulted into political prominence, too, for he was elected town clerk and treasurer and became a judge of probate. It seemed as if the heedless youth of yesterday was on his way to the kind of public esteem enjoyed by his father.

On Tuesday, January 23, 1900, however, editor Parsons looked out the *Press* office window to see little knots of people talking worriedly about a sign that had appeared that morning on the door of the Spencer bank. The bank had closed the previous Saturday evening as usual but—with no explanation—had not re-opened on Monday, causing some anxious talk. Confirming the worst rumors that had been swirling around town, the sign said, "Proceedings will to-day be instituted in United States bankruptcy."

Reassuring noises were quickly made by the *Press*, which extolled the integrity of the Spencers and reported that Rob was promising that all depositors would be made whole. What came out in bankruptcy court in Hartford three weeks later was not so reassuring. Rob Spencer spent the day being grilled by attorney T.M. Maltbie, who had been hired by the bank's depositors. At first the calm and collected Spencer impressed the large audience favorably, but as Maltbie's questions became more pointed, the depositors' hopes sank. How much money was left to cover the tens of thousands depositors had given the bank? About $400. Where had the money gone? To invest in western lands which had since become worthless. How much had the land been assessed for? Rob didn't know. On what had he based his expectation that the western lands deserved his depositors' money? "Faith." How long had the bank been short of capital? Since about 1892 (when a national recession wiped out land values). How, then, had the bank stayed open? By using new deposits to cover withdrawals. Did Rob's father, whose name was over the door, keep watch on the bank? No, he paid "little attention" and "never asked any questions." Did the bank ever compute an annual balance to determine its exact condition? "No," replied Rob, "we had no idea."

The crowd was aghast. Finally, an exasperated depositor stood up and declared to Rob, "Well, you're a fine specimen to run a bank." Then the hearing was over, the good name of the Spencers shredded. So, too, were their fortunes. Father, described in the newspapers as "very broken down by this matter," said "all will be sacrificed" to repay the depositors, that "he would have to begin life anew and when he did it would be without a dollar." But something worse was yet to come. A few days after the bank closed, Rob Spencer was arrested and charged with forging a depositor's signature on a $1,500 withdrawal order to another bank. In June 1900 he pleaded guilty in criminal court and was sentenced to two years in Wethersfield State Prison.

Shamed, his fortune gone, my great grandfather moved back down the river, this time to the tiny village of Hadlyme. He obtained a mortgage to purchase a small general store and moved his diminished family into the tenement upstairs. Despite his health, he gave up retirement and was still working when he died ten years later. With Rob in prison, Annie Bissland Spencer and her small children had to leave their comfortable home and move into her widowed mother's small tenement in Thompsonville. Every day she had to face the people whose faith in her husband and father-in-law had been violated.

But Annie settled down to wait out the long months as Rob served his time. Then, after his release from Wethersfield, Rob and Annie began a peripatetic existence as if he was searching the country for the road to redemption. For a while he supervised the shirt factory in the Indiana State Prison in Michigan City. There was, weirdly, a venture in the South involving the watermelon business, and then a small grocery store in Denver. Later in life, Rob and Annie moved to the Washington, D.C., area to be near three of their daughters, maiden school teachers all.

I don't think my uncle was a bad man, just an inept one, a charming doofus, as it were. Perhaps it had something to do with his upbringing. When Rob was a child, the store business took most of his father's attention, while his otherworldly mother, Helen, let her oldest daughter carry on the chores of the household. Then, in 1885, Rob's fifteen-year-old brother Herbert was drowned in a boating accident on the Connecticut River. As grieving parents often do, Roswell and Helen may have turned to spoiling the remaining children. Firm guidance, not spoiling, was what Rob needed and never got.

But he got something else instead, something that shows how we can be saved by grace. Through the whole ugly mess in Thompsonville and the lean years after, Annie stuck with Rob. She waited for his release, then ran a store in Michigan City with the hope it would grow into something for him, even followed him south for the watermelon venture. By the norms of the day she could have divorced a convicted felon, but she did not, and by that commitment alone he was redeemed.

I have tried to imagine what life must have been like for Rob and Annie in the years leading up to the bankruptcy. For years he would have come home from the bank every evening, smiled and hugged his wife and children, and given no hint of the desperation rising in his chest. But after closing the bank for the last time that Saturday evening in January 1900, he must have come home to tell her everything. With the children in bed, Rob and Annie would have stayed up late that night, the whole sad story pouring out of Rob as Annie Bissland Spencer listened.

On Monday morning Rob got up, steeled his nerves, and went to Hartford to confess to the authorities that his bank had run out of money. At the bankruptcy hearing several weeks later reporters were struck by how calm Rob Spencer was under the relentless questioning. Sarcastically called a "fine specimen," he quietly replied, "That's all right." He was just as composed later when, surrounded by petty criminals in another court, he was sentenced to prison. I think I know why. Rob knew that, whatever else he had lost, he still had his family. Spilling out the whole sorry story to Annie that Saturday night, he must have learned that she loved him still and that they would ride it out—together.

Together to the end, Rob and Annie died within a few months of each other in 1946. Then their maiden daughters retired from teaching and moved from the Washington area to a seniors' community in California. A few years ago the last survivor shipped me a suitcase filled with family memorabilia. Out of it spilled a cache of photographs.

One is of Rob Spencer only a few years after the scandal. Arms stiffly at his side, he squints into the sun with an uncertain smile that seems to be searching for direction. He looks like a man for whom the past isn't past. But the picture I like best is very different. It shows Rob and Annie many years later on their golden wedding anniversary in 1941. Dressed in fine clothes, they are the picture of respectability, their days of shame well concealed, if not forgotten. Standing before a handsome fireplace, Rob appears relaxed, gazing forthrightly into the camera while Annie sits comfortably in an upholstered rocking chair and looks into the distance. His outstretched arm reaches down to her. At each end of the mantle are their wedding portraits, taken fifty years before. Older and wiser and surrounded by more than a dozen bouquets of flowers from well-wishers, Rob and Annie look like a couple who had settled down for the long haul.

Gone Crackers

At a certain Connecticut Valley boys' school years ago the seniors used to choose a classmate for the honorary title of "Class Load." That unkindness—since abolished, thank heavens—was awarded the boy who most annoyed the others, someone seen as a sort of Howard Cosell in training. Something like this, but even worse, occurred in 1823 when Sylvester Graham was dealt rough justice by his classmates at Amherst Academy in Amherst, Massachusetts.

Sylvester Graham, originator of the "Graham System"

Graham stood out at Amherst Academy (which no longer exists) not only because he was so much older than the other students, but also because he was so assertive and arrogant. His irritated classmates circulated a false report implicating Graham in a criminal assault and he was quickly expelled. He had been at the school for only one term.

There are reasons, of course, why people turn into pills, and Graham had more than his share. Born in 1794 in West Suffield, a village a few miles north of Hartford, he was the youngest of seventeen children his father had had by two wives. Father, a Yale graduate, clergyman, and physician, was seventy-two when Sylvester was born but didn't have the sense to make a will. When Dr. Graham died at seventy-four, his widow was left without resources to care for the seven children still at home. The stress drove her mad, so Sylvester spent his childhood and youth being bounced among neighbors and relatives.

Assertive he may have been, but by the time he reached Amherst Academy he was deeply depressed as well. His expulsion triggered a complete mental breakdown. For reasons unknown, Graham made his way to Little Compton, Rhode Island, where the two maiden daughters of a sea captain nursed him back to health. He married the older of the two in September 1824.

Even before entering Amherst Academy he had given a public lecture on the evils of drink, apparently because he didn't like the taste of the stuff and was weary of being pressured to imbibe. After recovering his health in Little Compton, he trained for the ministry but soon became an agent for a temperance society, preaching the evils of alcohol. His interests gradually expanded to all of human physiology, which may have appealed to him as a system of clear-cut punishments and rewards for the practices of daily living. Graham began preaching the importance of healthful habits.

A gifted orator, Sylvester Graham was a tub-thumper in the grand tradition of fire-and-brimstone evangelism, a true believer in his own words and, like so many evangelists, a man driven by self-righteous indignation. The times were right for Graham's brand of oratory: the Jacksonian era in which he lived was one of rapid social change, so people were looking for guidance and meaning in a confusing world. Interest in science was growing as well, and soon Graham's prescriptions for better health were attracting audiences. Through the 1830s he lectured up and down the Atlantic Coast, developing the "Graham System" for healthful living as he went along.

Many of Graham's ideas resonate with our own. He urged regular exercise, whole-wheat bread instead of white, and a diet that included plenty of pure drinking water, rough cereals, and fresh vegetables and fruits. He inspired our modern dry breakfast cereals, as well as Graham flour and Graham crackers. Graham had other ideas for better health, which to our ears sound harmless if sometimes quirky: home baking, cold showers, looser and lighter clothing, open bedroom windows, hard mattresses, and cheerfulness at meals. But it is his ideas about sex that cause a neck-snapping alert among moderns.

Simply put, Graham frowned on sexual activity of almost any kind. He believed that the excitement, the stimulation, the excess of energy required by sex were debilitating to the rest of the body. Graham's ideas were heavily influenced by Benjamin Rush, the pioneering Philadelphia physician and statesman, who believed artificial stimulation—such as alcohol—weakens the body.

Until the 1830s Americans were a good deal more open-minded about sex than we realize. Even the Puritans were not especially puritanical about sex and a popular manual published in numerous editions between 1766 and 1831 advised that sex "eases and lightens the body, clears the mind, comforts the head and senses, and expels melancholy." Sexual abstinence, it warned, could harm eyesight in men and even turn women's complexions green. But all this was turned on its head by Graham and others leading what has been called "The New Chastity of the 1830s."

Graham said that intense, persistent sexual desire was not natural but rather an "aching sensibility," like a toothache. Although he did not claim that all sexual desire was a diseased state, he did argue that the sexual organs were "in their natural state, entirely destitute of animal sensibility" and that truly healthy people could easily "subdue their sexual propensities" for several months in a row. Ideally, Graham believed, sex was best performed no more than once a month and, really, a life could very well be spent with no sexual activity at all. Even erotic thoughts should be avoided, Graham argued: "Lascivious day-dreams, AND AMOROUS REVERIES" (Graham was prone to shouting) can themselves lead to disease and death "without the actual exercise of the genital organs!"

Graham believed that diet had a great deal to do with provoking an excessive demand for sex, because (in his view) the reproductive apparatus was connected not only to the brain but the digestive system, each influencing the other. Be careful what you eat, the evangelist warned, for "all kinds of stimulating and heating substances, high-seasoned foods, rich dishes, the free use of flesh . . . increase the concupiscent excitability and sensibility of the genital organs." In other words, Graham would warn us, eat a pepperoni pizza and, ladies, look out.

Graham was a forceful speaker but hindered, one observer noted, by "combativeness, extreme cautiousness, excessive ideality, and more than full self-esteem." Bakers and butchers were so angered by his entreaties against commercial bread and meat eating that they rioted in some cities. Some observers dismissed him as a crackpot, and Ralph Waldo Emerson called him "the poet of bran and pumpkins." And yet Graham got attention. Thousands attended his lectures and bought his books, Graham houses were opened in several cities, and his ideas were much discussed, if frequently ridiculed.

Graham's ideas were a reaction to larger social changes occurring in Jacksonian America. While his ideas were always expressed in terms of health and human physiology, Graham was really resisting industrialization of food and the breakdown of family ties, just as some of us object to the spongy concoctions of Wonder Bread or the obliteration of family time by Nintendo. Graham's crusade, like so many others, had deeply personal roots in his unhappy childhood.

One wonders about the interior life of Sylvester Graham's own family, of which little is known. The Grahams' two children—Sarah, born 1828, and Henry, born 1833—are evidence that sexual union did occur in their parents' marriage, although the family was smaller than typical of the time. Graham, so deprived of family life as a child, found some nurture at his own hearthside, though not in the form he—and we—might have expected. It turns out that Mrs. Graham "adamantly opposed his strictures" (according to a biographer), constantly subjecting him to a "table luxuriously spread with forbidden food and drink." Graham admitted to friends that he often gave in to these temptations.

To what other urges he succumbed is unknown. One of his followers said after Graham's death that the prophet could "see the truth clearly, and yet not have the self-government to practice it." In such matters, of course, he joins a long line of demagogues and evangelists who did not practice what they preached.

Popular interest in Graham's ideas dwindled and Graham effectively retired in 1839, buying the first and only house he ever owned, in Northampton, Massachusetts. He thought he was a failure, not knowing that some of his ideas, such as the value of fresh air, exercise, fresh fruits and vegetables, and whole grains eventually would become gospel for millions of Americans. Racked by a sense of lost opportunities as well as guilt over his inability to resist the forbidden fruits of home and hearth, he became increasingly eccentric and misanthropic, his mental health crumbling like a Graham cracker. He wandered Northampton's streets in his bathrobe, mumbling to himself, composing bad poetry and bitter screeds. Sylvester Graham died in 1851. The prophet of health was only fifty-seven.

Tears for Old Man River

When I was a small boy on a Sunday drive with my parents we'd occasionally pass a mansion with white pillars in Enfield, Connecticut. "That's Paul Robeson's house," my father would say to my mother, and I would demand—not for the first time—"Who's Paul Robeson?"

"A singer and a Communist," was the only answer I ever got, but the tone told me that Robeson, whoever he was, deserved no further consideration. It was only years later that I began to understand that Paul Robeson is worthy of a great deal of consideration and that my father's dismissive tone masked a sad episode in modern American history. There's enough shame in this story for everyone involved.

Paul Robeson was born in 1898 in Princeton, New Jersey, son of an ex-slave. Later, the family moved to Somerville, New Jersey, where Paul entered the integrated local schools. In 1915 he won a four-year scholarship to Rutgers, which had enrolled only two African-American students before "Robey." He quickly turned into one of

Paul and Essie Robeson found Europe more congenial than their native America

the most outstanding students in Rutgers history. At six-feet-two and one hundred ninety pounds, Robeson made the football team, despite harassment by teammates. He went on to graduate with fifteen varsity letters in four sports. He also became the school's star orator, a standout singer, and one of only four students elected to Phi Beta Kappa in the junior year.

Next, Robeson went to Columbia University law school, earning his tuition by playing pro football. He was hired as the only black at a prominent law firm, but quit the firm—and the law—when a white secretary refused to take dictation "from a nigger." In the meantime, he had been performing as an actor, at first as an amateur in Harlem. Soon he was appearing in the commercial production of *All God's Chilluns Got Wings*. Robeson was an instant success. In 1922 alone he took the lead role in *The Emperor Jones*, performed his first concert, and appeared in his first film.

Although Robeson's theatrical takeoff was rocket-like, fireworks accompanied it. His appearance opposite a white woman in *All God's Chilluns Got Wings* provoked threats of rioting and bombs. On the road, he was denied service at restaurants and accommodation in hotels. Robeson's career kept climbing, however, as his deep, rich voice and commanding stage presence riveted audiences. He was called back for twelve ovations after *The Emperor Jones* was presented in London; his concert tours in Europe included command performances before royalty. Meaty roles in major productions, such as *Porgy and Bess*, *Showboat*, and *Othello*, came his way. In *Showboat* Robeson's singing of "Ol' Man River" caused a sensation. The song became his signature piece and his singing of it can still be heard today on compact disks. Robeson's talents came naturally, for he had no formal training in voice or dramatics. He had learned singing in the small black congregations led by his preacher father.

Robeson's sense of social injustice, always strong, was inflamed by his tours in Europe, where he met political action groups. He was invited to the Soviet Union by famed film director Sergei Eisenstein, was accorded a lavish welcome, and was astonished at the apparent lack of racism there. "Here, for the first time in my life . . . I walk in full human dignity," he said. It wasn't long before Robeson was an outspoken advocate of communism, a defender of the Soviet Union, and an opponent of Nazi Germany. But his primary concerns lay with racism: he refused to sing before segregated audiences, launched a campaign against lynching, and urged lowering of racial barriers wherever they stood. "The artist must elect to fight for freedom or for slavery . . . I have made my choice," he said in 1937.

In the Cold War that followed World War II, many former friends of communism withdrew their support. However, a stiff-necked Robeson refused to back down. During the McCarthy hearings, Robeson was grilled by a congressional committee, which asked sarcastically why he hadn't stayed in the Soviet Union. His answer was vintage Robeson: "Because my father was a slave, and my people died to build this country, and I am going to stay right here and have a part of it just like you. And no fascist-minded people will drive me from it. Is that clear?"

But to the American mind at the time, communism had the appeal of the plague and Robeson's popularity plummeted. Concert managers blacklisted him. Occasionally he made a tour of Europe or in the Soviet bloc, and now and then he was able to stage a concert in the United States, although riots led by hooligans were apt to follow. His last years were a round of medical problems, harassment by McCarthyite witch hunters, surveillance by the FBI, calumny by newspaper columnists, and criticism from fellow black leaders. Gradually he sank into obscurity, even in the black community. He suffered several breakdowns, became withdrawn and dependent on drugs, and died after a stroke in 1976.

If only Robeson's life had been relieved by one of the classic love stories so beloved by Hollywood. You know, the kind in which a rising star falls for a sweet, pretty girl, whom he cruelly ditches after he becomes famous. Then the star falls, but in Part Three he and his original companion meet by chance, she forgives him, and he is redeemed. Something like that.

The Paul Robeson story includes, more or less, Parts One and Two— but Part Three is more complicated. And yet there is something to be learned here, something about the way two people can need each other, hurt each other, suffer greatly, and yet still have something to give each other.

Seriously injured when he was playing pro football to earn his law school tuition, Robeson was taken to New York's Presbyterian Hospital. During a long convalescence there he met a beautiful young woman named Eslanda "Essie" Cardozo Goode, a Columbia chemistry graduate and pathology technician who came from distinguished black ancestry. The two had different temperaments: in Essie's words, he was "literary . . . artistic . . . genial, easily imposed upon," while she was "essentially and aggressively ambitious."

Mapping her campaign to win Paul, Essie arranged "chance" meetings with Paul and studied sports so she could impress him with her knowledge. When Paul became interested in other young women, she "resorted to the old game," as she called it, conspicuously dating another man. Paul finally succumbed, appearing on her doorstep one morning of August 1921 to tell her that he loved her and wanted to marry her that day. Essie did not let the opportunity slip away. By nightfall a town clerk in Portchester, New York, had performed the ceremony.

Having landed the man she considered *almost* perfect, Essie set about finishing the job. She urged him to continue in law school, supervised his wardrobe, tried (unsuccessfully) to change his late-to-bed, late-to-rise habits, and persuaded him to join the Harlem amateur theater production which was to bring him to the attention of influential theater professionals. From there his career took off, with Essie as his manager. Soon she controlled almost all his finances, only giving him an allowance. Within five years, however, the personality differences began to tell. According to Paul's son, Paul Jr., "He made up his mind on the spot to prove to himself that Essie didn't own him."

And so Paul went on to an exhausting series of affairs, some of them conducted simultaneously. In 1930 Paul and Essie began discussing divorce after he decided he wanted to marry Yolande Jackson, a high-spirited, witty British actress. Essie consented to the divorce at first, but privately changed her mind after Yolande's brazen pursuit of Paul got under her skin. Meanwhile, Paul was having second thoughts about how the black community would view his breaking up with Essie and how the white community would react to his marrying a white woman. Furthermore, he realized, he needed both women: Yolande as lover, Essie as his manager and companion.

By early 1933 Paul decided to give up both Yolande and the plans for the divorce, although he continued his other extramarital affairs for several years. Essie and Paul worked out a new arrangement: she would no longer control his financial affairs (a professional manager would do that), each could have extramarital affairs so long as they were discreet, and Essie could continue to be "Mrs. Paul Robeson." Within a few years Essie was writing, "We get on marvelously, and I'm very happy, too." Well, maybe.

The Robeson marriage settled down to a state of accommodation, in which the old illusions were abandoned while the routines of daily living and business were maintained. A façade of respectability was erected for the benefit of the public. After World War II, when Paul's career, reputation, and health went into free fall, the extramarital affairs tapered off. Essie and Paul spent intervals apart, but she was frequently seen in public as his companion. Until her own health went into decline (she died eleven years before he did), Essie monitored his physical and mental health problems, making sure he got help when he needed it.

In 1941 Robeson bought a twelve-room Georgian mansion in Enfield, Connecticut. Robeson biographer Martin B. Duberman says that Robeson "essentially bought the place for Essie, as a place where she could pursue her careers" in writing and photography. Essie and Paul Jr. moved there and had friendly relations with the neighbors; Paul was seldom seen, although he did present benefit concerts in Enfield. Initially, the Robesons were made to feel welcome in Enfield, but Paul's Communist sympathies eventually soured the neighbors. In 1953 the house was sold.

Paul Robeson exemplifies the tragic hero, that archetypal creation of the ancient Greek dramatists, with elaboration by Shakespeare. Like Antigone and Othello (whom Robeson played so often), Robeson was hugely gifted and larger than life. Like them, too, he carried within him the *hamartia,* the fatal flaw that would be his undoing. His flaw was a naïve attraction to communism and the Soviet Union. Paul was not a traitor and communism for him was, I think, more symbolic than substantive, a means of expressing outage at American racism. In fact, he never joined the Communist Party, never wanted to abandon the United States, never saw the Soviet Union as more than a work in progress.

But in using his platform to preach what Americans feared and hated, he squandered an opportunity to inspire and to lead. To most Americans, black and white, Robeson seemed to be spitting on the flag. The African-American leader Walter White wrote bitterly about an NAACP event in 1945 at which Robeson made "a lengthy and vehement attack upon all things American and indiscriminate laudation of all things Russian," thus missing "a magnificent opportunity to make converts."

Of course, one can only go so far in blaming the victim. Robeson, like all American blacks, had suffered from American racism, even though he refused to quietly accept his victimhood. The torment of injustice racked and warped his career and personal life. The son of an ex-slave, he could not abide the idea of being "owned," and being "owned" was how Essie (admittedly, a controlling personality) made him feel. But instead of trying to work out the problems in his marriage, he tomcatted around for decades.

Today, the name of Martin Luther King, who led by peaceful example, can be found on thousands of schools, streets, and public places, as well as a nationwide holiday. The name of Paul Robeson, who tried to lead by outrage, is largely forgotten. One of the public tragedies of the twentieth century is how America lost a hero in Paul Robeson. One of the private tragedies is how Essie lost a husband.

A Stone for Jennie

While the ghosts of Thompsonville and its environs haunt me, I still find pleasure among the living. Since I began visiting there, my faithful guides and good friends have been Rose and Bob Sokol. Thompsonville natives, Rose and Bob laughingly admit to a "mixed marriage" (he's Polish Catholic, she's Italian Catholic; at one time their congregations did not mix). He worked in the carpet mills until they closed down; she was a nurse. Now in un-retiring retirement, they put their hearts and souls and backbones into the Enfield Historical Society, one of those flights of angels that hover over the Connecticut River Valley's history, preserving it for the rest of us. Historians to the end, Rose and Bob have already reserved their burial

A well-dressed and defiant Jennie Bissland (left foreground)

plot in the Enfield Street Cemetery, where Enfield's early pioneers and later magnates are buried. They say they're looking forward to the "good conversations" they can have with those worthies.

It was to the more humble Thompsonville Cemetery, however, that they directed me when I started looking for my great grandparents' burial lot. The size of their double lot there, when I discovered it, reminded me of the task Robert and Mary Hope Bissland set for themselves when they emigrated to Thompsonville from Gourock, Scotland, in 1871. They brought with them all eleven of their children, including my grandfather, James Hope Bissland.

My grandfather married three times, each wife taken from him by illness which the medicine and surgery of those days were powerless to cure. His first wife died after childbirth. As a widower of thirty-seven, he then married a Holyoke, Massachusetts, woman twelve years younger than himself. Her name was Jane Elizabeth Lade. She, too, was of Scottish ancestry, and she liked to be called "Jennie." For six years James and Jennie lived in Holyoke, where they were able to rent half a spacious duplex, clearly a move up for Jennie, who had been living with her family in a crowded tenement in a less desirable part of town.

Regularly, James and Jennie would take the valley train from Holyoke to Thompsonville and visit his parents and his brothers and sisters still living there. But there was something about Jennie that bothered the rest of the Bisslands. Although the Bisslands would have been unfailingly polite, they never fully accepted her. My mother, who heard the story from my late father, told me that. Why, she did not know. Perhaps it was because Jennie was so much younger than James. Perhaps it had something to do with the fact that in six years of marriage James and Jennie had no children. Perhaps it was something about Jennie's attitude or the way she carried herself.

I have only two pictures of Jennie Lade Bissland: in one, a portrait in a tiny locket, she is a sloe-eyed beauty. In the other, a Bissland family group, she poses in a dress that even to my untutored eye seems more elegant than almost everyone else's. Jaw set, she gazes at the camera with a look that is close to defiance.

Jennie must have known she wasn't fitting into the family and dreaded visits to Thompsonville. But in June 1889 there came an invitation she could not refuse: the wedding of her husband's youngest brother, John Knox Bissland. Once again James and Jennie traveled to Thompsonville but there she developed appendicitis. Appendectomies were barely understood at the time, and the one a Thompsonville doctor attempted on Jennie was a failure. Nine days after the wedding, eleven days before her sixth wedding anniversary, and seven weeks after her thirtieth birthday, Jennie Bissland died.

Having died in Thompsonville, she was buried in our family lot, to be forever close to the Bissland relatives who had not accepted her. But not too close. The Bissland lot was a large one, with a family obelisk in the center and a row of Bissland stones on the east side. In the far southwest corner, as far as one could go without straying into the next lot, Jennie was buried all by herself. She remains alone to this day, for my grandfather was buried beside his *third* wife in Chicopee, Massachusetts.

One day I called a man named Lade in eastern Massachusetts. I had figured out that he was a descendent of the Holyoke Lades and therefore some kind of nephew of Jennie's. He was friendly but he told me he had never heard of her. He was kind enough to send me notes the modern-day Lades had made toward a family genealogy. There was no mention of Jennie. She had been completely forgotten by her own family.

On visits to the cemetery, I began to contemplate Jennie's lonely stone, conspicuous by its isolation. It was a simple white thing, bearing only the name she preferred, "Jennie," in raised letters on the top. Looking closely, I realized the letters were washing away, worn down by more than a century of rain, snow, and ice.

I called a local monument company and asked about replacing Jennie's stone with an exact replica. "It's marble, that's why it's wearing away," the man told me. "Marble is softer than granite. Granite is a different color and it costs more, but it'll last just about forever."

I was thinking this over when the man asked me, "So what do you want? Marble or granite?"

"Granite," I said. "I want it to last."

————————

Starting in the 1960s, a scourge of urban renewal swept through America. In Thompsonville, a mini-scourge took away most of the retail heart of town, with empty lots replacing the store buildings my ancestors knew. The carpet mill had already gone south, leaving an empty shell where thousands of workers, including the Bisslands, had woven carpet for the nation. Some of the remaining mill buildings have now been turned into apartments and businesses, but Thompsonville's once bustling Main Street remains gap-toothed, the shoppers having fled to the malls. Surrounding the downtown, however, most of the old housing stock remains. Walk the lonely residential streets late on a winter's night, with snow and the dark masking what little modernizing has occurred, and your senses will tell you that you are back among the Spencers and the Bisslands. Editor Parsons is preparing tomorrow's issue of the *Press*, and the news will not be good. . . .

CHAPTER SEVEN

LOOKING FOR UTOPIA

The unofficial state motto of Massachusetts is "Politics ain't beanbag," a rough sentiment carved in high relief on the leathery hearts of Hampden County pols. Even politicians of the better sort get sucked into it. Mayor Michael J. Sullivan of Holyoke—said to be one of the good guys in these parts— slammed down his phone one wintry day in 2002 after talking with fellow Democrat and State Treasurer Shannon P. O'Brien. O'Brien, he charged, had called to "bully" him into supporting her for governor, promising reprisals if he didn't. Sullivan had fired back by calling her the B word. Sullivan later apologized for losing his temper, groaning, "I just made a lifelong enemy of a political powerhouse. This is plutonium politics. This is stuff you can't bury. It doesn't go away."

It was just another day at the office for a politician in Hampden County, the tough territory forming the lowest tier of the three Connecticut River counties in Massachusetts. Folks in Hampshire, the next county to the north, like to call *their* region "Happy Valley," a sentiment that goes no further than the county line shared with Hampden. Below that, Happy Valley it is not.

Chambers of Commerce assembled in posse formation will probably get me for this, but Misery Gulch would be a very good name for Hampden County's share of the Connecticut River Valley. This is, after all, a Yankee

Rust Belt. The county has the second highest poverty level of all the counties in Massachusetts. Housing values are down in the dumpster in two of Hampden County's major cities, Springfield and Holyoke, while their crime rates are among the highest in the commonwealth. Downtowns are shabby, the housing stock decaying, and it seems as if many of the politicians and other partisans who could be doing something about it burn up energy instead, fiddling or fighting. Maybe Slippery Dingle would be an even better name for this place, in recognition of all the opportunities that have slipped away and all the politicians who let them.

In Hampden's defense, the area is saddled with economic miseries that would try the patience of Job, and it does have many good people trying hard to do something (including those Chambers of Commerce and even a few pols). But too many backbone industries, ones that made the area famous, have closed down or moved. Almost all the paper manufacturers are gone from the "Paper City" of Holyoke, while in Springfield, which used to preen itself as the "City of Homes," such marquee industries as the Indian Motorcycle Company and the U.S. Armory are only memories. I was born in Springfield and spent my early childhood here, and the pleasantly prosperous city I knew has been replaced by a ragged stranger. Hampden County's historic prestige as the cultural and commercial capital of western Massachusetts is badly frayed, and its urban population has been dropping for years. *Sic transit gloria*; she found a better job somewhere else.

So it is in this place that we will search for utopia.

Edward Bellamy Had a Vision

New York State politician Roscoe Conkling would have been a thoroughly admirable fellow if he hadn't been such a rotter. A smart lawyer and a gifted orator, he became mayor of Utica, then a congressman (and strong supporter of Abraham Lincoln during the Civil War), and finally a senator. He was a mover and shaker in every circle he joined. But he also was a cruel scourge of the postwar South, a sticky-fingered boss of patronage (nicknamed "Boss Conkling"), an iron-headed opponent of reform, and a quarrelsome, bitterly partisan Republican party leader, inspired (as James Garfield observed) "more by his hates than his loves." A vain and stubborn man, Conkling was peacock-proud of his body, which wags called the "finest torso" in public life. Also, he cheated on his wife. Not a credit to the species *politician*. Oh no.

By 1888 he had retired to the private practice of law. On Monday, March 12, he awoke in his New York City rooms to a howling blizzard outside, with high winds driving a tsunami of ice and snow onto the city. Conkling was fifty-eight now, but tall and muscular and infused with a foolhardy spirit of Victorian manhood. On foot, he pigheadedly plowed through drifts for twenty-five blocks to reach a courthouse where he had a case. No one else showed up. Disgusted, Conkling spent the day at his office, then headed home through the storm. It took him two hours to go two miles, ice caking on his eyelashes and brows. Exhausted, he collapsed in a snowbank just short of his destination. The finest torso had come to earth and, as the snow collected around him like a shroud, Boss Conkling began to perish.

Edward Bellamy envisioned a better world

But very slowly. Instead of succumbing to a gentle death then and there, Conkling was rescued and taken home by some nearby hotel staff. Weakened by his ordeal, he developed mastoiditis and pneumonia and spent weeks in misery. The once powerful orator lost his voice. Racked by fever, he thrashed about on sweaty sheets. On the morning of April 18, as the last traces of the Blizzard of '88 melted away outside his window, he died.

More than a hundred miles to the north, in the mill village of Chicopee Falls (now part of the city of Chicopee, lying between Springfield and Holyoke), thirty-eight-year-old Edward Bellamy must have read the news of Conkling's death and pondered its meaning. You would have had to look very hard to find anyone more different from Conkling than Bellamy. Son of a long line of ministers, he was sickly and shy, a daydreamer and an intellectual who had not one whit of Conkling's will to power. He had tried careers in the law and in freelance writing in New York City before returning to his native Connecticut River Valley. Moving back to his parents' home, he became a book reviewer and editorial writer for the *Springfield Union.*

But Bellamy was not as wishy-washy as the Conklings of this world would have thought. Like Thoreau, Emerson, and others, he was a deeply introspective, highly independent thinker. "This life is a mystery," he wrote, promising himself to "say and do no other thing until I solve it in some measure at least." Sounding a bit like Thoreau, he wrote, "I will not live at random as men do."

In 1877 Bellamy took the risky step of leaving the *Union* to devote himself to writing novels and short stories, and was able to build a modest reputation for himself. He took another major step by marrying Emma Sanderson, a young woman well known to him although she was eleven years younger. The product of a broken home, she had lived in the Bellamy household as a ward of Edward's father. Having Emma marry him and bear two children was probably the luckiest thing that ever happened to Edward Bellamy, and it made a world of difference. But it almost didn't happen.

Bellamy was the quintessential klutz when it came to matters of courtship. Supporting the material needs of a family "makes men less generous, more grasping, and more unscrupulous," he had thought. Like a perfect booby, he had outlined all this in detail to Emma, declaring he would never marry. Here was another man who would not commit and could give you sixteen reasons why not. But Edward and Emma did have a deep friendship, one in which he had shown her many kindnesses.

At first, the naïve Bellamy did not realize that his friendship with Emma had become, in fact, "an absurd passion." He did realize it when, at twenty-one, the lovely girl began to keep company with other men, eventually becoming engaged to one of them. Edward sank into a deep sulk and became so poisonous toward her that Emma moved out of the house, coming back to the Bellamy home only to teach music and sing in the church choir.

The besotted Edward could stand it no longer. One Sunday evening, as Emma got ready to join her fiancé at church, Bellamy took her in her arms and declared, "You can't go out. You're my little girl, and I can't let anyone else have you." Apparently that was good enough for Emma and, in 1882, the two were married. It was a fortunate union. Their marriage and the birth of their two children brought Bellamy out of his self-absorbed cocoon, giving "the problem of life a new and more solemn meaning," as he put it. Responsible now for a family, he began to realize how important it was "to provide for and safeguard their future." He settled down to studying social conditions and ways of improving them.

The first results appeared four years later, in January 1888, when Edward published a new novel. Entitled *Looking Backward: 2000-1887* and described as "a love story reversed," the book became a sensation and the high point of Bellamy's career. It sold ten thousand copies the first year and eventually more than a million. It is in print today, still studied and discussed. Many regard it as one of the most influential books of all time and, in the words of one scholar, it "may well be the most influential work ever written by an American . . . [w]ith the possible exception of *Uncle Tom's Cabin.*"

But it is not a light romance, whether looked at forward or backward. The characters are two-dimensional and given to ponderous speechifying. Entertainment really isn't the point here. This is, instead, a vision of the future. It purports to tell the story of Julian West, who falls asleep for 133 years and awakens in Boston in the year 2000. An all-knowing character named Dr. Leete explains the amazing "post-revolutionary" world in which West finds himself. With remarkable prescience, the book forecast such features of modern life as credit cards and radios.

More significant, however, was the complete rearrangement of society and the economy Bellamy sketched in his novel. Hunger, war, conflict, and poverty had been eliminated in this new era, replaced by an egalitarian society served by centralized kitchens, warehouses, and laundries. Individuals and private capital no longer had economic power over people. Instead, an omniscient government, operating on scientific principles, made sure everyone was provided for. To those critics who argued that such an idea was irrational, Bellamy demanded to know how rational they thought unbridled capitalism was, with its boom and bust cycles, extremes of wealth and poverty, and class conflicts.

All that sounded good to a lot of people in America in the late 1800s, their souls seared by the depression of 1883, the Haymarket Riot in Chicago in 1886, growing labor unrest, squalid city slums, ruthless capitalists willing to let the public be damned, and politicians like Roscoe Conkling, who lived by the rule of dog-eat-dog. Within a few years, more than one hundred and fifty clubs inspired by Bellamy's ideas sprang up across the nation. *Looking Backward* was translated into more than fifteen languages.

Bellamy's book especially appealed to the middle classes, because it

promised that middle-class values of good character, work, and knowledge
would be rewarded, and that change would come through evolution rather
violent revolution. "He wasn't an agitator or a troublemaker. He was an
optimist, not a bomb-thrower," says Stephen Jendrysik, a Chicopee history
teacher and head of the Edward Bellamy Memorial Association, formed in
1972 to preserve the Bellamy homestead. He adds: "Even though he was a
utopian socialist, the town didn't take that seriously. He was a town celebrity and they were very proud of him. They thought of him as a writer."

Looking backward from our time, some of Bellamy's ideas may sound
terribly naïve. Less naïve, however, is the book's core idea: individuals have
an obligation to contribute to the common good, and society exists to
assure the security of its members. Put that way, Bellamy doesn't sound so
weird. He believed a society should be built on cooperation instead of competition and that sharing in community offered something that extreme
individualism did not. "Our souls are not islands in the void, but peninsu-
las forming one continent of life within the universe," he wrote. To thoughtful Americans of the 1890s, Bellamy was a refreshing contrast to the likes of
Roscoe Conkling or the robber barons, the highhanded pols and grasping
industrialists who were as emblematic of greed and indifference to others
in their day as the Dukes of Enron are in ours.

In our everyday language, a "utopia" is a thing that can never be achieved,
a place that can never be reached—something impractical and impossible.
But probably even Bellamy didn't think his utopia was possible just the
way he imagined it. It *was* possible, though, to aspire to something better
than the world as it existed then. It was Bellamy's genius to tell the beleaguered dwellers of Robber Baron America that they didn't have to settle for
the way things were, that the Morgans and the Vanderbilts and the
Rockefellers and the Conklings didn't have all the answers, that the
country—which, after all, was supposed be *for*, and *of*, and *by* the people—
offered other, and better, possibilities. People "read Bellamy with a thrill of
hope," one biographer wrote.

Never the healthiest of individuals, Bellamy died in 1898, only ten years
after Roscoe Conkling. Unlike Conkling, however, who has disappeared
into the footnotes of history, Bellamy and his ideas live on. As a people, we
move a little closer to "utopia" every time we undertake an act of selfless-
ness or a deed of caring, whether through legislation or private action. We
will never reach utopia. But it isn't the destination that counts the most . . .
it's the journey.

Follow That Rabbit

"Would you like a drink?" Peter Rabbit asked me and when I answered, "Cranberry juice," Peter bounded away to the kitchen, lipperty lipperty lip. Then I came to my senses and remembered I was talking with Frances B. Meigs, who isn't Peter Rabbit at all. Instead, she is Peter Rabbit's step-grand-daughter.

"Peter Rabbit" is what people often called Peter's very real and very human creator, Thornton Waldo Burgess, Frances Meig's step-grandfather. This is the *American* Peter Rabbit we are talking about here, a domestic shorthaired, long-eared, waistcoat-wearing white-haired mammal, *Sylvilagus transitionalis*, a creature with a Yankee accent. He is not to be confused with the little brown bunny Beatrix Potter brought to fame in England a long time ago.

Thornton Burgess's creatures charmed generations of children

I knew both critters when I was small, but vastly preferred the stateside version. Burgess had created a friendly world without end and I felt a certain comfort with it. Living there was a complete cast of engaging woods creatures, starring Peter and Mrs. Peter, safely domiciled in their Old Briar-patch. Co-starring were Peter's dependable pals, Jimmy Skunk and Johnny Chuck, wise observers of the passing scene such as Hooty the Owl, and enemies in endless but futile pursuit of Peter, such as Reddy Fox and Old Man Coyote.

They occupied a landscape made up of the Purple Hills, the Green Forest, the Green Meadows, Laughing Brook, Smiling Pond, and the Crooked Little Path, territory that became as familiar to me as my own bed. There was a morality here, too, giving the proceedings a most civilized air, because little lessons about life and nature were continually being taught. And most of the creatures seemed like such nice people, you'll pardon the expression, whom no one could mind having as neighbors.

Not too long ago lots of Americans felt that way. The Thornton Burgess Bedtime Stories ran six days a week in hundreds of newspapers. From 1910 to 1950, Burgess published thousands of stories, more than one hundred books, and had a weekly radio program. He became such a household name that mail addressed only to "Peter Rabbit, somewhere in the United States" would be delivered to the author at his homes, first in Springfield and then in Hampden, just east of Springfield. Because of his commitment to nature and conservation, Burgess was awarded the gold medal of the New York Zoological Society's Wildlife Conservation Fund.

But while many grandparents remember Burgess and his work, the world has moved on and today's children seem older and less innocent. Youngsters who years ago would have begged for their nightly Burgess bedtime story and looked forward to Burgess books for Christmas now play with battery-powered pinball machines and watch movies filled with endless explosions and scatological wisecracks. If Peter were to come hopping up to some of these kids, they'd probably make jokes about his butt.

Even Burgess, whose life was a Horatio Alger story in many ways, had his tragedies, something I didn't realize until recently. He had been born on Cape Cod in 1874, but his father died when Thornton Junior was only nine months old. The boy and his mother spent his youth scratching for a living. Still, Thornton Junior had plenty of opportunities to explore nature on the beaches and scraggly pine forests on the Cape, which in those days was mostly rural. "It was there the pattern of my life was set," he wrote later.

Young Burgess started work as a bookkeeper in Boston, but hated it and in his spare time wrote poetry to amuse himself. To his surprise, he began to get small assignments to write advertising verse. By his mid-twenties he had a job as an office boy at a publisher in Springfield, which by diligence he turned into an editorial position. The company published *Good Housekeeping* magazine and in one issue Burgess had stories under four different names. In 1905 he bought a house in Springfield and married Nina E. Osborne, but less than a year later she died while giving birth to their son, Thornton W. Burgess III.

Alone now, the widowed father had to send the little boy to his sister's care in Illinois, but he wrote nature stories and mailed them to the child.

Some were published in *Good Housekeeping* and caught the attention of Little, Brown and Company, a prominent Boston publisher of books. In 1910 the company published Burgess's first nature storybook, *Old Mother West Wind*. Next, a national newspaper syndicate invited Burgess to start writing six stories a week about the adventures of Peter Rabbit and his friends. In 1919 he published *The Burgess Bird Book for Children*, illustrated by the noted artist and illustrator Louis Agassiz Fuertes. When that book became a bestseller, Burgess was on his way to becoming one of the nation's best known children's authors.

Burgess was acquainted with many naturalists and wildlife scientists, among them Willis Grant Johnson, an editor and entomologist. Johnson, a good friend of Burgess, died of spinal meningitis and, in 1911, after two years of courtship, Burgess married his widow, Fannie. Fannie was a small, very pretty woman, who kept her long brown hair piled on her head with hairpins and combs. She had a quick sense of humor and a nature as kindly as Thornton's. And she shared her new husband's pleasure in fishing and camping.

Fannie brought two teenaged children with her, Chester and Helen. With a stepmother to look after him, Thornton III could now return to the Burgess home, but the six-year-old proved to be a rebellious and angry child. His tantrums were such a trial to Fannie that she briefly shut him out of the house on one occasion, only to attract the police and embarrassing publicity in the Springfield newspapers. Off the boy went to live with relatives again.

As the years went by, Burgess's popularity grew, and with it his influence. His "Green Meadow Club" enrolled two hundred thousand children who pledged to support wildlife sanctuaries. And book followed book. Some were devoted purely to the adventures of Peter and his friends, while in others Burgess used his characters as teachers who introduced youngsters to the wonders of nature, such as flowers and the natural life of the seashore. Early on, he became acquainted with a New York City illustrator named Harrison Cady, who also loved nature. The two became good friends and collaborators. Over the years Cady produced more than fifteen thousand drawings for the Burgess newspaper stories and books and became almost as closely identified with Peter Rabbit as Burgess himself.

For many years Mr. and Mrs. Burgess had as a summer home a farmhouse, which had been built in 1742 near the little Hampden County town of Hampden. Surrounded by eighteen acres of woods and meadows, the property had a brook ("Laughing Brook") and low hills nearby (the "Purple Hills"). Eventually it became their year-round home. Today the Burgess home is a 356-acre Massachusetts Audubon Society wildlife refuge and teaching center and is still called "Laughing Brook." The Burgess animal books are for sale in the shop, and the teaching staff regularly tell Burgess stories to the thousands of school children who visit. "The spirit of Thornton Burgess is very much alive here," says Jane McCarry, a member of the staff.

Thornton Burgess treated his stepchildren as if they were his own, calling Helen "my very dear daughter." Helen grew up, married, and then remarried after a divorce. Frances Meigs was one of three children born to her first marriage. The three step-grandchildren were largely raised by Thornton and Fannie. Frances recalls that Thornton was a very loving, tenderhearted and slightly naïve gentleman of the old school who couldn't dance or carry a tune and had little business sense. He was a bit old-fashioned, "a Victorian gentleman," concerned with good manners as well as sensitivity to the natural world. He wore rimless glasses or, sometimes, a pince-nez.

He cared deeply for his grandchildren but on rare occasions would cry out in anguish over his own son's never-ending problems.

The Burgess stories may have seemed whimsical, but they were laced with information about nature and framed with moral instruction about courtesy, kindness, and caring for the environment. Young readers often identified with one Burgess character or another (I was Peter Rabbit, while Frances Meigs preferred Jimmy Skunk) and lived vicariously through them. Peter, a lovable naïf, was forever bounding off (lipperty lipperty lip) on a harebrained mission that would end by teaching him—and his young audience—an important lesson. It was a near-ideal world in which danger sometimes threatened, but almost never took casualties. Kindness prevailed and selfishness or rudeness were never rewarded. It was a safe, comfortable place, filled with nature's wonders. It was utopian.

Today, Frances Meigs and her husband, Charles, live in a townhouse in a retirement community located on a narrow, winding road in Bedford, Massachusetts, a town northwest of Boston and an hour or so away from "Laughing Brook." While Mrs. Meigs and Peter have their white hair in common, she is tall and slim, while Peter is, well, a plump chap. All that sweet clover, you know. The Meigs picked their location because it looks out over a field framed by woods . . . rather like the Green Meadow and the Green Forest. Frances inherited her grandfather's love of nature and re-reads one of his books every few months. Reddy Fox, Johnny Chuck, and "lots of Peters" pass in front of their windows.

This, too, is an ideal place and I would have liked to stay longer. But after a pleasant conversation with Peter Rabbit's step-granddaughter, it was time for me to move on to my next appointment. And so away I went down the Crooked Little Path, lipperty lipperty lip.

Venice It Ain't

Anthony R. Scott's left thumb went missing in 1998, but the rest of him is still there, and then some. The man looks like a retired linebacker, with imposing height ("I'm six feet, two inches") and a certain poundage ("Overweight!"). An African American in his mid-fifties, with pepper-and-salt hair and skin the color of mahogany, he has the soft accent of his native N'awleans, despite years in the North and Midwest. He counts himself a "minority minority," by which he means he is one of the few blacks in the Republican party. He has a dry sense of humor. When a lawsuit against his appointment to the job he holds was thrown out of court, he drawled, "Well, I guess I'll be around a couple of more months." He also has a glare that can freeze a police sergeant in his tracks.

Police Chief Anthony Scott, scourge of criminals in the troubled city of Holyoke

That goes with the job, for Anthony Scott is the top cop in Holyoke, Massachusetts. And ought to be, from the looks of things. Holyoke, which lies at Hampden County's northern edge, is a rundown mill city that had a reputation for police scandals and drive-by shootings. It has long needed hard, smart policing and with Scott's arrival in mid-May 2001 started getting it.

Not that Holyoke was ever a rose garden. Planted in some riverside farm fields in the mid-1800s by Boston capitalists, it is said to be America's first planned industrial city. It became a place of spinning jennies, papermaking machinery, forges, blue collars and lunch buckets, saloons and street urchins. To make all this possible, a dam had been built to harness the Connecticut River and over seven miles of wide canals were dug, by hand, to channel the water power to factories. "The Flats," as Holyoke's lowlands became known, filled with brick tenements and mills. Yankee farm girls and then Irish, French, Italian, Polish, and German immigrants flocked to the jobs Holyoke offered, and the city became a polyglot of competing ethnic groups. Today, the "old ethnics" are being replaced by the "new ethnics": now nearly half the population is Puerto Rican.

At one point Holyoke had twenty-five paper mills and was the nation's largest paper producer. Today, only one paper mill remains and the old work forces of thousands are a distant memory. Holyoke is said to have peaked economically in 1917 when its population was sixty-three thousand, but it's been declining ever since. The population is now forty thousand, a twenty percent drop since 1970 alone. The older parts of the city show the decay. Mill and commercial buildings stand empty or under-utilized; vacant lots multiply as acres of shabby housing are demolished, High Street's fine stores are gone and trash fills the gutters.

So Holyoke became fertile ground for trouble, and in recent years has gotten it. *Public housing resident stabbed. . . . Bullets fired at van. . . . 2 arrested in drive-by shooting*, the headlines reported day after day. To the weary cops of the HPD, it must have seemed as if half the citizens left standing after the drive-bys were trying to give the other half a good whooping, and to throw in some cutting at no extra charge. Like packs of feral dogs, gangs marked their territories with spray paint: the "F.B." of the Flat Bush gang, a local outfit, appeared all over playground equipment in some neighborhoods. The Latin Kings invited themselves here, too. The street urchins of long ago turned into surly youths with baggy clothes and a surplus of attitude.

Making things worse in recent years was a police department that news writers got in the habit of calling "scandal-plagued." There were, of course, the garden-variety allegations of bunking and cooping, of racial and ethnic discrimination, of mishandling of confiscated property, of inappropriate and unauthorized use of overtime and compensatory time. But it was worse than that. A Holyoke officer was charged in Northampton with molesting a mentally retarded women. An officer who had been bypassed twice for promotion shot and killed himself. A lieutenant was acquitted of two larceny charges but the jury deadlocked on a third. Before another trial could take place, he died of liver failure. Then the city was stunned when John DiNapoli, an officer who was especially well liked, was shot and killed by a panicky drug dealer. To add insult to injury, one night someone stole a front-end loader and used it to pick up a police cruiser and drop it onto a police pickup truck.

That's Holyoke. Canals it may have, but Venice it ain't, and utopia it will never be. But in 2001 someone offered Holyoke a vision, which, if not utopian, seemed almost as wonderful.

In 1999, Michael J. Sullivan beat a two-term incumbent to win the mayor's office. Holyoke's crime wave, and especially Officer DiNapoli's murder, prompted Mayor Sullivan to lead a "peace march" through the city the next year. Symbolism only goes so far, of course, so then he did something else: using his power of appointment, he chose a new police chief, Anthony R. Scott. Things haven't been the same since.

"That took *cojones*," said Scott, using Madeleine Albright's favorite word for bravery. "For him to appoint someone who's an outsider and a black and not Irish took courage." And that isn't all: Sullivan, a Democrat in a Democratic city in one of the nation's most heavily Democratic states, appointed a Republican police chief who is not shy about his political philosophy. Scott's parents taught him one lesson above all others: "If you want something, work for it," so the chief is no booster of Affirmative Action. "Don't give me anything. All I ask is a level playing field. If I have that, I can compete with anybody. *A-ny-bo-dy*." The chief is ordinarily a calm, deliberate man whose underlying intensity pops up in his speech as *italics*, along with a generous sprinkling of hy-phens.

And he has no sympathy for the bad guys, especially those who complain that racism put them behind bars. "Don't give me that," Scott says. "You're in jail because you *robbed* somebody, not because you're black." Scott does believe that blacks get treated less fairly on lengths of sentences and probation. "But that's the courts' responsibility," he says. Whatever your color, if you break the law, Chief Scott wants *you*. "I *love* to put people in jail," is his mantra.

Scott knows something about courage. He's beaten cancer twice in the past few years, including one bout with squamous cell cancer which forced removal of his left thumb. He spent twenty-two years as a cop in New Orleans, starting out as one of only fifty black officers on a segregated force of 1,750. Life can be hard in the Big Easy, and Scott grew up in one of the city's roughest neighborhoods, one where many of his boyhood companions died young or went to jail. As a cop, he worked some of the police force's toughest jobs: vice, internal affairs, felony action. He was a candidate for lieutenant in the NOPD when he was appointed chief in Athol, Massachusetts. After that, he went to the chief's job in Rock Island, Illinois.

Scott spent ten years in Rock Island, shaking up the police department, beating down crime, and winning a slew of awards from a grateful citizenry. But Scott's wife, Helene, a New Orleans native of French and Italian ancestry, had fallen in love with New England. "That's the only reason I'm here," says Scott. "Because of her. I hate snow. I don't just dislike it. I *hate* it. I hate mountains. I don't just dislike them a *l-i-i-i-i-ttle* bit. I *hate* them." And that's how snowy, hilly western Massachusetts got itself a cop from the land of bayous and Mardi Gras. The things people do for love.

It's the height that bothers Scott about going up on mountains or mountain roads, but he doesn't seem to fear much else. It didn't take Holyokers long to learn that Chief Scott was blessed with Madeleine's jewels. Within a month of his arrival the new chief had launched TBOS (Take Back Our Streets) sweeps in which troublemakers were scooped up wholesale and hauled into court. Hundreds of street toughs found themselves in the docket, and some of Holyoke's officers took to calling their chief "Tee-Boss." Next, Chief Scott took on the local courts, which he asked to stiffen bail requirements and impose stiffer penalties. Police officers often grumble about "revolving-door" and "slap-on-the-wrist" justice, but seldom go public the way Scott did. When the chief couldn't get an answer from court officials, he promised to take his fight to the state capital. The western Massachusetts police chiefs association voted its unanimous support for his effort.

Then the chief announced a carefully researched eight-beat patrol system, a plan for community policing to get officers out of their cars, assign them to specific sectors of a city divided into eight beats, and put them in closer personal touch with citizens. All the while he was pushing his "broken-window theory," a corollary of former New York City mayor Giuliani's quality-of-life concept of policing: i.e., fix the windows, keep the streets clean, get rid of the graffiti, and people will begin to take pride in their neighborhoods—and crime will go down. By now the dust was flying, and even Republican governor Jane Swift took notice, coming to visit Chief Scott in his office. Afterwards, she jokingly said she should have considered him for the lieutenant governor's slot.

"He's like a rock star!" exclaimed Doris Ransford, president of the Greater Holyoke Chamber of Commerce. "People see something happening and they feel good about it." City councilman Diasdado Lopez, long a critic of the police department, says, "He's a good chief. You have to give him credit— he came out swinging." Only a few months on the job, the man was getting respect. Even the city council, used to calling other chiefs by their first names, addresses Scott only as The Chief. To the beleaguered citizens of Holyoke, it must have seemed as if the U.S. Cavalry and John Wayne were finally coming to their rescue.

John Wayne with a brain, that is. Chief Scott has a business administration degree, with a minor in management, from Loyola University New Orleans, a Jesuit institution. Policeman though he is, he often thinks in business terms. "Criminals are in business to make money," he says. "You drive up their cost of doing business and they'll go elsewhere. If I raise their overhead, they'll leave." Within a few months of his arrival, it was already happening: street crime began to drop. A favorite story circulating in town concerned a young drug dealer who decided to retrain in the construction trades. Chief Scott's crackdown, he said, had forced to him "to choose a different career."

But the police chief's eye is also on the city's bottom line. A few miles south of the decaying downtown is the handsome Holyoke Mall at Ingleside, a shopping destination for much of western New England and one of the Northeast's largest malls. Collectively, its nearly two hundred stores, ranging from Target to high-end Lord & Taylor, employ four to five thousand people and contribute enormously to the city's economy. While Holyoke's crime problem occurs miles away from Ingleside, the chief says, "It's the perception that counts. People hear about 'crime in Holyoke' and don't separate the two." With the city waiting breathlessly for a rumored expansion at Ingleside, no one wants to risk ruffling the feathers of the biggest golden goose the city has left.

Scott does what he does by putting in days that are twelve to sixteen hours long. "He's an inspiration to us," Lieutenant Marc Cournoyer says. "He's here when I get here in the morning at 6:30, and he's here when I leave. He takes his wife to dinner and then goes home to do police work on his computer. Someday his wife is going to put his picture on the side of a milk carton." Scott likes to say, "My hobby is my work and my work is my hobby." He does admit to listening to music or watching television occasionally. His favorite show? "'Law and Order.' I *love* 'Law and Order.'" Figures.

What did not compute is Scott's reception by his own department. As the cold wind of Scott's first autumn in Holyoke blew off the Connecticut River and whistled down the littered alleys of Holyoke, certain members of the Holyoke police force were trying to undermine him. Upset that this alien creature had been chosen for chief instead of one of their own, the old guard police unions launched a barrage of grievances and a volley of lawsuits challenging Scott's authority, his appointment, and even his eight-beat community policing plan. One union leader gave a speech that charitably can best be described as insolent. *We'll still be here long after he's gone,* the officer declared.

To the public, which was clearly moving into Scott's corner, it must have seemed as if the new chief was knee-deep in ducks determined to nibble him to death, one leg at a time. But Scott kept his own counsel, seldom saying much of anything in response. That is not only his way, it's also a strategy that leaves critics looking like ankle-biters. One admirer likened him to a smart politician who is media savvy without advertising it. "My mother always told me it was better to keep quiet and be thought stupid than open your mouth and prove it," Scott likes to say.

It is part of a strategy that has worked well for Southerners for years: the "aw-shucks, don't-pay-me-no-mind" façade that conceals a cunning mind. It worked well during the Civil War when the Union armies would dismiss the seemingly ragtag Rebels as beaten. Then, gray-clad cavalry would come galloping out of the woods and for a lot of Union officers would come the dawn. It's worked for generations of country lawyers, too. And it may well work for Scott, who likes to play himself down. "A chief doesn't have much power," he'll say, pulling his car into a reserved spot at the entrance to police headquarters, "but at least I have my own parking place." Aw shucks. Or he'll tell you that he's low man in the pecking order in his own house- hold. "My son comes first, then the dog, and then me. I *know* my place!" Yeah, right.

Strongly supported by the mayor, Scott is developing a powerful ally: the public. At one point, when Scott was under fire, Holyoke bumpers blossomed with the message, "We Support Chief Scott." Citizens seem to think he's a righteous cop and approach him wherever he goes to congratulate him and offer encouragement. The chief and I were at lunch when a woman he did not know walked up to our table and said, "I just want to thank you for all you're doing to clean up Holyoke. And keep up the pressure on those judges, too!" "That happens all the time," the chief said. He had been on the job only eight months.

In Holyoke, the effort to beat down crime and the struggle for control of the police department may go on for a long time. But as long as The Chief is on the job, things will be happening, not necessarily when you expect them. If you're a criminal or an obdurate cop, it would be a good idea not to underestimate this man.

Or someday the dawn will break.
And then your lights will go out.

Sons and Daughters of Erin

The most important community event in Holyoke each year is the St. Patrick's parade. It's trumpeted as "the biggest and best in North America," which may not be far wrong. A committee works year-round planning this mother of all pageants, which can include thirty floats, forty musical groups, and fifteen thousand marchers, and take three and a half hours to pass a given point. On a good day, police estimate, it can draw upwards of a quarter-million spectators—many times the city's population. Over the years (the first one was in the 1950s), the "Saint Pat" has spawned a bevy of side events—a race for runners, parties, receptions, and reunions—so every March Holyoke rocks to the rhythm of families reuniting, politicians stroking, and chips'n'dip disappearing.

For these few days Holyoke may forget its troubles, but one thing it cannot forget: the Irish still very much hold the balance of power around here, in local politics and in the police department. Other old ethnics—particularly the French and Poles—get some of the action, too, but the green shamrocks that blossom here each March carry a hidden reminder of who's in charge. It's not the Puerto Ricans.

And yet the Puerto Ricans are now the single largest ethnic group in Holyoke, counting over forty-two percent of the population. Since World War II, people by the millions have been leaving Puerto Rico for the mainland, pushed by the search for jobs and a better life. "We're just like everybody else—the French, the Irish, the Poles," says Diasdado Lopez, a veteran Holyoke city councilman who has had the guts to regularly confront the establishment. "We're looking for the American dream." But in Holyoke, the migrants' timing was bad, because the jobs began disappearing after they began arriving. Slowly parts of the city began turning into a ghetto of cheap and decaying housing.

So Lopez represents a troubled constituency and one that troubles the city. What Irish and the French and Poles sometimes forget, however, is that they themselves were the new ethnics once upon time, suffering their own problems and upsetting others in the community. The Puerto Rican experience is just the American story all over again, with variations. And yet there are signs of hope, even in Holyoke.

"I see more and more (Puerto Rican) students coming to college," says Manuela Pacheco, who has spent twenty years at the University of Massachusetts in nearby Amherst recruiting and helping bilingual students, persuading them education can help them get ahead. "I see the new faces here. There is hope. It's going to take a while . . . but we're going to be okay." There are other signs. In 2002, Holyoke got a new superintendent of schools, a Latino of Cuban extraction who could be expected to be sensitive to the needs of a school system where upwards of seventy percent of the students are Puerto Rican. The Greater Holyoke Chamber of Commerce is working with a Ford Foundation grant to offer job-training programs to unskilled youth. The city bought the Holyoke dam and the canal system, bolstering its municipal power plant's ability to offer cheap electricity that can attract new industry. And Councilman Lopez, who is keeping his eagle eye on doings in the City Hall and the HPD, pronounces the city's new police chief "great."

Hampden County's Puerto Ricans may not feel that love is all around them, nor are they ready, like Mary Tyler Moore, to toss their caps in the air. But the signs are there. *Luis and Maria, you're gonna make it after all.* It's both the journey *and* the destination that count.

Don't let the politicians scare you. There are things to see and do in Hampden County. Perhaps the best known is the Basketball Hall of Fame at 1150 West Columbus Ave., Springfield (www.hoophall.com; 877-4HOOPLA). Dr. James Naismith invented the game near here in the 1890s. There has been a basketball museum in Springfield for many years, but at this writing a new hundred-million-dollar-plus building—in the shape of a basketball, natch—was under construction.

Not wanting to be left out of the round ball sweepstakes, Holyoke hosts the Volleyball Hall of Fame, in Heritage State Park, and advertises itself at entrances to the city as "Birthplace of Volleyball." Heritage State Park, 444 Dwight Street (413-534-1723), is also the site of the well-regarded Children's Museum at Holyoke (413-536-7048).

Springfield also offers the Museum Quadrangle (State and Chestnut streets), which includes the Museum of Fine Art, the Smith Art Museum, the Connecticut Valley Historical Museum, and the Springfield Science Museum (www.quadrangle.org; 413-263-6800). The Springfield Armory National Historic Site, where the famed Springfield rifle was manufactured, includes one building converted to a museum (www.nps.gov/spar/; 413-734-8551). The Edward Bellamy House in Chicopee has been designated a National Historic Landmark, but call Stephen Jendrysik (413-594-6496) to arrange a visit.

Laughing Brook, the Massachusetts Audubon Society's wildlife sanctuary and education center, is located away from urban hustle and bustle, just as you'd expect, near the little town of Hampden at 793 Main Street (www.massaudubon.org/Nature_Connection/Sanctuaries/Laughing_Brook/; 413-566-8034). Of great interest on Cape Cod are two facilities maintained by the Thornton W. Burgess Society: The Thornton W. Burgess Museum in Sandwich and a nature center in East Sandwich (www.thornburgess.org; 508-888-6870).

Finally, for an experience you can't match anywhere else, visit the post office at 600 Suffield St. in Agawam, a pleasant suburb of Springfield. You are at the lowest-numbered ZIP code in the USA: 01001. Go crazy! Mail a postcard!

CHAPTER EIGHT

SOLITARY LIVES

In Hampshire County in western Massachusetts, the Connecticut River heading south takes a sharp right turn, then a hard left, straightens itself for the next few miles and then does a dipsydoodle—which locals call the "Oxbow"—before settling down to a more sedate course to the sea. This place of rights and lefts and twists and turns has attracted a lively population prone to similar gyrations, for this is the region of the Five Colleges: Amherst, Mount Holyoke, Smith, the University of Massachusetts at Amherst, and Hampshire, one little valley containing upwards of twenty-nine thousand students, a jiggly mix of molecules in an educational pressure cooker.

Pizza is the fuel of choice in this kind of atmosphere, and universities are magnets for pizza parlors. In or near Amherst alone there are thirteen, including one on Amherst's North Pleasant Street that just may be recognized around the world. A remote camera mounted outside its entrance snaps a digital image of customers every thirty seconds for the Web (www.masslive.com/campuscam). Pizza is academe's social lubricant, a business facilitator, the necessary fuel of much schmoozing and decision-making. Students flirt, cram for exams, or just hang while eating their pizzas, while faculty engage in weightier matters: they argue or swap campus gossip. Meanwhile, at any given time, at least a couple of the Five

Colleges' chief executives and their intimates are exchanging the latest news of berths at other institutions. They have been covertly studying the trade papers, searching for places where no fundraising is required, the students love learning for its own sake, and the faculty are as contented as cows, asking only to be milked daily. Remembering that, in reality, no such place exists, the presidents absent-mindedly flick dribbles of tomato paste from their trousers or skirts and chomp gloomily on their cheese plains, ordered unadorned to hold down the heartburn.

Curiously, all this curd-chewing bonhomie, or what passes for it, is built on a regional heritage that includes landmark instances of social isolation. That can be hard to recall in Five-College Country where you swim through tides of young humanity forever effervescing, but there they are, in history's pantheon: three remarkable stories of lonely hearts in Happy Valley. Sometimes we remember them over our pizza.

Lonely Angels

In January 1649, in the Great Hall in the Palace of Westminster, the floors and the galleries were filled with some of the kingdom's most important people, but all eyes kept returning to one man. He was a small, weary-looking gentleman of forty-eight, cheeks sagging and eyes pouched, his beard and long hair gone gray, a thoroughly unimpressive fellow, except for one thing. His name was Charles Stuart, but he was better known as King Charles, sovereign of England and Scotland. And he was on trial for his life.

The king—whom we know as Charles I—was not a bad man, but neither was he a wise one. Unimpressive in appearance, with a slight stammer and a Scots accent, he was brave, moral, and devout. But he lacked the common touch and, worst of all, common sense, so he commanded neither affection nor respect. As Puritan resentment against the Church of England and the monarchy rose, he stubbornly refused to restrain his Anglican attack dogs or yield one iota of what he considered his God-given power. Instead, he went to war to defend the divine right of kings and the established church, and when that failed and he was taken prisoner, he resorted to intrigue and smuggled messages.

By 1648, with the monarchy overthrown and Puritans in charge of the country, one hundred thirty-five men—a hodgepodge of men of conscience, zealots, and opportunity seekers—had been named to sit as a High Court of Justice. After a trial of only four days Charles was found guilty "of high treason and high misdemeanours." Swiftly he was sentenced to death by beheading. Nearly half of those named to the High Court of Justice never attended the trial and, in the end, only fifty-nine men signed his death warrant, some of them with great reluctance. These fifty-nine have been known ever since as the Regicides.

Charles bravely went to his death on the afternoon of January 30, 1649. That, ironically, was the beginning of the end for the Puritan Commonwealth. Even in revolutionary England, executing the king was more than many could stomach. The Puritan leader, Oliver Cromwell, a manic depressive who was never popular, died in 1658, and the Puritan Revolution soon unraveled. On May 29, 1660, Charles's son, King Charles II, entered London to public jubilation and the Restoration was underway. So also was a vengeful hunt for the Regicides.

The corpses of Cromwell and two of his lieutenants were dug up, put on public display, and then beheaded, with the bodies thrown into a common pit and the heads exhibited at Westminster Hall. Forty-one of the original fifty-nine Regicides were still alive at this point. A handful were able to make their peace with the restored monarchy and remain free, but many others were arrested. Pleas and excuses won some life imprisonment instead of the death sentence, but nine suffered the grotesque execution reserved for traitors ("half-hanging," followed by disembowelment). Fifteen other Regicides fled the country, three of them finding their way to New England, two to the Connecticut River Valley. And ever since they have been the stuff of legend.

New England was a fine refuge for the Regicides, having been settled by Charles I's historic enemies, the Puritans, and even during the Restoration the region was showing the independent spirit that would erupt a century later in the American Revolution. Two of the Regicides, Edward Whalley and William Goffe (or Goff), were prominent Puritan revolutionaries and were given warm welcomes in New England. Whalley, a cousin of Cromwell's, was a lieutenant general who ably led troops against the Royalists, then was in charge of guarding Charles for a time. His son-in-law, William Goffe, was a major general in Cromwell's army. A third Regicide who fled to New England, John Dixwell, was a minor official in Cromwell's government. He moved to New Haven, changed his name, and lived there openly and safely, reading and strolling, sustained by unknown sources until he died a natural death in 1689. (To this day New Haven has Dixwell, Goffe, and Whalley streets.)

Goffe and Whalley arrived in Boston in July 1660, scarcely two months after Charles II's return to London. In Boston they lived openly, although under false names. The story (and it may be no more than that) is that one of them challenged, and beat, a local fencing master, who cried out in astonishment, "Who can you be? You must be either Goffe, or Whalley, or the Devil, for there were no other men in England who could beat me."

Somehow, King Charles II learned where Goffe and Whalley had gone and sent a ship to Boston with an order for their arrest. But friends of the men back in England chartered a sloop, overtook the king's ship off the New England coast, and got to Boston harbor first. The sloop's captain rowed to shore and rushed to Governor Endicott's house, where the fugitives were being entertained. The governor ended the party and sent Goffe and Whalley out of town immediately.

The two Regicides fled to Connecticut, taking refuge in a cave in the vicinity of New Haven known to this day as "Judges' Cave." When soldiers came looking for them there, they fled again, hiding for an extended period in the Milford cellar of Micah Tompkins. It was said that Tompkins's children thought that "angels were in the basement." Eventually, the soldiers came again, and so an ancient poem goes:

> Whalley and Goffe in Massachusetts make their home,
> Then to Quinnipiac [New Haven region] in haste pursue their way.
> Nor know they where to rest or where to roam,
> Until in Hadley they concealed and lonely they stay.

In the 1660s Hadley, Massachusetts, was about as far as you could go before entering the wilderness. Somehow, in 1664, Goffe and Whalley found their way north to Hadley and Rev. John Russell, who concealed them in his own home. Supposedly, their presence was kept a secret from most townspeople, which would have been a remarkable feat in a village numbering no more than a few dozen families. Even in this lonely spot the Regicides must have had to lie very low, seeing little blue sky and fresh air, never enjoying the company of anyone outside the Russell home. On the Russell house's second floor there were loose planks behind the chimney, concealing a hiding place where the Regicides could wait out visits from the King's agents.

Whalley died about 1674 and probably was buried in Hadley, perhaps in the Russell cellar. Then, in June 1676, there occurred a major Indian attack, the event from which a legend grew. Although a large body of Connecticut soldiers was stationed across the river in Northampton, Hadley's townspeople were left to fend for themselves and were not doing well against their attackers, until (the legend goes) *suddenly, a grave, elderly person appeared in the midst of them. In his mien and dress he differed from the rest of the people. He not only encouraged them to defend themselves, but put himself at their head, rallied, instructed and led them on to encounter the enemy, who by this means were repulsed. As suddenly the deliverer of Hadley disappeared.*

The apparition presumably was Goffe but townspeople concluded it was an angel. The "Angel of Hadley" grew into one of New England's favorite legends and took on a life its own, re-appearing in James Fenimore Cooper's *Wept of Wish-Ton-Wish* and Sir Walter Scott's *Peveril of the Peak.* Nathaniel Hawthorne re-jiggered the story—same theme, different details—in *The Gray Champion.* For many years, historians assumed that the "Angel of Hadley" was as fanciful a story as Cooper's, Scott's, and Hawthorne's. More recently, however, Douglas C. Wilson published an article in the serious journal *New England Quarterly* arguing that Goffe may really have played an important role in the Indian attack in June 1676.

Another word on the subject comes from Libby Klekowski, who works in the Department of Biology at the University of Massachusetts-Amherst but fills Web pages with Connecticut River Valley historical lore. Ms. Klekowski doesn't believe General Goffe saved Hadley, but thinks she knows who the real angel is: "Perhaps both generals Whalley and Goffe would have thought the Reverend John Russell was their special savior and, therefore, could be called the Angel of Hadley."

I like both theories. When I drive through Hadley, I know this: once upon a time there were angels in this place.

Spiders and Rainbows

Born October 5, 1703, in East Windsor, Connecticut, he was the son and grandson of ministers and the only boy in a family of eleven children. He was tall and spare, solemn, quiet, and solitary. Never naughty himself, he was quick to tell others their faults. At age six he wrote a letter decrying materialism. (How many six-year-olds even know what materialism is?) He prayed "five times a day in secret." Some time between the age of eight and ten he and some other boys built a hut in a swamp to pray and discuss salvation. When he wasn't praying or correcting others, he was observing nature, writing carefully observed essays on spiders and rainbows.

Jonathan Edwards was a strange little boy.

He also was a brilliant one, interested in just about everything. Just before his thirteenth birthday, he entered Yale, where he was a somber, bookish loner, proud to be "free of the janglings" of some of his more frivolous fellows. He graduated jangle-free and first in his class when he was not quite seventeen years old. Having remained at Yale to prepare for the ministry, at age eighteen Edwards was called to the pulpit of a small Scots Presbyterian church in New York City. While there he became a convert to Calvinistic doctrine of absolute sovereignty of God, and would walk alone in the woods or on the river shore "to secretly converse with God." In between ministering and pondering, he wrote essays on both theology and science, including one on "flying spiders."

Jonathan Edwards preached terrifying sermons

So began the career of the man many call the first great American intellectual, one still studied today for his ideas on "the congruity of God's action to man's situations." The passionate toughness of Jonathan Edwards's mind helped Puritanism achieve one last flash of heat before fading from dominance, if not from influence. But if Edwards warned his listeners about descending into Hell, his own life was a descent into tragedy. He had a loving family, but in the community beyond his doorstep he trod a lonely path, one leading eventually to a stunning repudiation and then social isolation. As if that weren't enough, his life ended with a bitter irony worthy of a Greek tragedy.

In 1726, young Edwards moved to Northampton, Massachusetts, to become assistant and likely successor to his eminent grandfather, Solomon Stoddard, the "Congregational pope" who had been in the pulpit there for fifty-five years. Northampton was still a raw-looking and isolated frontier town, but for a minister it was a plum position nonetheless, perhaps the most important outside Boston. Within three years Edwards succeeded his grandfather.

In 1727 Jonathan married Sarah Pierrepont of New Haven, whom he had clumsily but persistently wooed for four years. The winsome Sarah was vibrant, happy, and graceful, everything that the socially inept Edwards was not, and he was helplessly, madly in love with her, the only woman he ever courted. She was, he wrote in a moment of rare but memorable poesy, a creature of "wonderful sweetness, calmness and universal benevolence of mind. . . . She will sometimes go about from place to place, singing sweetly; and seems to be always full of joy and pleasure; and no one knows for what. She loves to be alone, walking in the fields and groves, and seems to have some one invisible always conversing with her." Ever the Puritan, Edwards fought off "evil thoughts" during the courtship by doing "some sum in arithmetic or geometry."

Jonathan and Sarah not only complemented each other but also shared a seriousness of religious purpose as well. Hymns were the only music allowed in their home, and dancing and feasting were prohibited. Still, the Reverend and Mrs. Edwards were not quite as ascetic nor as stern as you might imagine. Sarah was a lively hostess (though Jonathan often seemed abstracted), and guests were frequent. The children could see how much in love their parents were, always treating each other gently, and the children themselves could count on one hour a day when father would give them his complete attention. Edwards enjoyed smoking a long pipe (although smoking was against the law) and the family's shopping lists contained constant reminders to buy chocolate. The Puritan divine also had a weakness for buying his wife a piece of jewelry now and then.

The softness stopped at his front door. Tall, thin, and delicate-looking, with a high forehead, Jonathan Edwards assumed a command presence when he stepped into the pulpit, one that could rivet the congregation. He had piercing eyes and a quietly intense way of speaking that was deliberate, clear, and very distinct, with key phrases accentuated by meaningful pauses. Neither a boomer nor a thunderer, Edwards did not try to overwhelm a room, but he filled it nonetheless.

In the early 1700s members of New England's clergy were bemoaning the "decline of religion" and remembering, wistfully, the lost golden age of Puritan theocracy. The Yankee parsons saw evidence of debauchery everywhere: swearing, drinking, husking bees, and, worst of all, the heretical belief that mere "good works," instead of faith alone, could earn one salvation. But then, from 1734 through the early 1740s, a religious fervor, known as the Great Awakening, spread through the Connecticut River Valley and New England. A rabble-rouser named George Whitefield, with motives no purer than certain modern televangelists, was imported from England to heat up the frenzy. Resident ministers threw away their notes and began exhorting their congregations to get right with an angry God who might have already made up his Calvinistic mind about who was going to burn in Hell, but who had to be appeased nonetheless.

Edwards was one of the revival's leading voices. On July 8, 1741, in Enfield, Connecticut, Edwards preached his famous sermon "Sinners in the Hands of an Angry God," a homily that has been called "the most famous example of 'the preaching of terror.'" Wicked men could slide into Hell at any moment, declared Edwards, pounding out his warnings with a calm yet relentless cadence that somehow was more unnerving than the bellowing other preachers preferred. No doubt God was angry with many in the congregation at that very moment, said Edwards, and nothing but God's pleasure kept them from tumbling into the fiery pit. Before the sermon was over, there was "a great moaning & crying through ye whole House," with listeners calling out, *What shall I do to be saved? Oh, I am going to Hell, and Oh, what shall I do for Christ?*

Jonathan Edwards has been called the "quintessential Puritan thinker and hero of the Great Awakening." Yet, paradoxically, Edwards also preached of God's love and, despite his cool intellectualism, he believed that religion was an affair of the heart. He stressed the need for an internal conversion, a change of heart, a physical and emotional upheaval without which a person's "good works" meant nothing. One of the most common words in his sermons was "sweetness," his word for God's grace.

Indeed, Edwards's life seemed to be one of dualities. He was warm, caring, and affectionate with his family, yet aloof with his extended family, the congregation. A brilliant intellect, he was uneducable about the practical politics of getting along in a small community. Stiff and solemn, committed to the straight and narrow path, he never understood the concept of the warm fuzzy. While he is most often remembered as the preacher of hellfire and brimstone, God's wrath and man's depravity, he also preached many sermons about God's love and the beauty of God's creation. He could paint a picture of Hell that would singe your eyebrows, and yet rhapsodize about "the beauty of trees, plants, and flowers . . . the beautiful frame of the body of Man, the beauty of the moon and the stars." His mind soared to the heavens, yet retained a scientist's fascination for the habits of nature's lowliest creatures. When I think of Jonathan Edwards, I think of polarities and paradoxes, the beautiful and the ugly, the harsh and the gentle. I think of spiders and rainbows.

An early riser "resolved never to lose one moment of time," Edwards spent up to thirteen hours a day in his study, working by candlelight. In the opinion of many congregants, he should have spent less time composing sermons and more calling on parishioners. He was apt to return from his solitary walks and rides covered with scraps of papers that he had pinned to his clothes, notes to himself that he could use later in his writing. The practice, of course, marked him as eccentric as well as unsociable.

At first, Edwards's Northampton congregation had been mightily impressed with their brilliant young minister, but deep affection never developed between people and pastor. Perhaps people could listen only so long to sermons warning them of their corruption and God's awful wrath. There were problems over payment of his salary and a continual tug-of-war over church authority and how to exercise it. Always ready to point out sin anywhere he found it, Edwards alienated one group after another. With nerves already raw, in the late 1740s Edwards tactlessly tried to impose church discipline on some youths who were sniggering over a mysteriously obtained book of instruction for midwives. Other issues arose, and for weeks in 1750 the town was in ferment over Edwards. On June 22 the congregation dismissed their minister of twenty-three years, voting 230 to 23 against him. At age forty-six, past his prime (in his opinion) and with a large family to support, one of New England's most prominent religious leaders was out of a job.

By the fall of 1751, however, an influential friend helped him obtain a new position: missionary to the Indians in Stockbridge in western Massachusetts. With only twelve white families and about 250 Indians, rough companions all, Stockbridge lay beyond the New England frontier line, a mere speck in the forest. This gritty position was also one for which the polished Edwards was monumentally unsuited, although he went to it uncomplainingly, attributing his fate to God's will. After more than two decades in one of the most prominent pulpits in New England, Edwards had been cast into the wilderness.

But Stockbridge also gave Edwards more of his precious thinking time, and the result was *A Careful and Strict Enquiry into the Modern Prevailing*

Notions of the Freedom of the Will, probably his greatest work. In it, Edwards granted man freedom to carry out his own choices, but believed the choices were determined by motives outside his control. Thus he asserted both man's freedom and God's omnipotence.

Edwards had had a falling out with his alma mater, Yale, and had developed ties instead with the College of New Jersey, known today as Princeton University. The ties were strengthened in 1752 when his daughter Esther married Rev. Aaron Burr, president of the college. (A later, more notorious Aaron Burr, the one who killed Alexander Hamilton in a duel, was Jonathan Edwards's grandson.) Then, after seven years in Stockbridge, came an invitation to Edwards to become president of Princeton. By then, Edwards had developed a fondness for Stockbridge—probably because he appreciated the solitude—and had qualms about the presidency but was finally persuaded to accept it.

He arrived alone at Princeton on February 16, 1758, was reunited with daughter Esther, and was formally inducted into office that very day. On the twenty-third he was inoculated for smallpox, but had an adverse reaction and soon was fatally ill. Being who he was, Edwards soon accepted his fate as the will of God—predestination, and all that—and died quietly, age fifty-four. He had been president of Princeton for little more than a month.

Generous to his wife and children but parsimonious with himself, Jonathan Edwards died leaving few possessions except books. He had been largely forgotten in his native New England and newspapers noted his passing with only a line or two. The Edwards family tragedy didn't end there. Within two weeks of his death Jonathan's daughter Esther (whom a family friend had described as being "in every respect an ornament to her sex") also died of smallpox. Racked with grief at the loss of both husband and a daughter, Sarah, his widow, died of dysentery that very autumn.

The life of Jonathan Edwards, scarred by repudiation and exile, loneliness and isolation, ended in sickness and loss. And yet he had spent much of that life appreciating the beauties of the world and the wonders of nature. Most important, at the very core of things he always had the devotion of his children and his beloved Sarah, to whom he left a message, dictated on his deathbed: *Give my kindest love to my dear wife & tell her that the uncommon union that has so long subsisted between us has been of such a nature as I trust is spiritual and therefore will continue forever. . . .*

An uncommon union and an uncommon life, filled with glimpses of both Heaven and Hell. A career of highs and lows, with the best and worst that life has to offer. It was a life of spiders and rainbows.

The Myth in the White Dress

One December evening in 1883, in the dining room of a stately brick house in Amherst, Massachusetts, one of the town's most prominent men fell into the arms of a woman not his wife and found comfort of the most intimate kind. While the two made love, the man's sister was upstairs in her bedroom. We do not know what she was doing at that moment, but writing verse is a strong possibility, for this was a poet. The gossamer strands of words she left behind would eventually make her one of our most celebrated literary lights. Her name was Emily Dickinson.

The man in the dining room was Emily's brother, Austin Dickinson, a bluff and craggy-looking lawyer of fifty-four years, the treasurer of Amherst College, and a man of substance. For the previous few weeks, however, he had suffered agony to the point of suicidal thoughts because of the unexpected death October 5 of his eight-year-old son, Gib. The woman who helped him through those dark days, and who, on this evening, became his secret lover for the rest of his life, was Mabel Loomis Todd, the pretty, big-eyed young wife of a quirky Amherst College professor of astronomy named David Todd.

In one of the twists of history that makes truth stranger than fiction, Austin's lover would later take the first important step that would make Emily famous. For much of her life, Emily had been the most secluded of persons, scarcely glimpsed by her Amherst neighbors. They took to calling her "The Myth." But four years after Emily's death, Mabel—who never met the poet face to face, despite being in her house many times—was able to organize some of the hundreds of poems Emily left behind and bring them to press as a book in 1890.

Before her death, fewer than a dozen of Emily's poems had been published, one at a time, in various periodicals. Her shimmering style differed from the ponderous poetic forms favored then, so she attracted little notice. However, the 1890 collection edited by Mabel, who was joined in the work by Boston editor Thomas Wentworth Higginson, had a major public impact. By 1892, the book had gone through eleven editions. A second collection edited by Mabel and Higginson appeared in 1891 and it, too, went through multiple editions. By 1894 Emily's work was attracting enough interest for Mabel to publish two volumes of her letters and then, in 1896, a third volume of poems.

So—posthumously—Emily gradually emerged into the limelight despite herself. Since then, she has achieved that rare kind of superstardom that not only dominates its own genre but transcends it. Among the literati, she has been pronounced a "patron saint" by William Carlos Williams and, by others, the "founding mother" of American poetry (Walt Whitman being the "founding father"). But, like Picasso, Beethoven, and Shakespeare, she has also become a public celebrity, with name recognition even among those whose taste in poetry runs more to limericks.

The reclusive Emily was a riddle to the townspeople of Amherst and a puzzle even to those who were allowed to get close to her. Her life and the meaning of her work are like the proverbial mystery wrapped inside an enigma, examined, analyzed, and worked over in a endless river of articles and books. Devoted as well to the reclusive poet are the Emily Dickinson International Society (EDIS), *The Emily Dickinson Journal*, and many Web pages, including the EDIS official site (www.cwru.edu/affil/edis/ edisindex.html), the Emily Dickinson Random Epigram Machine (www.io.com/~smith/ed/), and what appears to be the digital equivalent of a fanzine (www.geocities.com/edickinson2002/). All Emily, all of the time.

Sometimes it seems as if everybody is looking for Emily Dickinson, trying to catch a will-o'-the-wisp, a specter in ghostly white hovering just beyond reach. Among the most skillful of Emily watchers is Martha Ackmann, a professor at Mount Holyoke College, who has written that "although we clearly have learned much over the past century about the life of Emily Dickinson, we also recognize that much remains to be fully understood. As every biographer knows, Dickinson always remains a bit on the loose."

A bit on the loose. It wasn't always that way. Born December 10, 1830, the second of three children of Edward and Emily Norcross Dickinson, Emily Elizabeth Dickinson was descended from a long line of Yankee men of affairs, her lineage tracing back to Puritan days. Emily's father, Edward, was a country lawyer who was elected to Congress and the Massachusetts legislature, and also served as treasurer of Amherst College. He was said to be unnervingly stern—an impression underscored by his portrait, wherein he resembles none so much as Scrooge McDuck—but he is not believed to have been unkind to his children.

Emily attended Amherst schools (where her unusual creativity was noted), and went for one year to what is now Mount Holyoke College. At

Mount Holyoke she resisted pressure to convert to founder Mary Lyons's Christian orthodoxy, so she was classified with those for whom there was "no hope." There, and in Amherst, the stubborn Emily rebuffed Protestant formalism, declaring, "I stand alone in rebellion." That took nerve.

The young Emily did not stand alone socially, however. In 1849 she enjoyed Christmas frivolities with friends, noting at the parties that beaus could be had for the taking. In their twenties Emily and younger sister Lavinia ("Vinnie") visited Washington, D.C., toured Mount Vernon, and visited Philadelphia. In 1856 her bread won second prize at the local agricultural fair. In 1859 her father had to fetch her home at midnight from a "revel" next door at the Evergreens. In 1864 and 1865 Emily spent considerable time in Boston getting eye treatment.

Emily had begun writing poetry around 1850. She was prolific, in 1862 alone writing at least 366 poems, or one a day. In the 1860s a handful were published, most of them in the *Springfield Republican*. Most of her poems were short, often mystical and usually metaphorical. Her innovative style, sometimes with unusual cadence, was unlike anything else being written. Starting in 1862, she corresponded with Boston literary figure Thomas Wentworth Higginson about her work. Although he advised her not to publish, he was intrigued with her poetry and remained her literary mentor the rest of her life.

Historians are not sure when Emily's withdrawal from the world began, but it appears to have been a gradual process. In 1869, only four years after she had returned from eye treatment in Boston, she refused Higginson's invitation to visit the city again with the famous words, "I do not cross my Father's ground to any House or Town." In 1873, she did consent to receive Higginson in her home, an experience that left him shaken. He later admitted he had never met anyone "who drained my nerve power so much." Higginson described Emily as "a little plain woman with two smooth bands of reddish hair" and "a step like a pattering child's." He could only sit and watch as she talked "in a soft frightened breathless childlike voice," saying "I never see strangers & hardly know what to say," whereupon she talked continuously.

In 1874, Emily's father, Edward, died in Boston, where he had been serving in the state legislature. The funeral was held downstairs in the Homestead, but Emily remained in her upstairs bedroom, the door cracked open so she could hear the proceedings. In 1875 Emily's mother was stricken with paralysis, not dying until 1882, leaving only Emily and sister Vinnie living in the Dickinson Homestead, with brother Austin and his wife, Susan Gilbert, next door in "The Evergreens." Meanwhile, she continued to write poetry but since the 1860s had resisted publication. In 1876 an Amherst literary friend, Helen Hunt Jackson, wrote her, "You are a great poet—and it is a wrong . . . that you will not sing aloud." By 1882, as Austin and Mabel's illicit romance was deepening, Mabel was invited to the Homestead to sing for Emily. This she did without ever seeing her: Mabel stood in the dining room, singing, while Emily listened, out of sight, on the stairway to the second floor.

And so the young Emily, notably creative, sociable, but stubbornly independent, turned into the notably creative, unsociable, and stubbornly independent older Emily, a legend in her own time. Occasionally townsfolk would report a sighting. From time to time she would appear at her bedroom window and lower treats in a basket to children below.

From that day to this, the questions and the speculation continue. Did she have any love affairs? (She may have had romantic feelings towards certain individuals, but just who they were, and how strong those feelings were, continues to be debated.) Was she, in fact, in love with her sister-in-law, Susan Gilbert Dickinson, wife of the unfaithful Austin? (A recent book finds the evidence in Emily's letters to Susan, but the theory has not gained wide acceptance.) What inspired her poetry, and what are its meanings? (The scholars will be working on this forevermore.) And *why* did she withdraw from society?

This is for sure: Emily did not withdraw because she was shy or delicate. To the contrary, she seems strong minded and feisty, with husky appetites. While her poetry could capture the buzz of a bumblebee, it could also capture the sting. For many years her beloved pet was a Newfoundland named Carlo. Newfies are huge, phlegmatic creatures who, if they were human, would probably smoke smelly black stogies. A Newfie is not the emblematic lap dog of delicate lady poet. Nor was she cut off from world affairs: she carried on a voluminous correspondence ("My friends are my 'estate'") and was an avid consumer of the media of the day, from newspapers to literary journals. Among the newspapers, she and Vinnie seemed to savor a diet of crime, train wrecks, and natural disasters, once writing to an editor to encourage more such news. Emily's "withdrawal" was not so much a withdrawal as an engaging of the world on her own terms.

And then there's the white dress. She was wearing one when she met Higginson; townspeople spied her in one often enough to begin commenting on it, and she was buried in white. In our minds, Emily Dickinson (abetted by modern impersonators, like Julie Harris) is always dressed in white, ghost-like and ethereal. Which is the reason for Amherst's "white dress project."

Many years ago a white dress strongly believed to have been Emily's was donated to the Amherst Historical Society. After being on display for several years in the Dickinson Homestead, which is owned by Amherst College, it seemed clear that light, dust, and stress from hanging on a mannequin were straining the garment. It was decided the dress would have to be given a rest (it's now kept in a secret location) and to have a replica made.

Entirely of white, the original dress was made of cotton, mostly machine-stitched with some additional hand-stitching. It has a long row of mother-of-pearl buttons down the front and is embroidered, pleated,

Emily Dickinson's white dress   *Emily's dress, reproduced*

and full-sleeved, with a large, handy pocket on the right side. The dress was really a house dress, the kind of comfortable garment women wore while doing chores without their corsets. It was a simple dress.

But it was not simple to reproduce. No patterns and no materials like the original could be found. An English firm specializing in historic fabrics was found to reproduce the cloth. A New Jersey company reproduced the embroidery and Adrienne Saint-Pierre, a Connecticut costumer well versed in historic preservation, was employed to make the two replicas. The entire project cost $10,000, raised by contributions from a number of sources.

Quizzed about all this effort, the head of the Amherst Historical Society, Melinda LeLacheur, and the director of the Dickinson Homestead, Cindy Dickinson (no relation, but thank you for asking), say that the popularity of the original dress demanded it. Seeing an exact replica of Emily Dickinson's dress is a way people can "see" Emily. Standing in front of the display case, taking the measure of this white figure—short, with a mature waistline—noting the pocket where Emily may have stuffed scraps of poetry written between her household chores, one senses her presence.

But what does the white dress mean? Some have suggested it signifies purity, others the virgin bride, and still others, the mystery of life. Others say Emily favored white because it set off her reddish-bronze hair. Some ask why couldn't it simply have been a comfortable, inexpensive household garment? Why can't a dress just be a dress? But Melinda LeLacheur says that Emily's life was so filled with metaphors that it is hard to imagine a purely mundane explanation.

Certainly, Vinnie, who survived her and probably made Emily's funeral arrangements, saw significance in the white. She had Emily buried in a white casket lined with white flannel and fitted with white textile handles. As Emily had wished, six Irish workmen familiar with the family carried the casket through the fields "full of buttercups" to a nearby cemetery. A few days before her death, Emily had written her favorite nieces simply, "Little Cousins, Called back, Emily." Engraved on her tombstone are the words, "Called back."

One October I spent the night in a bed-and-breakfast just a few doors down Amherst's Main Street from the Dickinson Homestead. The house had been built in 1886, the very year Emily died. I stood on a second-floor porch gazing up the street, pretending it was 1886, and tried to find Emily's house, now hidden behind shrubs which have grown up since her day. I wanted a glimpse of the woman who rejected our company but had so much to say to us. In my imagination, she could have looked back from her conservatory, or perhaps peered out her bedroom window, and at that exact moment I might have seen her, a flash of white. But somehow the modern shrubbery kept me from seeing anything at all, even in my imagination. It's always like that with Emily Dickinson; we try to see her clearly, try to catch her, try to understand her mysteries absolutely. But, of course, we never do. And that's why we keep trying.

Life in College Town

Three of the "Five Colleges" (Smith, Mount Holyoke, and Hampshire) are located a few miles outside Amherst, but Amherst is the epicenter of the Five-College Region. The small town finds itself squeezed between polar opposites of higher education. Prestigious Amherst College (sixteen hundred students, nineteen percent acceptance rate, $34,000 in fees per year and rising) anchors the southern end of the village, while plebeian UMass, with its high-rise dorms, twenty-three thousand students, porous admissions, and $5,200 in fees (also rising), looms to the north. The town fermenting between them is the kind of yeasty, freethinking place that, as Tracy Kidder once put it, has a fine school system and its own foreign policy.

Amherst looks, sounds, and smells like a college town, exuding an exotic seediness that mixes with the aristocracy of fine old college buildings. As thousands of young hearts pound to a hip-hop beat, the brashness of youth and the wisdom of the ages meet and mix. In a bagel shop you see a bearded, potbellied professorial type wearing a sweatshirt with the message, "I think, therefore I'm dangerous." On the sidewalk a covey of college girls—"women" would be too strong a word in this case—flutters by, scattering Southie-flavored sentence fragments connected only by the sine qua non of teenytalk, the word *like*: "I'm like, *Go away!* You know? and she's like, *Wee-ahd!* So I go, Heath-ah, I am *NOT* loaning you my lab notes. So she's, like, all mad. . . ." Passing in the other direction is a herd of young bulls with attitude, apparently moving backwards until you realize it's only their baseball caps. In the window of one restaurant you see Indian students eating Chinese, in the window of another, Chinese students eating pizza. A couple pauses in a doorway to kiss. A dog barks, a sophomore belches, and a Beethoven sonata, played not badly on a single violin, drifts from an open window.

Ah, life in the Garden of Youth, a crowded place where it's hard to be lonely and easy to be silly . . . for a little while. All this shall pass, of course, and the Five-College Region's bouncing molecules will grow up to inherit the tuition bills of new generations of the callow, who, in one form or another, are always with us, bugging us sometimes but mostly charming us with their innocence, their enthusiasm, and a promise they have made without even knowing it: *they will become us and probably just a little better.* It's, like, wonderful, you know?

You can almost sense Hadley, Massachusetts, as it was during Goffe and Whalley's time when you visit the wide Hadley green. It lies along West Street, off Route 9 between Amherst and Northampton. Fine old houses line the green, but, unfortunately, Parson Russell's, with all its hidey-holes, is long gone. More information can be found on Libby Klekowski's Web page, "Angel of Hadley—Fact or Myth?" (http://www.bio.umass.edu/biology/conn.river/hadley.html).

More about the Northampton of Jonathan Edwards's day, and later, can be learned at the Historic Northampton Museum and Education Center, a collection of several historic buildings at 46 Bridge Street, Northampton (413-584-6011; www.historic-northampton.org).

The Five-College Region has excellent museums, their treasures ranging from ancient Greek ceramics to the photography of William Wegman and his Weimaraners. The Pratt Museum of Natural History on the campus of Amherst College has a collection of dinosaur fossils (413-542-2165; www.amherst.edu/~pratt/). Tours of Emily's house are offered regularly, but best booked in advance. The Dickinson Homestead is at 280 Main Street, Amherst; brother Austin's home, The Evergreens, is next door (413-542-8161; www.dickinsonhomestead.org). Jones Library, 43 Amity Street, also has memorabilia of Dickinson and Robert Frost on display (413-256-4090, www.joneslibrary.org/specialcollections). Nearby, the Amherst History Museum in the eighteenth-century Strong House at 67 Amity Street provides fine insights into local history (413-256-0678; www.amhersthistory.org). On the Hampshire College campus in the rolling countryside south of Amherst, there is, of all things, the National Yiddish Book Center, open to the public six days a week (413-256-4900; www.yiddishbookcenter.org). Still further down the road, in South Hadley, is the Mount Holyoke College Art Museum (413-538-2245; www.mtholyoke.edu/offices/artmuseum). At this writing, Smith College is renovating and expanding its art museum, which is scheduled to open early in 2003 (413-585-2760; http://www.smith.edu/artmuseum).

Elsewhere in the region, the Porter-Phelps Huntington House, 130 River Drive in Hadley, is a thoroughly engaging New England house museum with a long family history (413-584-4699).

CHAPTER NINE

THE REDEEMED AND THE UNREDEEMED

Just before my tenth birthday, we moved from the relatively urbane city of Springfield, Massachusetts, to the very un-urbane town of Charlemont. Straddling a tourist road called the Mohawk Trail and tucked in the lovely mountains of northwest Massachusetts, Charlemont dozed beside the Deerfield River, one of the Connecticut's many tributaries. Charlemonters farmed or sold souvenirs to the tourists, who were viewed with pity for their eagerness to pay good money for rubber tomahawks, musical toilet paper dispensers, and aromatic pillows carrying such messages as "I pine for you and balsam."

It was the era just after World War II when thousands of veterans were flocking to the countryside to start chicken ranches. My father bought a Charlemont farm (right next to a chicken ranch) and started a nursery business, sure to be a winner when all those veterans began landscaping their new Cape Cod–style homes. Accustomed to a big-city school system, I now found myself in the Charlemont village school, which housed grades one through twelve in one ancient building.

Elementary grades, two to a room, occupied the first floor, while a high school enrolling about forty students was on the second. The basement was divided into three areas. At the eastern end was a tiny cafeteria equipped with a bottomless reservoir of chipped dried beef. At the western end, a chemistry lab combined with the boys' latrine to produce odors capable of clearing any sinus. Deep in the bowels of the building was the boiler room where the custodian, Baldy Bill, maintained a delicious gallery of nude calendars that students liked to study while Baldy was busy elsewhere. Here we boys received some of our first anatomy lessons, or did until little Dolly Higgins wandered in one day and ran squealing to her parents.

Memorable among our high school teachers was one I will call Miss Jones, because she's probably still out there somewhere. Newly hatched from a nearby teacher's college, Miss Jones completed dressing for work each day by thrusting a supply of tissues down the front of her blouse, the better to dab her nose as she struggled through another day with Charlemont High's reluctant learners. This appeared to give her one more bosom than the normal quota of two ("bosom" being our most refined term for a single breast). After thoughtful contemplation of this phenomenon, we students divided into two camps. The more-is-better crowd held that a woman could never have too many breasts. Opposed were the minimalists, who considered three bosoms an affront to the American Way. And so time passed at Charlemont High School.

Presiding over the entire school was the principal, a testy gentleman I will call Mr. Dilworth, because he's probably out there somewhere as well. Probably his workload made him cranky. As well as supervising the whole building, Mr. Dilworth was expected to teach high school classes, substitute at a moment's notice in any grade from one through twelve, and coach basketball and baseball. Mr. Dilworth did his best, but his coaching strategy for basketball boiled down to three words: "You gotta hustle" (delivered somewhat testily, as I recall). One day Mr. Dilworth summoned two of us junior boys to the principal's tiny office. He told us that our scores on the latest statewide ability tests differed noticeably from our classmates, but whether our scores were higher or lower than theirs he cagily kept to himself. The point, Mr. Dilworth said, was that more was expected of us and we had better start hustling.

Our parents took this as a wakeup call and promptly removed us from Mr. Dilworth's care in favor of nearby boarding schools. I was sent to Mount Hermon School for Boys, in Gill, Massachusetts, on the western bank of the Connecticut. My classmate went to Deerfield Academy a few miles south. After seven years of being sequestered in the hills of Charlemont, I was back in the Connecticut River Valley. I felt as if I had been redeemed.

The Girl Who Never Came Home

One September I spent a pleasant night at a bed-and-breakfast in the southern part of Deerfield, Massachusetts. The next morning I happened to mention the famous Deerfield massacre of 1675, and my hostess, Edna Stahelek, exclaimed, "It happened right here!" It turned out that her yellow gabled home fronts on Bloody Brook and a monument to the catastrophe is just across the street.

Deerfield is an intersection of tourism, preppie education, historical preservation, and sorrowful memories. Surrounded by farm fields, it is set in the Pocumtuck Valley, not far from where the Deerfield River flows into the Connecticut. Repeated flooding by the Deerfield has given the Pocumtuck plain extraordinarily rich soil, while nearby hills shelter it from extremes of climate. For both Indians and, later, the white settlers, the Pocumtuck Valley had location, location, location.

By 1675 more than two hundred white people lived here in a frontier village they called Pocumtuck. But then King Philip's War erupted. A wagon train and soldiers were sent to save the town's valuable crop of grain. On September 18, 1675, as the loaded wagons were slowly crossing Muddy Brook four miles south of Pocumtuck, the Indians attacked, killing most of the company. The little stream flowed with blood, forever changing its name to Bloody Brook, and the last demoralized handful of Pocumtuck's English defenders fled.

In 1680 settlers began to return, changing Pocumtuck's name to Deerfield. By 1688 the frontier town's population had swelled to about 235, mostly adventurous young people moving a few miles up the valley from older towns. They voted to call Rev. John Williams to minister to them. The precocious Williams was just twenty-one and already three years out of Harvard. He answered the call to Deerfield and within a year had married Eunice Mather, daughter of a late minister in nearby Northampton.

The Rev. John settled in to be Deerfield's spiritual leader for more than forty years. Deerfield's residents formed a close-knit little community sharing a hardscrabble but promising existence on the outermost edge of New England life. They laid out roads, built a grain mill and also a new meetinghouse for the Reverend Mr. Williams, and hired a schoolteacher. Poor but proud, Deerfield entered the 1700s with cautious optimism, turning quietly in its own orbit. But in the woods nearby the wolves howled.

Beginning in 1688, nearly two and half decades of conflict between the British and the French and their Indian allies brought still more attacks in

*Old Deerfield's Indian House door,
scarred by attackers in 1704*

the Connecticut River Valley. Deerfield quickly built up its defenses, creating a log stockade on Meetinghouse Hill that enclosed perhaps ten acres, the meetinghouse, and about a dozen houses, including Williams's own. In late February 1704, Deerfield felt relatively safe, for it was thought the bitter cold and heavy snow would discourage invaders from trudging the three hundred miles from "New France" (Canada). No one would have guessed that two hundred Indians, mostly French Mohawks and Abenaki, plus fifty French soldiers, were already moving on snowshoes in Deerfield's direction.

Studying the stockade, the French and Indians could hardly believe their luck. Snow had drifted against the ten- to twelve-foot palisade, giving the attackers an easy path over the stockade wall. As the night wore on, the watchman (whom Williams would later call "faithless") was no longer seen on guard. About two hours before dawn, forty of the raising party went over the wall, opening the north gates for the rest. "With horrid shouting and yelling," Williams later wrote, the enemy fell "like a flood upon us."

The minister was awakened by the sound of axes and hatchets breaking open his doors and windows. He ran back to his bedroom, where he grabbed his pistol and tried to fire it at the first of about twenty Indians, who, with "painted faces and hideous exclamations," rushed after him. The pistol misfired, so three of the invaders disarmed Williams and "bound me naked." Then the shivering minister watched the Indians ransack his house and murder two of his eight children: six-year-old John and little Jerusha, who had been born only six weeks before.

Shortly after dawn, Williams and the rest of his family were marched out of their home and past Deerfield's burning houses for a rendezvous with other prisoners. Then began a long, brutal trek through snowy woods, north to Canada. Of the 291 persons who had been in Deerfield that night, fewer than half escaped death or capture.

Once settled in Montreal and the nearby Indian village of Kahnawake, the Deerfield people were treated fairly well, although they were pressed to convert to Catholicism. Slowly and in bunches, many of the captives were "redeemed" (i.e., ransomed) and on November 21, 1706, nearly three years after his capture, the Reverend John Williams stepped ashore in Boston. By then all of his children had been redeemed as well. All, that is, but one.

While her father was being welcomed in Massachusetts, little Eunice Williams remained in Indian hands, as did about twenty-eight others, mostly children. In some cases, their new Indian families had developed affection for them and refused to let them go. Even the French governor Vaudreuil, who sympathized with Eunice and respected her father, could not persuade Eunice's Indian master to give her up.

Back in Deerfield, Williams returned to the pulpit, wrote an account of his experience, called *The Redeemed Captive of Zion*, and remarried within a year (his first wife had died on the trek to Canada). In 1707, word reached Williams that one Schuyler, a Dutch merchant in Albany with dealings in Canada, had seen little Eunice, and had news both reassuring and shocking. Eunice was in good health, but now, at age ten, "seemes unwilling to Returne." The years dragged on. Occasional sightings and rumors reaching Deerfield kept Eunice alive but floating ghost-like, tantalizingly out of reach. Hopes were repeatedly raised, then dashed.

Then, in 1713, came very bad news indeed, news not quite as terrible as death, but to the Puritan way of thinking, very close to it: Eunice, born a Christian and destined to be a Puritan gentlewoman, had now, at age sixteen, married an Indian and a Catholic one at that! Within weeks the Dutch merchant Schuyler was able to visit Eunice and her new husband at Kahnawake and, speaking through interpreters, plead with her to come back, or at least make a visit to New England.

But Eunice "proved harder than Steel," remaining absolutely silent almost to the end. She gave her visitors one terse answer: *No, not even a visit.* She would say nothing more. A few years after this, another delegation came to see her, this one from New England and including the father who had not seen her in a decade. But John Williams was completely rebuffed by his daughter, reporting later, "And yet she is obstinately resolved to live and dye here, and will not so much as give me one pleasant look."

Her Indian family had given Eunice Williams both a French name—Marguerite—and a Mohawk Iroquois name, A'ongote, meaning, roughly, "She who has been placed as a member of the tribe." At some point she acquired a second Indian name, Gannenstenhawi, meaning "She who brings in corn." Her husband was Francis Xavier Arosen, the first two names being his baptismal name, the last a Mohawk word meaning squirrel. Arosen came to Kahnawake as an outsider as well, for he belonged to the New York Mohawks, not the Canadian. Eventually Marguerite A'ongote Gannenstenhawi and Francis Xavier Arosen had two daughters, Catherine and Marie.

Meanwhile, back in Deerfield John Williams and his family were prospering. His three oldest sons became ministers and his daughter Esther married one. All four adult children named one of their own children Eunice. Then, in July 1729, Rev. John Williams died of a stroke. To the end he had prayed for the "redemption" of his daughter, now in her early thirties and still refusing to return to Deerfield or even visit it.

Since mid-childhood in Canada, Eunice/Marguerite had been determinedly hostile to her father. John Demos, a Yale professor who told her story in a prizewinning and highly readable book, *The Unredeemed Captive,* thinks she felt she had been abandoned. Even as a small child in Deerfield she must have sensed her father was a powerful man, one to whom others deferred. Yet she had been dragged from her bed, carried by strangers on a terrifying journey through the woods, and, when she begged her father for rescue, offered nothing but reminders to pray and remember her Scriptures. Then he had walked away from her, not to be seen again for years.

Meanwhile, new bonds of affection had quickly sprung up to replace the old. The Iroquois were extremely fond of children and they undoubtedly indulged little Eunice/Marguerite, whom they adopted into their family. As the girl grew older, her tribe and family no longer insisted on holding her but repeatedly told visitors she could choose to leave if she wished. Of course, she did not, as they must have guessed.

While one of the meanings of "redeem" is to "to release from captivity," another is "to remove from blame." As the years wore on and Eunice Williams turned into Marguerite A'ongote Gannenstenhawi, she was transformed from captive into a beloved member of another family and another community. Nevertheless, the searing memory of capture by strangers and then seeming abandonment by her father caused her to wrap him in blame. Looked at this way, who now was the redeemed and who was the unredeemed?

Not long ago I was noodling around the World Wide Web when I came across some pages posted by an Ann Favret of Worthington, Ohio. I was astonished to find that the pages presented the genealogy of the very same Williams family I had been researching. With all the Williamses in the world, it turned out that Ann Favret had been born Ann Elizabeth Williams, and she was directly descended from the Reverend John.

Mrs. Favret knows the whole story of the redeemed and unredeemed captives and has visited her ancestor's grave in Deerfield. And Mrs. Favret had a little surprise for me: not only had she married a man with roots in France, the ancient enemy of her New England ancestors, she had converted to Catholicism, the religion her Puritan forebears despised. "Get used to it, John," she laughed when I asked her how she'd explain that to the Reverend John Williams. "It's okay. I'll be in heaven beside you."

She grew serious as we continued to talk about her distant aunt, Eunice/Marguerite, and John Williams, her grandfather many times removed. She didn't fault either one. "No, I don't regret what she did [choosing not to return home]," Mrs. Favret said. "She seems to have been happy. She was loved. Why wouldn't she want to stay?" And she has some kind words for John Williams as well. "I understand why he was upset. He had a right to be indignant, back then. But I think he's found out since that the doors to heaven are open to people of every faith. Probably in today's world he would be much more understanding. I think he would value any Christian religion."

Redemption.

"Crazy Moody" and the Un-Prep School

There was a neighborhood in Chicago so dirty and dangerous that it was called "Little Hell." Even the police would not go there. But on almost any Sunday in the late 1850s and early 1860s a respectably dressed young man could be seen riding a pony through Little Hell, one or two ragged urchins riding behind him and a crowd of others tagging along. The man's name was Dwight Lyman Moody, but for his daring to enter Little Hell to conduct Sunday School classes people called him "Crazy Moody."

Moody was a prosperous if poorly educated shoe salesman who had grown up on an impoverished New England farm and left home at age sixteen. As years passed, Moody added avoirdupois—plenty of it—so that later in life, with a beard turned white, he resembled nothing so much as Santa Claus with a Yankee accent. By then no one called him Crazy Moody. Instead, they called him the most important evangelist of the nineteenth century. He packed huge auditoriums in both England and America and captivated audiences—in an age that had no electronic amplification—with his locomotive of a voice and his charismatic personality.

Evangelist Dwight L. Moody made a powerful impression

"Sometimes he's called the Billy Graham of his time," someone once said to me. "But, really, you could call Billy Graham the Dwight Moody of our time." Still, Moody has wound up in the dustbin of history, scarcely mentioned in the standard textbooks. That makes sense, according to the late William G. McLoughlin of Brown University, a noted historian of religion: for all the excitement Moody caused and for all the individuals he "converted," he achieved no real change in the beliefs and values prevailing in his day.

One fall day I arrived at a big white farmhouse in Northfield, Massachusetts, a place I had been before and where I was going to spend a couple of nights. Country plain and worn around the edges, the old house sits on the crest of a hill overlooking the Connecticut River Valley. Low green hills with the first touches of autumn color rose softly nearby, and the river itself could be seen gleaming through the trees. In this house Dwight Lyman Moody was born in 1837, so it is called as The Birthplace. It hasn't changed a lot since he lived there.

But something has changed: instead of the fields and pastures of Moody's boyhood, the old house is surrounded by one of the two campuses of Northfield Mount Hermon, the largest independent boarding school in America. Nearly twelve hundred boys and girls from throughout the United

States and around the world come here each year to prepare for college. This is a place that many in the outside world would call a "prep school."

The term "prep school" conjures up images of Biff and Muffy, pretentious little prigs in blazers, scions of old wealth who can afford to study the dead poets and other froufrou matters. In reality, the nation's independent schools—which educate about 1.5 percent of our children—are less exclusive than they used to be and more diverse (although, like the best liberal arts colleges, they are still selective and far from cheap). And, like Moody and the old farmhouse that symbolizes him, Northfield Mount Hermon turns out to be a school of few pretenses.

I arrived in time for Northfield Mount Hermon's opening convocation, a long ritual of welcome-backs, awards, and uplift. In orderly rows, the students marched into an old auditorium dating from Moody's day, neatly scrubbed and trimmed and wearing their "special occasion dress"— jackets, ties, dresses or dressy slacks and tops, altogether a sight for parents' sore eyes. But they were still kids. When the sheriff of Franklin County, in top hat and tails, ritualistically tapped his staff of office on the stage floor three times, they exuberantly stamped their feet three times. When, in rich New England tones, he bawled, "Gawd save the Commonwealth of Massachusetts," they chorused back, "God save the Commonwealth of Massachusetts!" Everyone smiled.

Then I set out to explore Northfield Mount Hermon, a name compressed in daily discourse to "EnEmAitch." I was curious about this school, for my future wife and I had graduated from it many years before and knew it had changed. Most of all, I wanted to find out this: was this still the school envisioned more than a century ago by its founder, Dwight L. Moody, Christian evangelist? More pointedly, did Moody himself still mean anything to anybody?

Moody's greatest successes as an evangelist came during the period 1875-1885, but after that the times seemed to increasingly pass him by. A shrewd reader of audiences, he began to develop other strategies for saving souls. One was to establish two private secondary schools, Northfield for girls and Mount Hermon for boys. The girls' school opened on the old Moody farm in Northfield in 1879. At first the girls were housed upstairs in The Birthplace in an area they called "Penny Alley." Two years later, on farmland purchased in Gill, five miles away, Mount Hermon was opened for boys.

Established in America's Gilded Age, these were private schools with a difference: they welcomed poor children as well as others and they were diverse in their admissions. An American Indian and a Chinese student were among the members of Northfield's entering class. Moody's sympathy for the less advantaged, for educating "calico girls" and not just "velvet girls," sprang from his own impoverished childhood and his work with the poor of Chicago. But these schools were also supposed to serve the Gospel, preparing workers for Christ.

From Penny Alley, Northfield and Mount Hermon have grown into a physical plant many colleges would envy. Merged into one coeducational school in 1971, NMH's two campuses cover more than three thousand acres and include over 160 buildings. There's even a maple sugar house, for the schools have always had their own farm operations. But the core of EnEmAitch is its educational program, which since Moody's day has called for educating "The Head, the Hand, and the Heart."

To educate the head, students can choose from about three hundred courses, ranging from art to multivariable calculus. They take only two major, or college preparatory, courses per term (the year has three terms). NMH students also typically take one minor class per term, with no homework or exams, in which they can develop their creative side or explore moral or social issues. In the late afternoon are sports (NMH has over sixty-five sports teams for boys and girls, ranging from field hockey to football), music practice, or some other activity. From 8 to 10 p.m. is required study time. And, as they have from the founding, "all students participate equally in the daily work of the school." About four and a half hours per week are spent on the student's work assignment. Every student has a job, from picking raspberries on the school farm to sorting socks in the laundry.

Moody could probably accept most of today's curriculum and certainly he'd recognize the work program as well as the school's strong tradition of music, but his famous temper might flare at NMH's approach to spirituality. Moody's school no longer tries to save souls for a Protestant heaven and chapel is no longer required, although spirituality is still valued. Viewing spirituality much more broadly than Moody did, NMH requires instead that all students take nondenominational religious study courses. In addition, required assemblies on each campus introduce different religions monthly. "If we tried to require students to attend [Christian] chapel, we'd have a riot on our hands," Rev. Betty Stookey, school chaplain, said. "We have Buddhists, Muslims, Catholics, Jews, and others, and in significant numbers. We should not force them into one religious mold."

Death of a Headmaster

Every school, large or small, has its legends, its secrets, and its mysteries. At my school, Mount Hermon School for Boys (now Northfield Mount Hermon School), all three were wrapped up in one man: Elliott Speer.

Speer, who was headmaster for scarcely two years in the 1930s—long before I got there—is a legend because of what he accomplished. To this day, men who were students during his brief administration call themselves the "Speer Boys" and remain devoted to his memory.

But, looking back on it, the story of what happened to Elliott Speer was a campus secret, one that I never heard when I was there. In fact, I roomed in the home of the assistant headmaster, a man who had been a participant, though a minor one, in the drama, and he never mentioned it. Not once. Nor did anyone else. It was as if the adults had taken an oath never to discuss it in front of the boys.

Which is understandable, because the Speer story is also a mystery of the worst kind, the kind moderns would call an "O.J. Simpson case," where the mystery lies not so much in who did it (because we think we know), but how on earth the apparently guilty party was able to evade justice.

Speer, a Presbyterian minister, came to Mount Hermon in 1932, succeeding Henry Franklin Cutler, a strict disciplinarian who had ruled the boys' school for forty-two years. Right away Speer began loosening the constraints, introducing dances for Northfield and Mount Hermon students and allowing students to read the *New York Times* on Sunday. The students and many faculty quickly became devoted to him, but one who did not was Thomas E. Elder, a dean who had long been a key figure in the previous administration.

On Friday evening, September 14, 1934, with students scheduled to return on Monday to start a new school year, Speer retired to the library of Ford Cottage, a large brick Georgian house still used today as the head's residence. Shortly after 8 p.m., someone standing in the rainy darkness outside the library window fired a shotgun blast, mortally wounding Speer. He died a few minutes later.

Newspapers across the country headlined the story as the

shocked trustees tried to figure out what to do. Then Elder, whose position made him one of the candidates to succeed to Speer, produced two letters that he said were an exchange of correspondence between him and the late headmaster. In the one supposedly from Speer, Elder was praised extravagantly and made many promises of salary and pension benefits. In his purported reply, Elder stressed how "loyal" he was to Speer. The letters are puzzling in light of the tensions that had existed between Speer and Elder. The state police were more than puzzled: they declared the letters to be forgeries. They concluded something else as well: given the maze of paths and woods on the Hermon campus, the killing was almost certainly an inside job, committed by someone intimately familiar with the area.

Suspicion quickly enveloped Elder. However, the murder weapon was never found and a ten-day inquest failed to produce an official suspect. Elder had become such an anathema to the community that he was asked to resign. He spent the rest of his life in New Hampshire, eked out a living as a cattle classifier, and died in 1947.

Who killed Elliott Speer . . . and why? Officially, the mystery remains to this day. But it isn't ready for the cold-case file yet. In Columbus, Ohio, Craig Walley, a 1956 graduate of Mount Hermon and a lawyer, is researching it, with a book-length examination of the case in mind. If you have any information that could help, contact him by e-mail at speerbook@aol.com.

Victim in an unsolved mystery, Elliott Speer (in car)
followed Henry Cutler (left) as headmaster

Ironically, this religious diversity is a natural result of one of Moody's founding principles, that each school view itself as an opportunity school for diverse peoples. The opportunity extends to less-advantaged youngsters: NMH grants financial aid to nearly half of its students, a higher percentage than its peer schools. It also seeks students from throughout the world as well as minorities from this country. International students, coming from as many as forty or more countries, typically make up a fourth of NMH's enrollment; ten percent is more typical of independent schools.

Fittingly, Richard W. Mueller, head of the school, was a thirty-two-year veteran of the U.S. Foreign Service when NMH's board of trustees tapped him. Consul general in Hong Kong at the time, Mueller had no professional experience as an educator ("It never occurred to me"), but the NMH trustees liked his leadership skills, conditioned by years of diplomacy, and his belief in collaborative decision-making.

"This place has changed a lot in the past three years [since Mueller arrived]," one faculty member told me. Hopefully, though, history won't repeat itself. In the 1930s another new headmaster with ideas, Elliott Speer, was about to begin his third year at Mount Hermon when he was murdered in one of America's most famous campus crimes. It is still unsolved. "I pray a lot," says Mueller with a grin.

NMH faculty, all of whom coach sports or advise activities as well as teach, also serve *in loco parentis*. New faculty must live in dormitory apartments for their first seven years, although some choose to stay longer. Their job is to shape the whole person. For Lorrie Byrom, dean of the faculty, the ideal graduate of NMH is a person who "is willing to take a stand, is not easily influenced by peers, is articulate in writing and speaking, and has international and environmental perspectives." And any EnEmAitcher should be "comfortable with diversity," she says. Byrom recalls raising small children when she and her husband lived in an NMH dormitory. "They'd open the door to anybody," she remembers. "It didn't matter if they had green hair or wore a coat and tie."

Asked why they chose NMH over other schools, most students told me that it is more "liberal." They mean different things by this, "without limits" not being one of them. Some students, already politically aware, feel the school is more supportive of their social values. Some dislike the pressures for conformity at some other independent schools. Toniness has never been a Northfield Mount Hermon hallmark, either. Inspired by the school's farm program, students have made a cherubic pink pig the school mascot and call their teams the Hoggers. Not very preppie.

The place may be "liberal," but not everything goes. The man charged with the thankless task of applying just the right amount of discipline to 1,160 bright and frisky adolescents is Randy Stevens, a jovial bear of a man with an uncanny resemblance to Garrison Keillor. One September when I was there, Stevens/Keillor was managing, as usual, to sound good humored in the face of the latest student kerfuffle. Taught by NMH to stand up and make their cases, Stevens's young charges were moaning about their Constitutional right to go bra-less and bare-naveled. "I've never heard so much about midriffs in my life," sighed one administrator. A junior girl on the Mount Hermon campus grumbled to me, "If you got boobs, you got boobs, they're still a distraction, bra or no bra." The Stevens position was compellingly simple, however: "When you have fully developed young women with no bras in the same room as boys with raging hormones, it's not conducive to learning." At last report, both Stevens and the students were holding firm.

NHM staffers don't doubt that Dwight Moody might be disconcerted at first by what his schools have become. But, says Lorrie Byrom, "We'd expect him to stand on his own two feet and make his case, like any good EnEmAitcher." That said, most think Moody would come to realize that what he created had to grow with the times. "I think he would be very proud," says Meg Lyons, the school's alumni director. "What we're doing is very close to his vision. He was saying, 'Stand up for what you believe.'" Lyons, who taught at several schools before coming to NMH, says, "What we say to teenagers is, 'Go out and make a difference. You have that responsibility, to make the world a better place.'"

One morning, shortly after 7:30, I happened to walk into the octagonal parlor Moody had added to The Birthplace as a gift to his elderly mother. As usual, early morning river fog enveloped the campus, but it would lift soon, raising the curtain on a tapestry of fields and soft hills where Moody liked to roam. Running through my mind was music from yesterday's convocation, a thousand young voices rising in the school song, William Blake's "Jerusalem":

> I will not cease from mental fight
> Nor shall my sword sleep in my hand
> Till we have built Jerusalem
> In every green and pleasant land.

There is redemption in this place. It has forever graced Dwight Moody, whom some might consign to oblivion but who turns out to be alive here, on the hilltops and in the halls, the woods and water, and in the hearts and minds of NMH's twenty-five thousand alumni of all races and creeds, all around the globe. Moody's belief that *everyone* is worth saving and his commitment to making a difference in the world are ideas that guide NMH today, although the school defines them in more secular terms. And the NMH idea is a renewable resource, a belief that education is a journey, not a destination. The burden of being human is that we need salvation, secular or spiritual, again and again; the glory is that it is always available to us. Moody's not finished with me yet.

It's Great to be Green!

The portion of Deerfield, Massachusetts, which is off the beaten path and known today as Old or Historic Deerfield, has a main street that stretches for a mile, sheltered by ancient trees and an honor guard of handsome old houses. Locals call it, simply, "The Street." In 2002 The Street doesn't look very different from how it did in 1902—neater, if anything— or even 1802. Some of its houses date back to the early 1700s. It's a place with ancient roots, long traditions, and its own way of doing things.

In August, 1902, a stranger walked down The Street, bringing *his* way of doing things to the little farm town. At the time, no one would have bet a nickel on his chances. Five-foot-four, 120 pounds, wearing spectacles and greased-down hair parted in the middle, twenty-two-year-old Frank Learoyd Boyden looked like a wet-behind-the-ears pip-squeak. What no one could see was the iron in his spine and the wiliness wired into his neurons.

At first, Boyden didn't realize this himself. His only goal was to earn enough money as head of Deerfield Academy, an academic backwater, to get out of town and go to law school. But, gradually, Deerfield took over Boyden and Boyden took over Deerfield, and today mentioning the name of the town in educators' circles will usually prompt the name of the man. Once again we learn Napoleon's First Law: underestimate pip-squeaks at your own risk.

Today, Frank Learoyd Boyden is a legend and his school the kind of place that the news media unfailingly refer to as "the elite Deerfield Academy." When Boyden arrived, Deerfield Academy was a quasi-public rural day school enrolling only fourteen students. "It's a tossup whether the academy needs a new headmaster or an undertaker," one of its trustees said. But in the next few years Boyden proved surprisingly resourceful. Threading his way through a mare's nest of local politics, he boosted school performance and brought in new students, many of whom he had recruited personally on horse-and-buggy trips through the countryside. From serving rural youngsters fresh from the field, Deerfield Academy gradually turned to the city youth who had the talent, the money, and the ambition for college.

Eventually, Deerfield rose to an eminence that got the prominent and the wealthy pressing for admission (though not always successfully. Boyden turned down the sons of the president of Amherst College, his alma mater, because they were "too small in size"). The students' confidence in themselves rose as well and took on a *noblesse oblige* flavor: an early student publication proclaimed, "It is the inevitable rule of life that the strong and able shall lead those not so gifted. It is the purpose of this school to turn out primarily only those who should in some way become leaders in our national life." Since then, Rockefellers, the King of Jordan, many educators, lawyers, and business executives, and countless children of governors and congressmen have attended Deerfield. When Boyden retired in 1968 after sixty-six years as headmaster, the academy was in the front rank of American private schools.

Boyden employed an arsenal of talents to take it there. He turned out to be a natural educator. He was a wily politician with a knack for cultivating allies. With the face of a "grumpy Labrador" (according to writer John McPhee, a Deerfield grad), his diminutive size and rumpled appearance led opponents to underestimate him. He knew how to tell a good story with the right amount of embroidery. He could flush out wealth and tree it: *Newsweek* magazine said he had "a genius for persuading people to part with their money." So determined to do everything for "my boys" (the school was boys-only for much of his tenure, but now is coed), he resisted taking vacations and expected his faculty to work long days, just as he did. He also expected them to do as he said.

Today, Deerfield Academy (which its members call DA, pronounced "DeeYay"), enrolls about six hundred students, about half of whom attended private schools in their earlier grades. Despite this indicator of a privilege, Deerfield admits on a need-blind basis; once admitted, about a fourth of its students are granted financial aid. The school admitted its first black in 1959 and now has a significant minority population. Like Northfield Mount Hermon, essentially one hundred percent of Deerfield

grads go on to college, a significant percentage of them
to the Ivies and other highly
selective institutions. After
that, the emblematic career
choice is finance.

Frank Boyden has been
dead for more than a quarter-
century, but his presence is
seen everywhere. Deerfield's
instructors are demanding and
the sports program intense,
involving every student in
competition. That's the way
Boyden always wanted it. The
campus is immaculate: John
McPhee wrote that Boyden
would personally summon a

*A horse and carriage became trademarks
for Deerfield's Frank Boyden*

custodian when he spotted so much as a scuff mark on a stair riser. And
although the title of the administrator of some other private schools has
evolved into "head of the school," Deerfield's Eric Widmer is still called
headmaster. That's not without significance.

Widmer, Deerfield '57, was a professor and administrator at Brown
University before being called to the academy's top post in 1994. He is
plainspoken and deliberate in his manner, carries an air of authority, and is
unfazed by Boyden's ghostly presence. When Boyden built the Academy
Building, an administrative center that also has classrooms, he ordered a
large lobby at the building's main intersection. There, out in the open, he
placed his desk, so he could keep his eye on students and his finger on the
school's pulse. The desk is still there, a silent memorial occupied only by
Frank Boyden's spirit.

Widmer has a more conventional office down the hall and says that DA
is not slavish in honoring Boyden's memory. Since Boyden's tenure, the
academy has gone coed, which he probably would have opposed, and
strengthened programs in the arts, in which Boyden had little interest. But
in maintaining some of the traditional hallmarks of prep school education
from Boyden's day, DA has resisted the liberalization seen at other schools.
For example, a code requires dress-up clothes in all classes and on certain

other occasions. Students are expected to learn social skills, including good manners. Rules are strict, but surprisingly brief in the student handbook. Asked why, one administrator simply grinned and said, "We keep them too busy to get into trouble." Boyden said DA was "the last bulwark of the old discipline." Widmer calls the school's conservative values "The Deerfield Way" and says, "Students seem to like it; it works for us."

Deerfield Academy students do seem to have the pride and spirit of the Marine Corps. They work hard, play hard, and tell themselves they and their velvet-lined Parris Island are the best. It can make for insularity: one administrator observed, "Our world ends at the campus boundaries." And, as in all elite populations, there is pressure towards conformity. "You have to be very sure of yourself to be different here," a student told a national magazine doing a story on boarding schools. Nonetheless, DeeYayers seem to be having an excellent adventure. The school's selectivity and the intensity of its expectations bind students into a fervent brother- and sisterhood, so devoted to the school that DA graduates are apt to do things like lug a green-and-white academy banner to a rugged mountaintop, then send a picture back to the alumni magazine.

A week after I attended NMH's opening convocation, I went to its counterpart at DA. After an inspirational talk by a guest speaker, a student leader gave a stirring speech of his own. "You're the cream of the crop," he told his fellows, an assessment with which Patricia Gimbel, the academy's dean of admissions, concurred when I met with her the next day. Deerfield interviews all applicants (Ms. Gimbel keeps a bowl of green and white M&Ms in her office to buck up the candidates). Only a fourth are accepted, and their standardized test scores are among the highest of the New England private schools.

After convocation we all repaired to the dining hall, students still in their dress clothes, which ranged from the blazer-and-chinos uniform of preppies to micro-minidresses. There were faculty member at all the tables (which are round, to facilitate conversation) and the tables were set with white tablecloths and flowers. Sit-down meals are one way Deerfield teaches social graces: the new students at my table were becomingly bashful, but third-year student Hilary, an old hand at this sort of thing, chatted happily, agreeing with the convocation speaker that DA grads would become America's leaders.

Meanwhile, some members of the table carried out their rotating dinner assignments, carrying in the food to their table or removing dishes.

The dinner was tasty and ample, although, truth to tell, the main course looked like the same Mystery Meat served up the road at NMH. (You find it everywhere. There must be a huge factory some place making this stuff.)

Deerfield and Northfield Mount Hermon do, in fact, have more in common with each other than either does with public high schools, but it doesn't take a lot of ethnology to reveal the differences. Historian Gertrude Himmelfarb could easily find her "two American cultures" here: a rela-

tively traditional, more structured view of life at Deerfield; a more communitarian, service-oriented society at Northfield Mount Hermon. These are the service academies of the Two Cultures, echoed in the schools' mottoes. Deerfield's: "Be worthy of your heritage." Northfield Mount Hermon's: "Education of the head, the hand, and the heart."

Such are the redemption stories of two Connecticut Valley Yankees. Dwight Lyman Moody has been redeemed by his school; Frank Learoyd Boyden was his school's redeemer. The two created schools that today offer educations that are among the

Dwight and Emma Moody still watch over the Northfield Mount Hermon campus

best to be found anywhere in America, schools that impress you with the dedication of their staffs and the depths of their resources, schools that send your confidence in youth soaring when you see the fresh-faced enthusiasm of their eager-to-learn, eager-to-achieve students. There is no adolescent world-weariness here, for these students are fired up and busy.

"Not that we're perfect," DeeYayers sometimes say without, however, seeming to really mean it. To a visitor, Deerfield's self-satisfaction could benefit from a dose of humility, while NMH could take some lessons in esprit de corps from Deerfield. Deerfield seems to be telling its students how wonderful they *are*, while NMH is telling them how wonderful they *can be*. DeeYayers are the anointed getting anointed even more;

EnEmAitchers see themselves as works in progress. DeeYayers like to cheer ("Oh-Two, Oh-Two, Oh-Two," members of the class of 2002 spontaneously chanted at a school assembly); EnEmAitchers like to argue. And if Deerfield people can seem a little smug and boola-boola, Northfield Mount Hermon folks can seem a little solemn and self-righteous. As one of my Hermon instructors used to say, Could we have some moderation, please?

The Education of Young Gentlemen

In my day, Mount Hermon was strictly a boys' school making many of the usual prep school efforts to prepare young gentlemen. We wore coats and ties to dinner, slicked down our cowlicks, and pined for the girls of Northfield, who were safely sequestered on their own campus five miles away. Although most Hermon students lived in dormitories, four of us were assigned to two bedrooms in the third-floor garret of none other than the assistant headmaster, Arthur D. Platt. In return for overseeing our moral development, Mr. and Mrs. Platt were assigned the services of two of us as household helpers. I'm not sure they got any bargain.

Deprived of ordinary female companionship, we wasted time ogling the Platts' college-age daughter. Cut off from the usual outlets for teenage mischief, we thought up new ones. We bought gallon jugs of cider, added raisins and sugar, and tried to ferment the stuff. What we got were ominous-looking heads of foam and an odor that could stop a train. We hurriedly poured our noxious brew out the third-floor back window. It soaked the ground and shrubbery just outside the living room of Mr. Platt, who, of an evening, liked to sit near the window with his pipe and newspaper. Soon we were summoned to the great man's study. Solemn as an owl and clearly disappointed that we had once again failed to act like gentlemen, the assistant headmaster searched our faces in silence, then asked the crucial question.

"All right, men," he said wearily (he really did call us men, in spite of all the evidence to the contrary). "Who's been taking leaks out the window?"

To visit Historic Deerfield is to discover once again the studied perfection for which its southern soul mate, Colonial Williamsburg, became famous (413-774-5581; www.historic-deerfield.org). Old Deerfield's tree-shaded main avenue, "The Street," is lined with beautifully restored early American homes, many open to visitors. Deerfield Academy's campus crosses The Street (413-772-0241; www.deerfield.edu). Adding to the experience are the Flynt Museum, Deerfield's fascinating "attic," and Memorial Hall. Among other things, Memorial Hall holds mementos of the Raid of 1704 and the Unredeemed Captive. Best of all is the front door from the Sheldon House with the hole hacked in it by the Indian raiders that terrible night. Here also are gifts presented by Arosen, who, with his wife, visited New England several times after Rev. John Williams died (413-772-0845, www.memorialhall.mass.edu). A few miles north of Deerfield is its companion frontier town, Northfield. It suffered the horrors of war and was abandoned several times. It, too, has a long, tree-shaded main street, crowned at its northern end by NMH's Northfield campus. While Deerfield is beautiful because of what humans created there, the Northfield and nearby Mount Hermon campuses, set on river valley terraces, are beautiful for what nature created there (413-498-3000, www.nmhschool.org). "The Birthplace," where NMH alumni often stay, is available for overnight accommodation (413-498-3361), but for all the romance of sleeping in the same house where Dwight Moody was born, visitors will find these guest quarters to be decidedly humble. Or perhaps—like Frank Boyden's shabby overcoat ("That coat's raised millions for Deerfield!")—that's the point.

CHAPTER TEN

A SHADY CORNER
OF VERMONT

Periodically, an unseen force turns New England upside down, gives it a shake, and drops huge numbers of ConnYorkers into Vermont. Suddenly, thousands of people from Down There—wealthy Connecticut shore towns and nearby New York places—are Up Here among the hills and cow pastures, sucking in lungfuls of quaintness and wondering why their cell phones don't work. Outfitted by Barney's and Bloomie's, Prada and Rossignol, the visitors are très jolie themselves, but they bring an honest sense of wonder at the peace and beauty of this land, and they are right to do so. It's mostly a gorgeous place, a four-season Eden for the rest of us. Summer brings the theater (oops, theatre) crowd, autumn brings the leaf-peepers, and in winter the skiers schuss in by the thousands. Spring—which locals used to call the Deep Mud Season until the tourism people shushed them—brings burnt-out brokers who dream of opening a country inn, à la Bob Newhart, so they can rusticate with Darryl and Darryl instead of rat-racing with Gordon Gekko. A few of these escapees from Gotham really do open inns, but even fewer last very long before burning out all over again. Running an inn is a 24/7 thing.

Vermont is part of a pair. Imagine you are a highflying goose, on your way to Canada and following the Connecticut River Valley to get there. As you cross the northern border of Massachusetts, the river points north and straight ahead, with New Hampshire lying on the eastern bank of the river and Vermont on the western. The two states look like giants in twin beds, a hard-edged, flinty character occupying the right, while something softer and rounder is on the left. These are the Yankee Twins, seemingly joined at the hip but not at the head, for they have different outlooks on life. New Hampshire is on the conservative side of the scale. It is one of only two states with no sales or income tax. That's partly the product of years of editorializing in the Manchester *Union Leader* by its late publisher, William Loeb, legendary for his front-page anti-tax and anti-lots-of-other-things hissy fits printed in boldfaced caps. In that cranky spirit, New Hampshire, despite all reason, still does not require drivers to buckle up for their own good and its license plates snarl *Live Free or Die.* (Is that an order?) Vermont, on the other hand, is gentler and more pastoral, a place where the nurturing cow is the perfect symbol for the state, a place of surprisingly liberal social tendencies, including the recently enacted first-in-the-nation right of gays to civil unions, the closest thing to marriage.

Of course, the issue of civil unions was fought out first in public with opponents trumpeting *Take Vermont back!* and proponents arguing, *Don't take Vermont backwards!* I have an honorary aunt—actually my wife's relative, but I'm fond of her—who still lives in the same house in Townshend, Vermont, that her late husband's family lived in for generations. Aunt Ginny Chamberlin just snorted when I asked her about the warning from some that Vermont would become a magnet for gays. "If they can stand the cold and the snow, let 'em come," she said. It's not that Vermont and New Hampshire are either conservative or liberal, she said. "We're *independent*," she said. "We don't like to be told what to do." Well, yes. Vermont is home to the U.S. Senate's only declared Independent, "Jeezum Jim" Jeffords, as well as the House of Representatives' first Independent in forty years, Bernie Sanders. But New Hampshirites tend to be Independent-*Right,* while Vermonters are Independent-*Left.* The left-and-right geography fits them very nicely.

Vermont's curves are so seductive, the green dress she wears so bewitching, and the very air so fecund, that creative people of all kinds are drawn here. There are the usual crafts people with their natural fibers and clay pots, but there are many others. Each summer, tiny Marlboro College, a few miles west of Brattleboro, hosts the distinguished Marlboro Music School and Festival, which was co-founded by Rudolf Serkin. Throughout the state, painters zero in on views while sculptors explore other dimensions. The famous Bread Loaf Writers' Conference takes place each summer near Middlebury in northwest Vermont, and draws both name writers and wannabes. *Book* magazine offers the thought that Vermont "may well have more writers per capita than any other state." The spirit of Robert Frost still hangs over the place and, over the years, Pearl Buck, Robert Penn Warren, Sinclair Lewis, and Aleksandr Solzhenitsyn have lived here, as John Irving, Galway Kinnell, Ron Powers, Tasha Tudor, Archer Mayor (see below), and many others still do. And there are poets! O yes o yes o yes.

Driving Beemers or SUVs the size of main battle tanks, the ConnYorkers flow up the Connecticut River Valley on Interstate 91 and start peeling off at Brattleboro, the first town of any size in Vermont. Brattleboro (named for land speculator William Brattle, who never set foot here and later joined the Tory side in the Revolution) and Windham County, which surrounds it, hold down Vermont's lower right corner. This encourages boosters to call the area the Gateway to Vermont or the Hub of New England. Actually, this place is more interesting than those Chamber of Commerce banalities. For one thing, "Billy Brattle's Borough," though settling down now, is still kind of a hippy-dippy, geeky-freaky, retro-Sixties kind of a place, with a funky downtown of bookstores, interesting restaurants, and intriguing shops. "A college town without the college," as someone once put it, although some natives like to call it Granola Town. Brattleboro makes for a piquant introduction to the Green Mountain State, but there's more: this is a region brimming with old mysteries and mischief past. As we shall see, it isn't just the trees that make this a shady corner of Vermont.

Captain Thunderbolt

A long, long time ago, a strange man came to the southern Vermont village of Brookline and did a strange thing. Exactly how he accomplished this, and for exactly what reasons, we do not know. But to this day you can see what he did.

Brookline is just a splinter of a town lying on both sides of a brook called the Grassy, all hidden in a valley in northern Windham County. Perhaps five hundred people live there now, but in 1821 there were about a thousand. Or there were until that terrible June. First came a swarm of grasshoppers that destroyed almost all the crops. Then, on June 20, a torrential thunderstorm turned placid Grassy Brook a vicious cataract, destroying a schoolhouse, carrying away every bridge in town, washing out roads, and turning rich farm fields into beds of gravel. It was too much for some folks. Farmers gave up and moved away. Stores closed and houses were abandoned.

Then something wonderful happened. A doctor who was also a schoolmaster in a nearby town came to Brookline with an offer. He would build a new school for the town and even teach the first term . . . so long as he could design the building. Despite his professional standing, the man was considered rather strange and bit mysterious, and so was his plan. But that was about the only way the battered little town was going to get a new school, so nobody wanted to look this gift horse in the mouth. Even after he submitted plans for a schoolhouse that would be . . . *round.*

Aunt Gin checks out the round schoolhouse built by Captain Thunderbolt

Probably no one in Brookline had seen or even heard of a round building, let alone a round schoolhouse. But the stranger was obviously an educated man, a good talker, and self-confident. He called himself Dr. John Wilson and he seemed to know something about medicine, education, and just about everything else. He had been living in nearby Newfane and before that, Dummerston, and while people in those two places thought him oddly secretive, they also were impressed with his erudition.

So a building committee composed of two leading citizens approved the strange plan in August 1821. The curious structure was built of brick the next year. It had one room, five windows, and one door. The stove was in the center, a canny layout that kept everybody equally warm. For over one hundred years the building was used as a school and then, for many years, as a town hall. It is thought to be the only round schoolhouse in the country, and you can see it there today, although it is no longer used for much of anything.

So Brookline got a very good deal, although Dr. John Wilson soon moved on to the bright lights of Brattleboro. But the good "Dr. Wilson"—teacher, benefactor, and healer—was not who he said he was. In fact, Brookline's angel was no angel at all, but a man with a dark past. To understand who he really was, we have to travel through time to Cambridge, Massachusetts, in the year 1821 . . . the same year that was so eventful for Brookline.

On the twentieth of December that year, at Lechmere Point in Cambridge, a handsome young Irishman with blue eyes and muscular body calmly helped an executioner place a noose around his neck. He took a handkerchief and, after he was hooded, raised it to his chest three times and then let it fall—the signal that he was to be dropped into eternity. He appeared to have died quickly.

His name was Michael Martin, and he had been condemned to death for highway robbery. He left both his body and a tell-all confession to a local newspaper reporter.

Martin told his interviewer how he had been a young ne'er-do-well and petty thief in Ireland until he met an older man there, who was tall and muscular, who dressed well, who had "a good gift of the gab," and who claimed to be an English clergyman.

The stranger turned out to be John Doherty, a Scotsman better known throughout the kingdom as Captain Thunderbolt, a notorious highwayman. Doherty liked the cut of Martin's jib and made him an offer: *Join me, and become a professional. We'll have a fine old time, scaring the loons and taking what they don't need anyway.* Martin accepted, and was dubbed "Captain Lightfoot." For the next few months Thunderbolt and Lightfoot kept busy robbing stagecoaches and hunting parties, staying one step ahead of the king's dragoons, and scaring the wits out of the gentry. Now and then they'd toss some of their loot to the poor and they liked to round out their robberies by kissing the ladies.

British authorities had about as much success pursuing the pair as Wily

Coyote has in pursuing the Roadrunner, but by 1819 things were getting too hot even for Thunderbolt and Lightfoot. They split up, Martin going to Salem, Massachusetts, and Doherty to the West Indies, or so he said. Martin tried honest labor for a while, but it didn't agree with him. Drunkenness, fighting, and public carousing required a more lucrative career path, and so he slipped back into crime, conducting a string of highway robberies in New England, then Quebec, and then New England again. Captured in Springfield, he was convicted of highway robbery in October 1821, and sentenced to die. He passed the time until execution day planning an escape (unsuccessful) and narrating his memoirs (highly successful, selling over ten thousand copies throughout New England after his death).

As copies of Martin's confessions filtered through New England in 1822, they aroused unusual interest in Windham County, Vermont. There, the mysterious Dr. Wilson had arrived about 1819. He had boarded with a Dummerston family who noticed that he left the room whenever a stranger came to the door. Wilson taught school and practiced medicine, but was unusually reclusive. When he did converse with others, however, he was impressive for his erudition, for he could quote Shakespeare and other authors at length. Then he moved to Newfane, where he was living when nearby Brookline was ravaged. After he built the round schoolhouse and taught a term, he moved to Brattleboro, where he practiced medicine but lost thousands in a sawmill venture.

Vermonters were struck by how closely the mysterious stranger in their midst resembled the British highwayman described in Martin's memoirs. Not only was Wilson of a size, age, and manner that matched Thunderbolt's, but also he had arrived some time after the highwayman had left England, had revealed little about his past, and had some curious practices, such as wearing a heavy muffler in summer and winter and refusing to try on new footwear anywhere but in the privacy of his own home. So a lot of talk went on over the cracker barrel, but no one did anything.

On April 13, 1834, Dr. Wilson married Abigail Chamberlain, daughter to a highly respectable family in Brattleboro. She was nineteen; he was more than twice her age. They soon had a child, a son, but it wasn't long until she obtained a divorce, charging "tyrannical treatment" by her husband. She also alleged, vaguely, that "he had been a robber or some such infamous character."

The loss of his wife seemed to mark a turning point for Dr. Wilson. Perhaps he thought his young wife's repudiation of him signaled the failure of his effort to become a new man. He had been more sociable of late, but now he returned to his solitary ways. Only an unsavory class of cronies were allowed in his house; to others, his door was closed. As he drank more and more, his medical practice declined and so did his health. In 1846 or 1847 he became seriously ill, but refused to allow his clothing to be removed while he was being cared for. Shortly before his death, on March 22, 1847, he asked that his body not be undressed after he died and that he be buried as he was.

As you might expect, the request was not honored. He was found to be wearing several suits of clothes, as if to bulk up his form. A long scar was found on the back of his neck, where he had always worn a scarf. The calf of one leg was withered and built up artificially with cloth. Another scar, such as might have been made by a musket ball, was found in the calf, reminding onlookers of the wound that Thunderbolt was

Relics of Captain Thunderbolt, including an artificial heel and a sword cane

known to have suffered there. And part of one heel was missing, so Wilson had an artificial heel to give the leg the appearance of proper length. The wounds matched those in the British authorities' description of Captain Thunderbolt. In executing Wilson's estate, the late doctor was found to be worth several thousand dollars—far more than might be expected in his circumstances. Numerous swords and guns were found, too. All in all, it seemed clear that "Dr. John Wilson" was none other than Captain Thunderbolt . . . just as his neighbors had long suspected. Mystery solved.

The old highwayman was laid to rest in Brattleboro's Prospect Hill Cemetery, his long run from the law over at last. Although we think we know who he really was, he stubbornly remained in disguise, for his stone was engraved "Dr. John Wilson." Even though his artificial heel, sword cane, and other tools of a secret life are on display in the Brooks Memorial Library in Brattleboro, a bit of a mystery still clings to the man. Almost everyone will tell you that the schoolhouse he built in Brookline is round so the highwayman "could see in all directions" if the authorities were coming for him. It's a story we'd love to believe. But visit the school yourself and you can see that explanation makes no sense. With only one door—facing the road, no less—where would the fugitive go when danger loomed? In fact, the round schoolhouse would be the perfect place for "Dr. Wilson" to be . . . *cornered.*

And *why* had this scoundrel been so generous? Was he trying to atone for his crimes? Were the school and his teaching and his medical practice all part of a changed man? Maybe, maybe not. Certainly, he did not appear to die in a state of grace, at peace with himself and the world. And he made no confession, nor left one.

And so, in some small way, Captain Thunderbolt eludes us yet. We still wonder about him, and we wonder about his round schoolhouse. Heroes and villains die, but some mysteries never do.

They Called Him Jubilee Jim

There are scoundrels and then there are *scoundrels.* The first are those whiny sad sacks of little wit who abscond with the church treasury, abandon their families for the office blonde, or commit any of a thousand other cheesy crimes and misdemeanors. How boring. But then there are those scalawags we secretly admire, if only a little bit, even though we shouldn't. They are the charming con artists and cat burglars who prance through life with a bawdy song in their hearts and a sneer on their lips, robbing, lying, and cheating with panache, stealing the jewels of Topkapi and thumbing their noses at the conventions the rest of us are stuck with. They are the Thunderbolts and Lightfoots of this dull old world, the rakes who kiss the ladies after robbing their gentlemen, then ride off into the night, scattering gold pieces to the poor and buying drinks all around.

Jim Fisk, Jr., was like that. He was a generous, funny, charming, talented, and likable louse. He was—and I say this with all due respect—a *scoundrel,* "as absolutely devoid of shame as the desert of Sahara is of grass," according to a prominent clergyman of his time. And he was southern Vermont's gift to the world, although it is mostly Brattleboro that is obliged to claim him, even if it would rather not.

Fisk was born on April Fool's Day in 1835 in Pownal, a Vermont hamlet on the other side of the Green Mountains, and was a healthy, chubby, high-spirited child. His father was a shrewd Yankee peddler who moved his family to Brattleboro when young Jim was still a schoolboy—a schoolboy with little use for lessons, but a talent for making friends.

When the boy gave up schooling he showed so much talent for salesmanship that his father sent him on the road. Fisk Senior stayed in Brattleboro to open the Revere House Hotel in 1850. Fisk Junior scored his first breakthrough in business by applying circus showmanship to peddling. He painted a wagon in bright circus colors, dressed in top hat and striped pants, and laced his sales patter with jokes, making himself a hit with bored and lonely farm families. Always jovial, Fisk flattered the farm wives, flirted with the younger women, and scattered candy among the children.

Jubilee Jim Fisk, at his desk, and Josie Mansfield

Business boomed, so he was able to buy out his father's business and pay Fisk Senior a handsome salary to work for him. Now that the business was his, young Jim Fisk bought more wagons and hired drivers for them. His sales territory spread throughout southern Vermont and New Hampshire, western Massachusetts, and eastern New York State. In later years, Fisk declared, "By George, them was the happiest days of my life! I had everything I hankered after. . . ."

But of course, he hadn't, because nothing was ever enough for Jim Fisk. After a few years of peddling he became a wholesale dealer for Jordan, Marsh and Company, then a rising Boston dry-goods company. When the Civil War broke out, Fisk won a number of government contracts by lavishly entertaining and bribing army supply officers at a hospitality suite he set up in the nation's capital. Then he headed south, where he was able to develop a huge business illicitly buying Southern cotton and smuggling it to Northern mills, although both the Union and the Confederacy banned trade with the enemy.

His methods made a fortune for Jordan, Marsh, but he did more. After the battle of Antietam in 1862, in which twenty-two thousand men on both sides were killed or wounded, Fisk almost single-handedly led the churches of Boston in a massive relief effort, gathering blankets, medical supplies, food, and other aid for the battered troops. Said one astonished observer, "Never in my life have I seen anyone throw his whole soul into his work as that man did. He seemed to do more in an hour than any other three men."

After the war, Fisk left Jordan, Marsh on good terms and headed for New York City to seek new challenges. He opened a brokerage office and tried to run it the way he had his hospitality suite in Washington. But jokes, free food, and champagne didn't work, and soon his fortune was wiped out. Fisk was not cowed. As he bade farewell to the stock market, he swore that, since Wall Street had ruined him, "Wall Street should pay for it."

With the help of some old friends and some new ones, including a notorious old sharpie named Daniel Drew, Fisk soon got back in the game, this time as a well-financed insider, connected to some of the slickest operators of the Robber Baron era. Thanks to some successful corporate finance deals and a lot of fancy footwork, Jim Fisk became rich and now began to live life with the style that would make him famous.

Several years earlier, he had married Lucy Moore of Springfield, Massachusetts. He was nineteen, she was only fifteen. It was a curious marriage, filled with mutual admiration and respect, and while there was certainly love in it, that love carried with it a peculiar sense of devotion. "She is no hair-lifting beauty," Fisk said years later. "[She's] just a plump, wholesome, big-hearted, commonplace woman, such as a man meets once in a lifetime, say, and then gathers her into the first church he comes to, and seals her to himself."

Fisk set up Lucy in a handsome house in Boston while he established himself in luxurious New York hotels. There he began to pursue "hair-lifting beauties," showgirls and camp followers of the rich. Chief among them was Helen Josephine Mansfield, better known to the press and public as Josie Mansfield. Josie had no interest in dull domestic life, preferring life in a women's boarding house that probably was an elegant bordello. Josie was "statuesque," meaning tall, shapely, and more than a little plump, but more importantly, she had an irresistible appeal to men. Fisk was bewitched by her. He bought her a fine brownstone house near his office and moved in with her, grateful that his wife never paid him surprise visits.

Women weren't Fisk's only diversion. He loved to eat and he put on the pounds, which in those days signified prosperity and power. With his expanded waistline, florid complexion, auburn hair, bright blue eyes, sharply pointed moustache, and fancy dress—for Jim Fisk was a dandy—he cut an imposing figure in New York City. A stickpin with a five-carat diamond blazed from his chest like a locomotive's headlight and became his personal trademark. He rode in an elegant carriage with four footmen who laid down a carpet whenever he disembarked. He bought theaters and opera houses and underwrote productions at them. Fisk's flamboyance, bad manners, and wretched grammar gave New York high society and old money a perpetual case of the vapors, but the Vermonter didn't care, for he was as full of life and wit as a happy-go-lucky boy, "continuously boiling over with jokes, good, bad and indifferent." The press called him Jubilee Jim.

In fact, he was very much like a youngster playing with expensive toys. He bought a steamship company and wore an "admiral's" uniform to dockside. He became a benefactor for the down-at-the-heels Ninth Regiment of the New York State Militia and, although his only wartime experience was as a cotton smuggler, he became the regiment's colonel. Reportedly, he spent $5,000 for his own uniform.

He was something else again in the privacy of his office, where he worked hard and efficiently, employed cunning and daring, and was unburdened by tiresome scruples as he finangled his deals in high finance and low. He was at his best behind the scenes: bribing judges, watering stock, and jiggering the bookkeeping whenever it suited his purposes. The press called him the Prince of Erie (and his offices "Castle Erie"), because of the highhanded way he ran the Erie Railroad, with little regard for passenger safety but a great deal of regard for his own profit and pleasure. In a failed effort with Jay Gould to take over the Albany and Susquehanna Railroad, he employed a crooked New York judge, gangs of goons, and a variety of other unscrupulous methods. Bloodied but unbowed by failure in that direction, Fisk and Gould, joined by Daniel Drew, turned their attention to trying to corner the gold market by inflating the price and then spreading false rumors about President Grant's intentions. The result was the financial panic that started on September 24, 1869, and became notorious as "Black Friday." Speculators were wiped out and the nation's economy badly damaged. Even Europe felt the effects.

Fisk's relationship with Josie Mansfield was equally tumultuous. Fisk was madly in love with the plump Ms. Mansfield, but she was in love only with his money. About 1869 Fisk made a substantial investment in a Brooklyn refinery managed by a slim, unbalanced young man named Edward S. Stokes. Stokes caught the eye of Josie, and soon he was calling on her whenever Fisk was occupied elsewhere. By 1870 Josie had sent Fisk packing, but he continued to long for her, giving her money and writing her letters that grew more and more anguished. Josie's reply was to brazenly demand a large cash settlement. He refused and buried himself in work.

But matters involving the Mansfield-Stokes-Fisk triangle were coming to a head. Discovering that Stokes was milking the refinery's funds for his own pleasure (something Fisk no doubt would have preferred to do for himself), Jubilee Jim had the young man arrested for embezzlement. Stokes counterattacked with a lawsuit charging malicious prosecution. The cases dragged on, with Josie testifying against Fisk, but ultimately the judge found in his favor. The frustrated Stokes went hunting for Fisk. He found him on a staircase at a hotel, drew a pistol, and shot Jubilee Jim twice, fatally wounding him. Before Fisk died the next day, he dictated his will (leaving most of his estate to Lucy), and called for his wife. She arrived from Boston after he had lapsed into unconsciousness and when he died, she kissed him and exclaimed, "My dear boy! He was such a good boy!"

Thousands paid their respects while Fisk lay in state in the New York State Opera House and thousands more witnessed his funeral cortege as it moved up Fifth Avenue, escorted by one hundred policemen and the entire Ninth Regiment. Fisk's rosewood coffin with gold mountings was carried by train from New York to Brattleboro, and was met by crowds at every station along the way. He had always regarded Brattleboro home, so he was buried in Brattleboro's Prospect Hill Cemetery.

If you're in Brattleboro, you can visit Jim Fisk today. As in life, he's hard to miss. The Fisk monument is an ostentatious affair, one of the largest in the cemetery. It includes, at each corner, a life-size human figure. The four figures represent aspects of Fisk's interests (railroads, water, the stage, and commerce), but from Fisk's point of view, they're something better and even more appropriate: they are four shapely, mostly nude, women.

How Jim Fisk would have loved that.

The Plotter

The fog was draped over the trees like gauze that January morning as I left Brattleboro and pointed my unmarked VBI car north on Route 30. I was a cop on the trail of a mystery man in Newfane, someone who had been causing trouble for the police for a long time. Usually the drive is a pleasant one, for the road hugs the gentle bends of the West River and tourists like to follow it search of scenic Vermont. On this day, though, it was anything but scenic. Patches of dirty snow alternated with clumps of ugly brown grass, and the black limbs of trees were like long, skinny arms, reaching eerily out of the mist as if they were trying to goose me. That made me uneasy. With the police radio muttering ominously in the background, I kept thinking of the last words from Vermont Bureau of Investigation headquarters: *Gunther, watch out for this guy. He's got more plots up his sleeve than a sugarbush has taps.*

Archer Mayor lives near the Newfane courthouse

That was about the worst simile I'd ever heard, but I knew what I had to do. Something ugly was going on in tiny Newfane, something I had to expose to an anxious world. I found my quarry's driveway on a side road, but as I rolled into it, the "cruiser" I was driving turned into my old Volvo wagon and the police squawk box began broadcasting Vermont Public Radio. Suddenly, I was Joe Gunther no longer. A tall, whippet-slim man with piercing eyes loomed up in front of me and I thrust my only weapon at him: a box of Dunkin' Donuts. "Boy, you know how to grease a palm," he laughed and within minutes Archer Mayor was telling me about the kind of plots he likes to create: murder mysteries that are investigated by a Vermont cop named Joe Gunther. As we say in this business, Mayor spilled his guts.

Except that what he writes are more than murder mysteries. Archer Mayor, never a great fan of the mystery-story medium, thinks of himself more as a social anthropologist than a mystery writer. It's just that he has chosen to report his findings in nearly a dozen "Joe Gunther" police procedurals that mystery fans love and critics rave about.

They're usually set in Vermont, too, although they explore darker sides of the state that tourists seldom see: drug traffic moving on Interstate 91, cops gone bad, financial chicanery at a ski resort, tension between a cult and townspeople. Maybe it's the contrast between these surprisingly ugly doings and the idyllic backdrop of the Green Mountain State that intrigues people. Or perhaps it's the classic appeal of a well-told mystery story with a satisfying denouement. The high-protein informational meat built into Joe Gunther stories can't hurt, either. In any case, Mayor has written a well-received Joe Gunther mystery novel almost every year since 1988.

Joe Gunther is a Brattleboro cop who has risen to a top investigator's job with the fictional "Vermont Bureau of Investigation." He is the hero as played by Everyman. Among his crime-fighting assistants is the talented but ill-tempered, perpetual-pain-in-the-caboose Willy Kunkle, whose off-putting personality hasn't kept him from developing useful contacts in almost every dark corner of the Vermont landscape. Gunther has a long-time, off-again-on-again love interest with Gail Zigman, a former hippie turned lawyer, while Kunkle has developed a relationship with Sammie Martens, a female cop who we can only hope will mellow him, but probably won't.

In the past few years this trio of small-town cops has ranged over much of Vermont, with occasional forays into nearby Massachusetts, New Hampshire, and Quebec, although their home base of Brattleboro has, and will probably remain, the center for much of the action. Thanks to Mayor's imagination, since 1988 the fictional crime rate has shot up considerably in Brattleboro and shown some interesting spikes in other parts of the Green Mountain State as well. Of course, the quartet's cases-cleared rate has gone up just as fast. And yet the Joe Gunther mystery novels derive their appeal less from car-chase/.38-caliber/face-punching action than from the fascinating interplay of lives exposed.

"You don't see Joe Gunther busting people so much as he visits their lives and gets them to open up," explains the author. "He's in the *confessional* business. His strengths are in the dogged pursuit of the truth and also in his easy ways. He can get people to talk who normally would be ill-inclined to do so. He's avuncular, pleasant, soothing, supportive, even though he's basically trying to pick your pocket if you're a bad guy."

Mayor grew up in Europe, child of parents who moved constantly in the world of international business, and somehow his lack of rootedness endowed him with an insatiable curiosity about other people and their lives. He was fascinated by a book called *Le Diable Boitu* ("The Limping Devil"), in which a devil takes a mortal as an apprentice and, flying through the air, shows him the secret lives of people by lifting off their roofs without their being aware of it.

"That concept of peering into people's lives almost unnoticed has always been a fascination for me," Mayor says. "That curiosity fuels me as a writer." Mayor has long served as a volunteer on local ambulance squads, and remembers, "We'd do late-night runs and on returning from the hospital, or perhaps just making an ice-cream run, we would cruise the streets of Brattleboro. I used to be just entranced, much like the limping devil's apprentice, watching the lights in the windows. You'd see shadows passing and you'd think, what are they doing? What are they up to? What are they thinking?"

So Joe Gunther is Mayor's primary tool in getting behind the window shades, but Gunther is carefully drawn to bring his audience with him. In Mayor's first successful mystery, *Open Season*, we catch a few glimpses of Gunther: he's in his fifties, paunchy, with thinning hair. But most of the time we are not looking *at* Gunther, we are looking at the world *through* Gunther. Mayor usually writes in the first person, so that his stories unfold as Gunther's stream of consciousness.

Mayor books are meticulously researched and filled with facts. "That's the level of detail people have come to expect of me, that I will not put a door where it doesn't belong," Mayor says. "They won't forgive me if I make an error in science or jurisprudence or police procedure. Those things I try to get right because a lot of people read my books to learn how things function. There's a lot of information in there; that's the historian in me."

Mayor came to Vermont in 1980, hoping to find a hometown, determined to write novels after a peripatetic career as researcher for Time, Inc., a scholarly editor in Texas, and sundry other jobs that more or less drew on his degree in American history from Yale. Over the next few years he wrote seven novels ("exercises in typing"), none of which sold. A literary agent sent back one with the comment, *You killed off the only really interesting character in the book.* The character was Joe Gunther. Mayor tried again.

He drafted what became *Open Season*, his first successful mystery, in three totally different versions. One had something to do with the U.S. Senate and another involved an Arab plot. By the third version, Joe Gunther was a Brattleboro police officer and Mayor was writing in the first person. "It took me only three months to write," he recalled. "I knew I had found my voice, I had found my platform, and the bloody book wrote itself." And Mayor had learned how to vanish as effectively as one of his own villains. "If you write well, the reader will never think about the author," Mayor explains. "Good writers will let readers possess the tale. The reader becomes the teller of the story. The 'movie' of the book unfolds in the reader's brain. The writer's job, when he or she best understands it, is to disappear."

"A fine first thriller," the *Wall Street Journal* said of *Open Season*, while the *Washington Post* called the book "absolutely mesmerizing" and the *New York Times* called it a "distinctly American murder mystery—not for the faint-hearted." Says Mayor, "I was terribly pleased and scared to death. It made the second book incredibly difficult to write. I thought, 'I've got to do this again?'"

But, of course, Mayor has done it over and over, exploring the social anthropology of Vermont in such books as *Borderlines* (cultists), *Scent of Evil* and *The Dark Root* (the drug trade), and *Tucker Peak* (the ski industry), more than a dozen in all. And every one carries razor-sharp portraits of Vermonters in their natural settings: medical examiners, merchants, state's attorneys, cops, selectmen, news reporters, and natives of every kind, high and low, good guys and suspects, angels and swindlers, all moving across a Vermont landscape that is both beautiful and, in Mayor's hands, occasionally threatening.

Mayor follows the professional author's Iron Law of Writing ("First, apply ass to chair"). He writes seven days a week, using a laptop computer while moving around his studio, from Barcalounger to couch to desk (feet up). "Various books have been written in various sitting positions," he says. The author's day starts with a little fruit for breakfast and no lunch (Mayor is a tall, thin drink of water). When he's not on the road doing research, giving lectures, or meeting his fans at book-signings, he spends his mornings with the mundane chores of an independent businessman (which is what Mayor says a writer has to be). Afternoons and evenings, sometimes until midnight or 1 a.m., are spent writing. Mayor works wherever he goes. His car is fitted with plugs and lights so he can write in the few minutes he may have before a speaking engagement.

In his spare time, Mayor serves as a volunteer EMT, as an assistant medical examiner, and as elected town constable for Newfane, a position he laughingly dismisses as "more dog officer than anything else. I'm the bottom of the law-enforcement barrel." He deals with trespassing dogs, noise complaints, and neighborhood problems, and occasionally serves papers. "I don't see myself as a law enforcement officer. I don't see that as a strength of mine," he explains. "I'm not an enforcement type. I'm not hard enough or tough enough or determined enough or whatever it is to be a good police officer."

But, like Joe Gunther, he is a dogged information seeker, and, like Joe Gunther, he has an easygoing way that, in the author's own words, "can get people to talk." And, like Gunther, he prowls the Vermont landscape, trying to find out the truth about people. Think about that, if you're a Vermonter. Archer Mayor may be just outside your window.

Or lifting up your roof . . . and peering in.

Crooked Sticks

Ah, Brattleboro. So many rascally tales to tell (yes, there are others), so little time and space. But all good things must come to end.

And so they must for Vermont's seasonal visitors as well. With the waning of each season, the ConnYorkers pack up their SUVs to return to The City and other points Down There. Reluctantly, we take our leave also, heading north while blowing air kisses to Captain Thunderbolt, Jubilee Jim Fisk, Archer Mayor's rogues' gallery, and all the other shadowy denizens of this shady corner of Vermont.

Ciao, you guys.

Granola Town's hippies may be aging and swapping their tie-dyes and love beads for Lands' End, but they haven't lost their social consciences. Archer Mayor calls Brattleboro "the crankiest town in Vermont. You can't propose painting a traffic circle without someone protesting." That extraordinary social conscience, that caring, really caring, about the community is one thing Mayor loves about the town. These are people who are engaged with their community, who have civic-mindedness tattooed on their foreheads, and who haven't given up on government the way too many others have. To those wing-nuts who claim government is the enemy, the answer from the Brattleboro citizenry is, "No way, man. *We are the government.*" So you may find a protest parade on Main Street when you come to town. It may even be (as it was once) women marching bare-breasted.

But if you missed that spectacle, there are other things to see. Take Exit 2 off Interstate 91 for the most direct route to old downtown Brattleboro. Visiting Boho-boro can be like going down the rabbit hole if you haven't seen the town since the 1950s. By contrast, taking Exit 3 further up the road is déjà vu all over again: it delivers you to the same old commercial claptrap and fast-food horrors you can find in a thousand other places. In honor of Archer Mayor's quartet of intelligent action heroes, however, you may want to visit the Dunkin' Donuts there and have a "creme-filled." Or three. Less dangerous to your cholesterol level would be a visit to his web site, www.archermayor.com, where you can learn all about the Plotter of Newfane, or to your local bookstore, where you'll find his work in the "Mysteries" section (works of social anthropology though they may be).

Relics of Captain Thunderbolt are on display in the local history room of Brooks Memorial Library, 224 Main Street, Brattleboro (802-254-5290; http://www.state.vt.us/libraries/b733/brookslibrary). Prospect Hill Cemetery, where both Captain Thunderbolt (as "Dr. John Wilson") and Jubilee Jim Fisk are buried, is easily located further south and just off Brattleboro's Main Street. Ask anyone.

An especially interesting source of information about "Dr. John Wilson," and a lot of other things, is the fascinating "Brattleboro History Scrapbook" web site maintained by independent historian Thomas St. John: www.geocities.com/seekingthephoenix/home.htm.

Now that you've finished this chapter, you can say it's been "sugared off." That's how you talk like a Vermonter.

CHAPTER ELEVEN

Aspects of Love

well boss

you may have noticed
that devilmaycare
air no longer effervescing
from the back alley
thereby hangs a tail
ha ha exclamation point

archy the cockroach
and vers libre bard
and moi
feline belle of new york
and reincarnation of cleopatra
tho less regal now
but toujours gai wotthehell toujours gai
thot some country air would do us good
so off to vermont we went
conveyed to the land of sap and cheese
by the kindness of strangers

it s amazing how much
respect a girl can get
when she stands by the side of the road
and wiggles her fanny
we got a ride with a yokel
altho the yokels up there aren t what
they used to be
this one had a latte in his left hand and a
cell phone in his right and seemed
to steer with his knees
he dropped us in st johnsbury
at the dog chapel
it s a place for canine contemplation
i have contemplated dogs for years
without learning anything
but no dog should contemplate anything
except an eternity in hell

pardon my french
but if not
wotthehell

love and smackers
mehitabel

Many years ago, Mehitabel, a raffish New York alley cat ("but always the lady") claimed to be the reincarnation of Cleopatra. She was brought to the attention of newspaper columnist Don Marquis with the help of Archy, a cockroach. A particularly hardheaded vermin and free verse poet ("vers libre bard"), Archy typed late at night, painfully, by diving headfirst on the typewriter keys, one by one. Like e.e. cummings, he couldn't manage the shift key.

Marquis has long since passed away, so the vers libre here is just a Fig Newton of my imagination, but Vermont's Dog Chapel is not. You can find it at Dog Mountain on Spaulding Road, just off U.S. 2 north of St. Johnsbury. With its steeple, colored windows, and white paint sparkling in the sunshine, it looks like a small country church. Look closer, though, and you'll see that the winged figure on the steeple is a Labrador retriever, the

All breeds are welcome in the Hunecks' Dog Chapel

stained-glass windows depict dogs, and the pews are supported at each end by carved retrievers. But the best part about the dog chapel is the story of how it came about. It is all about love.

A few years ago, Vermont artist Stephen Huneck contracted adult respiratory distress syndrome while in a hospital. In a coma for two months, he once stopped breathing for more than five minutes and doctors expected him to die. Throughout the ordeal, his wife, Gwen, never left his side. She slept on the floor and talked to him in his coma, often about woodcuts he had been planning to make of their beloved black Labrador, Sally.

Miraculously, Huneck recovered and, as he gained strength, began producing woodcuts about life from a dog's point of view, the first being "My Dog's Brain," a phrenological map of a Labrador retriever's mind. Then came a series of lighthearted illustrated books: *Sally Goes to the Beach, Sally Goes to the Mountains,* and so on. Huneck's work hit the *New York Times* bestseller list and what had been a country farm grew into the Dog Mountain complex: workshops that help Huneck produce furniture with dog themes; a gallery shop selling Huneck books, calendars, and arts; a pond (retrievers like water, after all), and a rearranged hillside, with flowers, walks, and a lovely view of the valley.

Most of all there is the Dog Chapel, which Huneck built at a cost of $200,000 as a tribute to the natural world, the value of love like Gwen's, and, of course, the "incredible love" dogs give us. It is a place where people (and their dogs) can sit and meditate on what's important in life. The walls of the chapel vestibule are covered with snapshots and tributes to dogs deceased. Outside, a sign welcomes "All breeds, all creeds, no dogmas allowed."

Huneck, a husky man whose black hair, dark eyes, and skin speak of his partly Native American ancestry, feels strongly about the spiritual connection between man and nature. "We need nature to be fulfilled as people," he says. "I think that's what my artwork is about." In his art, dogs are messengers from nature. Sentiments we think of as exclusively human are expressed with a canine flavor, the so-called secret life of dogs revealed in a way that touchingly suggests that other forms of life may not be so "other" after all.

Dogs surround Huneck wherever he goes; he has four. As he works in his studio, carving a chair in the form of a dog, Molly the golden retriever snoozes nearby in a beam of sunlight. The original Sally has passed away, but Huneck says he still feels her presence. "The local Indians believed there was a heaven and the only animals that would go there with them were their dogs," Huneck says. "I know Sally is up there waiting for me."

When a Woman Loves a Man

Ethan Allen was not a piece of furniture. He was a hot-tempered, hard-drinking, hellfire-and-brimstone fighting man who probably wiped his nose with the back of his hand, and *that* on the back of his pants. But take care what you say about Ethan Allen when you're in Vermont, where he's remembered as one of the gods of the hills. Without him, there might not even be a Vermont—just a bigger New York State or New Hampshire. And that's a thought to make any Vermonter gag on his crackers and cheese.

Ethan Allen looms over Vermont's early history like a giant. It's often said that he stamped the Green Mountain State with the independent spirit for which it is famed. Although he was born in Connecticut and spent his last years on his farm near Burlington, his influence was felt on all sides of Vermont's mountains, including those sloping down to the Connecticut

*Even in stone, Ethan Allen leads the way
in Green Mountain country*

River. And one of the best stories about him—what might be called "The Taming of Ethan Allen"—began in the Connecticut River Valley.

In his younger days, Ethan liked to court trouble. In 1764, he had himself inoculated with smallpox in full public view in front of the Salisbury meeting-house, although Connecticut had outlawed the procedure. When a minister intervened, Allen responded with language so sulfurous it brough a charge of blasphemy. Allen had already outraged the conventionally religious by loudly proclaiming himself a deist. And all too often, the hot-tempered, hard-drinking young man, whose legendary strength concealed a high intelligence, would settle arguments with his fists. "You lie, you dog," a well-oiled Allen would bellow, stripping off his shirt and lighting into the other party. Finally, he was forced to leave Salisbury, resettling in Northampton, Massachusetts, where his loud mouth and hard fists got him "warned out" of town all over again.

By age thirty, Allen seemed to have failed at almost everything he had tried and gained a reputation as a troublemaking eccentric as well. He needed a fresh start. Then a new frontier—the region we call Vermont today—beckoned. Having moved there, however, he discovered that Vermont had a very big problem: New Hampshire's royal governor, Benning Wentworth, had blithely issued grants to tracts of land in Vermont on nobody's authority but his own. Then the Crown had given *New York* real authority over the area, meaning those who had settled the "New Hampshire Grants" might have to buy their land all over again.

Until now, Ethan Allen's two-fisted irreverence for authority had gotten him in trouble wherever he went—but his toughness was exactly what the worried settlers of the New Hampshire Grants wanted. In 1770, with no significant military experience, the charismatic Allen was elected colonel-commandant of the raw country militia that would become known as the Green Mountain Boys.

What followed for the next six years was one of the most remarkable, even brilliant, examples of leadership in American history. Alternating between hard bargaining and guerilla warfare, Allen was able to terrorize the Yorkers into retreat, but with surprisingly little real violence on either side. Ethan Allen was tough but much of his sound and fury was just theater, laced plentifully with loud "God damns!" "Damned rascals!" and "Infernal scoundrels!" His most effective weapon was his ability to portray himself and the Green Mountain Boys as ruthless savages who would stop at nothing—yet, in six years of conflict, Allen and his men took not a single life. Time and again, New York land surveyors and other authorities were chased home with the warning that Allen's bloodthirsty gang had murder on their minds. A New York sheriff's posse was frightened away after Green Mountain Boys paraded behind a hill with their hats on sticks, simulating a larger force.

With rebellion against the Crown spreading across the American colonies, Ethan Allen expanded his hostility from the Yorkers to the British authorities in general. In 1775 he achieved his most dramatic military victory when he and the Green Mountain Boys captured the stone fortress of Ticonderoga, the first royal stronghold to fall to the colonists. In the predawn hours of May 10, 1775, Allen and about eighty of his men swarmed over the sleeping fort screaming "No quarter!" (As usual, no one was killed.) When a half-dressed royal officer demanded to know by what authority Allen had entered the fort, Allen famously replied (or so he later said): "In the name of the Great Jehovah and the Continental Congress!" In later years he avoided mentioning what he had shouted at the commandant's door: "Come out of there, you damned British rat!"

"That sounds more like him. He was rather a blunt fellow," Dr. Ethan Allen Hitchcock Sims told me with a smile. A retired professor of endocrinology at the University of Vermont's medical school, Dr. Sims is a direct descendent of Lucy Caroline Allen, second daughter of the old warrior and Allen's first wife, Mary Brownson. Physically, he is nothing like the colonel. Dr. Sims is tall and slim, a thoughtful, soft-spoken man, more interested in his ancestor's intellect—which was considerable—than his blood and thunder. He is the kind of gentleman who will offer a visitor a glass of wine and good conversation about music, history, and Ethan's views on religion.

Dr. Sims lives in a retirement community a few miles south of Burlington, minutes from Ethan Allen's last home on the city's north edge. There, the original Ethan Allen homestead is preserved much as it must have looked in his day, and, along with a museum and gardens, it hosts endless streams of schoolchildren and other visitors. And it is there that part of Ethan Allen's life is preserved, a part quite unlike his earlier years.

David Bryan is director of the homestead's education programs. He researched and wrote a pamphlet called "Fanny and Her Children," probably making him the world's authority on Fanny Montresor—Ethan Allen's *second* wife. It turns out that the story of Ethan and Fanny Allen is as striking in its own way as the story of Ethan versus the Yorkers.

With the bloodless capture of Fort Ticonderoga in May 1775, Ethan Allen was suddenly the hero of the American colonies and his Green Mountain Boys were transformed from frontier outlaws into allies of the cause. Fired with success, Allen led a pitifully small force into Canada, hoping to capture Montreal. He and his force were captured instead, casting him into a humiliating, and at times brutal, captivity at the hands of the British.

He was released late in 1777 and returned to Vermont, where he slowly worked his way back into public affairs, becoming one of the leaders of the Republic of Vermont, which the region called itself when the other former colonies did not initially accept it for statehood. In 1783 another crisis occurred in Allen's life. Mary Brownson Allen, who had carried the burden of raising their five children and running the farm while Ethan roamed the landscape, died at age fifty. It had been a drab, unhappy marriage, not helped by Allen's frequent absences. The forty-five-year-old widower, by now the most influential man in Vermont, nonetheless continued defending the little republic against forces without and within. However, another force was moving in his direction, and soon he would surrender to it.

In New York City more than twenty years before, a baby girl had been born out of wedlock to Catherine Schoolcraft and a young British soldier of Huguenot heritage, John Montresor. The mother died in or shortly after childbirth. But then another Schoolcraft daughter, Margaret, married a widower named Crean Brush and the newlyweds were given custody of the infant, who had been named Frances but was commonly called Fanny. Brush, a lawyer and official in the royal government of New York, was granted thousands of acres of land in the New Hampshire Grants, specifically in the Connecticut River town of Westminster. That made him an enemy of Ethan Allen.

With the American Revolution over, Fanny—by now a high-spirited, twenty-three-year-old beauty who had already had one brief, unhappy marriage to a man named Buchanan—came to Westminster, Vermont, to see what she could do to secure the Brush land grants, which she had inherited from her late stepfather. Not much, it turned out, but she secured something else: the heart of Ethan Allen. Fanny and her stepmother had been renting a room in the Westminster home of Stephen Bradley, an Allen ally who hosted many Vermont leaders when they came to Westminster on government business. That Fanny was the stepdaughter of an old enemy of Allen's proved no impediment, for not only was she uncowed by the crusty, overbearing Allen, but also she had a talent for prettily teasing him in a way that kept him coming back for more. When an acquaintance noted Allen's interest, saying she could become "the queen of Vermont," she saucily replied that she could just as well marry the Devil and become the queen of Hell.

Ethan's proposal to Fanny is one of Vermont's legendary stories, subject, as legends are, to variations in the telling. Nonetheless, it goes something like this. On the morning of February 9, 1784, Ethan Allen walked in on Fanny as she was standing on a chair to arrange china in a cupboard, and declared with no preliminaries, "If we are to be married, now is the time, for I am on my way to Arlington." Fanny replied, " Very well, but give me time to put on my joseph." (A joseph was a kind of coat.) Ethan led Fanny by the hand to the Bradley kitchen, where the chief justice of the Republic of Vermont just happened to be finishing his breakfast. "Judge Robinson," Allen bellowed. "This young woman and myself have concluded to marry each other, and have you perform the ceremony."

When the startled judge asked, "When?" Allen barked "Now!" And so it was, out of a "decent respect for the opinions of mankind," Ethan and Fanny were married, though the two felt they could have lived together without a marriage ceremony. The newlyweds bundled themselves into a sleigh, crossed the Green Mountains, and settled temporarily in the Bennington area. On November 13, they became parents of their first (of three) children, a daughter who also was named Fanny. The same year, Ethan published his book on philosophy, a defense of deism and attack on organized religion which he titled *Reason, the Only Oracle of Man.*

Ethan and Fanny's marriage was a happy one. Regretting, perhaps, how he had gallivanted during his first marriage, he now stayed closer to home. In 1785 he and Fanny had moved to the Onion River region of Burlington, where he settled down to farming his large landholdings, emerging into the public forum only occasionally. The adventurer had become a home-body, staying close to his pretty wife. The one-time god of the hills quietly farmed his "choice river intervale," raised children (he and Fanny had two sons, Hannibal and Ethan Alonzo, in addition to Fanny), and wrote an appendix to the *Reason* which reflected the happiness he was finding in marriage and private life. But on February 17, 1789, almost exactly five years after marrying Fanny, he died, probably of a stroke. He was only fifty-one.

Fanny would re-marry four years later to Dr. Jabez Penniman, have three more children, and spend much time developing a masterly knowledge of plants, herbs, and botanical Latin. She would die in 1834 at age seventy-four. David Bryan points out how the spirited Fanny left a final message to the world. Plagued throughout her life by unkind curiosity about her origins, she decreed that her tombstone would carry the names of neither Montresor, Buchanan, Allen, nor Penniman. Instead, she borrowed the name of the last emperor of the Aztecs and sleeps to this day in Burlington's Elmwood Cemetery under the name *Fanny Montezuma.*

Someone else wrote the words that could serve as her epitaph. Shortly after they were married, Ethan gave Fanny a copy of his newly published *Reason, the Only Oracle of Man.* It was the product of four years of effort and he was so proud of the book—perhaps because of how it contrasted with his rough-and-ready image—that he liked to sign letters, "The Philosopher." He gave a copy to his young wife, inscribing it this way:

> Dear Fanny wise, the beautiful and young,
> The partner of my joys, my dearest self
> My love, pride of my life.

When a Man Loves Many Women

Brigham Young, who was born in 1801 in Whitingham, Vermont, had more than twenty wives and fathered forty-seven children. Joseph Smith, born in 1805 in Sharon, Vermont, may have had as many as fifty wives, although he admitted only to his first, with whom he had nine children. But in the marrying department, John Humphrey Noyes, born in 1811 in

Brattleboro, beat them all. He had a *hundred and fifty* "wives," though only—only!—fourteen to sixteen children.

John Humphrey Noyes had a hundred and fifty wives

What WAS it with these guys, all Vermonters born in the same generation?

An answer lies in the religious impulses of the nineteenth century, impulses just as powerful as those that drove some men and women westward into the teeth of Indian country and others onto clipper ships to open up the Orient. It was a time of new frontiers, with the intoxicating freedom to build not only a new land and a new economy but new social orders.

Collectively, the nineteenth-century religious movements had the power and heat of a volcano, pouring out Protestant sects in profusion and endless variety, each with the urge to spread the word and convert lost sheep to the One True Way. All had their own road maps for getting there. Revivalists with burning eyes and come-to-Jesus voices crisscrossed the countryside, exciting people to the point of exhaustion. Spiritualists tuned into heavenly frequencies for divine advisories, faith healers promised the lame they could walk if they *only believed*, and millenarians computed the time left—not much, usually—until the end of the world. Whole communities of people withdrew from the world to live by their own divinely inspired rules: Shakers, the Eben-Ezers of Amana, Harmonists, the Zoarites, the Icarians, Inspirationists, Economists. It was just a coincidence that Young, Smith, and Noyes all came from Vermont, for divine lightning was striking everywhere in the nineteenth century.

While Joseph Smith was busy in western New York State laying the foundation for the Mormon church as Brigham Young waited in the wings, a young man from Putney, Vermont, was graduating from Dartmouth

College with no thoughts of religion at all. The son of a successful Brattleboro businessman, John Humphrey Noyes was a conflicted youth, racked by mood swings and periods of bashfulness that alternated with ones of boldness. He flayed himself for appearing "a stupid dunce" because of his shyness, writing that it would easier facing "a battery of cannon" than "a room full of ladies." Bashful or not, he graduated Phi Beta Kappa and began to study the law, where once again his shyness proved torturous.

Before he could start a second year of legal studies, however, Noyes experienced a religious conversion and so escaped the law to become a student at Andover Theological Seminary. Religion seemed to help him with his personal problems, but the contentious, worldly atmosphere at Andover displeased him, so once again he fled. He enrolled at Yale Divinity School and joined one of New Haven's "free" churches, a place fired by the revival spirit. He discovered the doctrine of Perfectionism and proclaimed his belief in it. Perfectionism is the idea that an individual can become free of sin through religious conversion and will power, an idea that was an anathema at Calvinist Yale. When he refused to recant, Noyes was expelled from Yale and stripped of his preaching license.

That wasn't all he lost. In the free church he had fallen desperately in love with Abigail Merwin, who was thirty years old to his twenty-two, had dark hair and eyes, and "was beautiful and talented." At first she strongly supported his claim to Perfectionism, but after his expulsion she became engaged to another. It was a crushing blow to Noyes, who continued to worship her from afar. Years later, he tried again to renew the relationship when he heard that Abigail's husband had died, and once again he was rebuffed.

Noyes wandered the Northeast after his expulsion, then returned to his home in Putney, where in 1836 he organized a group of "Bible Communists," believers in sharing their worldly goods. As he used his powerful mind to attract followers, he gained confidence in himself. In 1837 he wrote the so-called Battle Axe letter, in which he advocated what sounded like free love. However, it took until 1846 for his Putney community to adopt his idea of "complex marriage."

Sex was not the centerpiece of Noyes's community, but it was of a piece with his other ideas. He was building a utopian socialist community in which selfishness in all things, material, social, and even emotional, would be replaced by a perfect state of community with God. Like many other separatist communities, the Noyes Perfectionists gave up private property.

Likewise, the exclusive attachment of two people for each other, instead of for the community, was thought to be selfish and sinful. Therefore, among Noyes followers, every man in the community was "married" to every woman, and vice versa, an arrangement called "complex marriage." This did not mean free love in the most promiscuous sense, nor did the community sanction sexual orgies. The members were God-fearing, quiet, and sincere, and a number of controls were built into the community. For example, if a man was attracted to a woman, he had to request what was politely called an "interview" by speaking to a third party. The request would be relayed to the woman, who could accept or decline, as she wished.

Those members having sex were expected to take care to avoid unplanned pregnancies and, in fact, over the three decades in which complex marriage was in place, the community experienced averaged only three births a year. In the experiment's last decade, something called "stirpiculture" was practiced, in which pregnancies were planned by a committee. It was a form of eugenics, in which only members of good character and spirituality were allowed to produce children. After children were weaned, they were taken from their birth mothers and raised as a group by designated caretakers.

Noyes's followers were honest and hard-working and his Vermont community lived quietly. No matter. Putney residents were outraged by "complex marriage" and Noyes was soon arrested and charged with adultery. He jumped bail and by 1848 was able to re-establish the community in Oneida, New York. But, gradually, external pressures from opponents of complex marriage and, more importantly, internal dissension from the younger second generation of community members forced the end of complex marriage in 1879 and the shutting down of the entire community in 1880. At its closing, the Oneida Community had about three hundred members, equally divided between men and women.

The Oneida Community's highly regarded workshops were transformed into a joint-stock company, developing into today's publicly traded corporation known as Oneida Ltd., the world's largest manufacturer of stainless steel flatware, as well as silver-plated products. The old Oneida Community Mansion House built by Noyes still stands, operated by a nonprofit organization. It houses a museum and thirty-five apartments, some occupied by descendents of the original Oneida Community.

Complex marriage has been called everything from a pure search for spirituality in community to a thinly disguised excuse for promiscuity. It was, rather, another all-too-human quest, idealistic but impractical, both altruistic and self-serving. Oneida's Perfectionism was always less than perfect. Men and women were supposed to initiate "interviews" equally, but old habits died hard: the men did all the initiating. Moreover, a woman was not supposed to repeatedly refuse a male of higher standing in the "ascending fellowship" of spirituality. And, conveniently, John Humphrey Noyes was judged most perfect of all, for the Oneida Community permitted him to father thirteen children by women of ages ranging from twenty-one to forty-three (in addition to one he already had with his only legal wife, Harriet Holton, plus one or two others by a member in Putney).

Mansion House curator Kerry Keser gives credence to the view that if it hadn't been for Noyes's loss of his beloved Abigail Merwin, he might not have come up with the idea of complex marriage. And while the Oneida Community was not quite the hotbed of unregulated sex some imagine, "I don't doubt there was lot on the side," she says with a laugh.

The Face in the Stone

In 1876, while Giacomo Puccini was just starting to think about writing the kind of romantic operas that would make him famous, a young sculptor named Augustus Saint-Gaudens was leading a *La Bohème* life in New York.

"Gus" Saint-Gaudens wasn't desperate enough to burn his own work to warm his hands *La Bohème*–style, but the rest of the script was pure Puccini. Burdened by debt, the American sculptor lived in his shabby studio, hoped for a big commission, and was in love. That was why he needed that big commission. He had promised the parents of his fiancé, Augusta "Gussie" Homer, that they wouldn't marry until he had financial security.

In December 1876 a committee made the decision that young Saint-Gaudens had been waiting for, but it was not the one he wanted. By a six-to-five vote they chose another sculptor, the well-known John Quincy Adams Ward, to create a public memorial in New York to the late Civil War hero Admiral David Glasgow Farragut. Then came a startling announcement from Ward. He generously withdrew from the competition, saying, "Give the younger man a chance." So, in an ending worthy of the stage, runner-up Saint-Gaudens was granted the prize after all.

Within a few months Gus wed Gussie in a Unitarian ceremony at the Homer residence in Roxbury, Massachusetts, and the couple sailed for Europe, where they could live economically while he worked on the Farragut. In Paris, Saint-Gaudens found a former dance hall to use as a studio. He let artists he knew set up their easels in the orchestra gallery and the sculptor and his friends would sing back and forth to each other as they worked. Puccini would have loved it.

Both Gus and Gussie had been in Europe before. They had met for the first time in Rome in November or December of 1873, at a party of American expatriates. Gus Saint-Gaudens, who had curly, reddish hair, a sharp profile, and a talent for making friends, had been leading the life of a starving artist in Europe. He was the son of a New York shoemaker of French extraction and had shown an early talent for making cameos, an ability that was to grow into sculpting. Augusta Homer was the daughter of an old New England family who had sent her abroad to study and practice painting. She was tall, slim, with compelling dark blue eyes, hair piled high on her head, and a pretty smile. She had inherited the family deafness, which made her seem aloof in social gatherings, yet pleasingly attentive to Gus when she hung on his every word. But she also was prone to depression and hypochondria. During their courtship, Gus had called her his "own darling Dimply" and himself "your own fond, loving Gus who loves you so truly, deeply and well," promising "we shall never be separated again."

In July 1880, three years after the marriage, the sculptor returned to New York and the Farragut monument was unveiled the following May. Gussie had already returned to Roxbury to await the birth of their first and only child, Homer, who was born September 29, 1880. Departing from the stuffy classicism of the time, the Farragut Memorial won wide praise for what was to become the sculptor's hallmark: realistic detail combined with idealism. Saint-Gaudens's reputation grew steadily after that. Commissions for other public works followed, among them the General William T. Sherman Monument in New York's Central Park, the "Standing Lincoln" in Chicago, the Adams Memorial, and the famous Shaw Memorial in Boston, a tribute to the Union Army's first African-American regiment and its colonel, Robert Gould Shaw. Saint-Gaudens also liked to do portrait reliefs in different media, as well as commemorative medals. In 1904 President Theodore Roosevelt asked him to design three U.S. coins. To this day, his twenty-dollar "double eagle" gold piece is said by many to be the most beautiful of all American coins.

For a summer's vacation in 1885, the Saint-Gaudens family rented a large, old house in Cornish, New Hampshire. The property had a stunning view of Vermont's Mount Ascutney across the Connecticut River and the sculptor fell in love with the place. In 1892 he purchased it for a summer home, naming it Aspet, after his father's birthplace in France. Attracted by the gregarious Saint-Gaudens, a colony of artists, including Maxfield Parrish, gathered in Cornish. In 1900, after a diagnosis of cancer, the sculptor made Aspet his permanent home, turning out a steady stream of work despite his declining health. He died in 1907, only fifty-nine years old, and he and his family are buried there.

Gussie lived until 1926, devoting herself to preserving the memory of her famous husband. She turned Aspet into the "Saint-Gaudens Memorial," with admission charged. In 1965, the Memorial was designated a National Historic Site; the Saint-Gaudens residence, its studios, and other buildings are beautifully preserved by the National Park Service. More than forty thousand visitors tour the grounds each year.

But there is another side to all this, a counterpoint to the opera-like story of the shoemaker's son who won his bride only after winning a contest and then became famous. It is the story of a secret love affair that wasn't so secret after all. And it has a twist with an outcome that you can see on the World Wide Web.

Gussie, troubled by her health, spent much of her adult life making pilgrimages to spas and other places she thought would help her. When at home, the strong-minded and strait-laced Gussie handled her husband's financial affairs and their household and studio staffs brusquely, and was cordially disliked by them. Her absences and imperious manner must have soured the marriage as well, so Mr. and Mrs. Saint-Gaudens spent long periods apart from each other. In those days, divorce would have been unthinkable.

Instead, the double standard ruled. Sometime around 1881, not long after his son was born and when he was in his early thirties, Saint-Gaudens fell in love with a beautiful model at least ten years his junior. She had been born in Sweden and was named Albertina Hulgren or Hultgren, but he called her Davida, perhaps in tribute to Michaelangelo's *David*. Eventually she changed her name to Davida Johnson Clark. The relationship turned into a twenty-five year affair, secret at first, that lasted until he was no longer well enough to travel from Cornish to see her.

Saint-Gaudens biographer Burke Wilkinson believes the sculptor was always looking for a feminine ideal, someone tall and slim, with the classic face of a Greek statue. Gussie had some of those characteristics, but Davida, with her straight nose, heavy lids, and high forehead, apparently had more. Probably, she first modeled for Saint-Gaudens when he was working on angels for the tomb of Governor Edwin Morgan. But characteristics of Davida appear in other works, perhaps the most famous being the head on the figure of Diana the Huntress, which Saint-Gaudens first created in 1891 (and later re-created) as a weathervane for Stanford White's new Madison Square Garden.

A thirteen-foot version of the weathervane—Saint-Gaudens's only female nude and a *cause célèbre* in its day—can be seen today in the Philadelphia Museum of Art, as can a six-foot, six-inch reduction in Saint-Gaudens's "Little Studio" in Cornish. Many other copies exist; a number of smaller reductions were made and sold by Tiffany. Other versions of Davida *qua* Diana can also be seen at the Cornish studio, and

Augustus Saint-Gaudens

glimpses of Davida can be found in works elsewhere, such as the angelic *Amor Caritas,* now in the Musée d'Orsay, Paris. The Diana figure has acquired an emblematic association with the Gilded Age.

To a visitor, it seems that Davida's face is almost everywhere you go in Saint-Gaudens's studio and gallery in Cornish.

By contrast, there is only one bas relief of Gussie, and it is intriguing. Though the sculptor had been inspired by Davida's image for much of his professonal life, he began his one and only sculptural image of Gussie shortly before his death, and it can be seen today at the historic site in Cornish. In this shallow relief, he has hidden a heart in Gussie's sleeve. The family sheepdog, "Doodles," stands beside her. Only roughly sketched in, the dog has a man's face—the face of Saint-Gaudens. Even the experts don't know what all the imagery means or whether there is even more hidden in the work. "Who knows?" says Gregory C. Schwarz, chief of interpretation at the site. "Someone could write a master's thesis about what's in there."

It is not certain just when Gussie learned of her husband's affair with Davida, although some evidence suggests it was in 1892. Characteristically, Gussie then departed on a prolonged trip, although she did not leave the marriage. By then, Gus and Davida had a child of their own, named Louis Clark and nicknamed "Novy." He had been born September 23, 1889. Davida died in 1910. Louis Clark moved to California, where he had a son, Louis John Clark, who in turn had a daughter who was named Valerie Clark.

Valerie Clark knew little about her ancestry except that her grandfather, "Novy," had been bitter over Gus's failure to marry Davida and rarely talked about him. As a young woman, Valerie was persuaded by a friend to visit a psychic, as a lark. The psychic told Valerie that a tall, slender man with an aquiline face and a goatee could be seen standing beside her "in spirit." He had long fingers and apparently worked with his hands, because he was holding beautiful tools that looked like "dental tools, but bigger." The resemblance between that image and her great grandfather startled Valerie. The psychic told her that she and the man were two souls with an agreement that "while one of us was in the body, the other would remain in spirit, helping from the other side. And then we'd reverse that.

"I don't get it, but I believe it. I believe in reincarnation." Valerie says. "I can feel him around me and when I ask for help, it comes." Valerie launched her own business, designing fine jewelry in the form of fish and other images from the sea. Promoted on the World Wide Web, her business grew and she now publishes a thirty-two-page catalog of sea-themed jewelry. She married and has two teenage daughters. When she was in her twenties, she made one other major change in her life: she legally changed her name from Valerie Clark to Valerie Saint-Gaudens.

Valerie Saint-Gaudens (above)
Davida as "Diana" (right)

Today, on another coast and a century after the famous sculptor's death, three-dimensional art—sculpture on a smaller scale—is being created once more by a Saint-Gaudens. And, for the first time, the relationship between Augustus Saint-Gaudens and Davida is being publicly, and proudly, acknowledged.

The Naked Bride

On a wintry day in the West River Valley town of Newfane, the snow-covered common and its buildings are so perfect that you can only think of heaven and degrees of perfection usually reserved for the celestial. Sunlight glitters on the snow and plays off the fluted columns of the Greek Revival county courthouse and a nearby inn. The spire of the beautiful old Congregational Church reaches up to heaven and the Union Meeting Hall nearby (built 1832) points four finials in that direction as well. Surely, nothing but righteousness can prevail here.

And, mostly, righteousness has prevailed. But that doesn't preclude a little Yankee ingenuity when a situation calls for it. And, around 1790, the situation of Major Moses Joy and the beautiful widow Hannah Ward called for a lot of it.

Not long after the Revolution had been fought and won and Vermont was still an independent republic, Major Joy fell in love with Hannah. Hannah's late husband, William Ward, had been an early settler of Newfane and landowner in the area and the adjacent town of Wardsboro is named for him. But he had died on a fur-trading trip to Canada, leaving his widow and estate with debts. And that's what threatened Major Joy's courtship of the comely widow.

Newfane attorney Obediah Martin, a friend of Joy's, had told him the hard truth. Were he to marry Hannah Ward, he would inherit her late husband's debts. Few Vermonters had much money in those days and then, as now, even fewer fancied spending it. While Major Joy's heart ached for Hannah, his purse trembled with anxiety.

The old law was complicated, but it came down to this: the late husband's debts were part of his estate and so were all of Hannah's clothes. If he married Hannah while she was wearing clothes furnished by her late husband, Major Joy would acquire both the estate and the debts. And, under the law, trying to furnish her new clothes would just get Major Joy into more trouble.

Tension mounted. The hearts of the discouraged lovers thumped to a funereal beat. But then Major Joy had an idea. Suddenly, plans for the wedding went forward. Lawyer Martin fretted, but Major Joy just smiled. The great day in February 1890 arrived, a crowd trudged through the snow to gather at the Field Mansion in Newfane, and the bride arrived—wearing the shabby old clothes from her late marriage.

To the guests' amazement, she began to disrobe, at a crucial moment stepping behind a door into a closet, from which rustling sounds could be heard. The door opened briefly when one of her bridal attendants emerged, carrying all of Hannah's clothing. Then a bare white arm appeared through a small hole that had been cut in the door. Major Joy took Hannah's hand and the minister began the ceremony, uniting the young man and the naked widow, who was ninety-five percent out of sight in the closet.

When the ceremony was over, a bridal attendant returned to the closet and soon Hannah emerged in a fine silk gown, to receive the congratulations of guests on the fine marriage she had made to a man who could not only appreciate beauty, but economy.

And that's how two thrifty Vermonters were able to make love in a very cold climate.

To visit the Dog Chapel and the Huneck Gallery (802-748-2700), take U.S. 2 two miles north of St. Johnsbury, Vermont, and turn onto Spaulding Road. (See also www.huneck.com). You can get a little closer to crusty old Ethan Allen, if you dare, by visiting the Ethan Allen Homestead, gardens, and exhibits in Riverside Park just off Route 127 north of Burlington, Vermont (802-865-4556) or visit the web site www.ethanallenhomestead.org. Fort Ticonderoga, site of Allen's greatest military triumph, is a historic landmark open to the public in Ticonderoga, New York (518-585-2821) or visit www.fort-ticonderoga.org. The Mansion House Museum in Oneida, New York, preserves the history of John Humphrey Noyes's Perfectionist community (315-363-0745 or visit www.oneidacommunity.org). The Saint-Gaudens National Historic Site, open seasonally, is located just off Route 12A in Cornish, New Hampshire, across the river from Windsor, Vermont (603-675-2175; www.nps.gov/saga). The artistic work of a modern Saint-Gaudens can be found at www.saint-gaudens.com.

CHAPTER TWELVE

A Collection of Heads

Driving north from Brattleboro on Interstate 91 on a spring day is like driving into the front cover of *Vermont Life*, the state's official magazine. Overhead, the sky can be so blue that it hurts just to look at it. On the left, a gentle caravan of the Green Mountain's foothills, dressed in the light green of budding trees, rolls northward, while on the right are glimpses of the glittering Connecticut and, just beyond it, the softer side of New Hampshire. The towns are invisible from the highway but you know they are out there, small, white-clapboarded places like Putney, Rockingham, Hartland, Walpole, Windsor, Hanover, places named by our ancestors more than two centuries ago. As you look away from the empty highway, gazing in your aloneness at an undulating forestscape unbroken by house or meadow, signs or smokestacks, you think, *This is how it must have felt to them.*

In 1740 a man named Farnsworth came to what is now Charlestown, New Hampshire. A few families joined him and they put up a fort, really only half a dozen reinforced houses joined by a stockade. Called "Fort Number 4," it wasn't long until it came under attack by Indian raiding parties from Canada who killed or captured anyone they found outside the walls. Among their captives in 1754 was a very pregnant Mrs. Susanna Willard Johnson. Returning to Canada, the Indian raiding party and its captives paused in Vermont so Mrs. Johnson could give birth to a daughter, whom she named "Captive." About four years later, Captive Johnson and her family were allowed to return to the Connecticut River Valley. Captive's older brother, Sylvanus, came back from captivity speaking only the Indian tongue. He settled in Walpole, New Hampshire, and worked as a fisherman, but he never gave up all of his Indian ways, insisting until the end of his days that the "Indians were a far more moral race than the whites."

But he did stay. The Upper Valley countryside from Brattleboro to St. Johnsbury contained a river teeming with fish and a rich bottomland lying between terraced hillsides, fertile territory for people who knew how to use their heads as well as their hands. Most of Vermont is a great place for raising rocks, children, and side-hill mountain goats, but generations of canny agriculturists made good livings from the Upper Valley; some still do. Some did other things. Captain Samuel Morey of Orford, New Hampshire, was called "the Edison of his day." Robert Fulton gets all the credit for inventing the steamboat, but around Fairlee, Vermont, and Orford, just across the river in New Hampshire, they'll tell you it was Cap'n Morey who really invented the contraption and tried it out on the Connecticut River fourteen years before Fulton's *Clermont*.

That Cap'n Morey was a nautical genius in landlocked Vermont isn't that surprising. Yankee heads were good for many things besides counting cows and planning stone walls. Most rural New Englanders had to do a great deal with very little, so they were forever concocting inventions and finding new ways to stretch a dollar. The qualities of thrift, common sense, and flinty reserve for which Yankees are famed were forged from life on a land that gave up its rewards only grudgingly. Fortunately, many of the first settlers were up to the challenge. Unfortunately for those of us trying to polish the family escutcheon, a few of our ancestors left gentility behind in the process.

One such story touches my household. It begins in 1630, when an irascible carpenter from Suffolk named William Knapp arrived in Massachusetts Bay and settled a few miles inland, in Watertown. He must have been a virile sort, for he was about fifty years of age—old for that time—and yet his brood of seven children included a babe in arms. Knapp lived among Puritans, but he was no puritan. Until the end of his days Old Knop, as he was dismissively called in town records, gave local officialdom heartburn as he dodged debts, swore in public, slandered the governor, and brewed beer illegally. He was a randy old goat, too: in his seventies he paid one Phoebe Page, a known slattern, five shillings for a "cleaveing kiss," and then demanded another free. (Having her limits, Ms. Page refused.)

And yet I have a certain regard for Old Knop, rough edges and all. That he was willing to abandon what little he had in England for a journey to the edge of the earth showed courage. There he stuck, loudmouthed and unrepentant in the face of starvation, storm, and stern Puritan solemnity. He may have turned the air blue with his profanity while brewing beer on the sly, but all around him neighbors were folding in the face of New England's harshness and fleeing back to Old England. Whatever else you could say about William Knapp, he was a survivor.

Joseph Bemis, a young blacksmith from Essex, arrived in Watertown a few years after Old Knop. Like Knapp, he stuck, but unlike him, Bemis mostly stayed out of trouble, prospered modestly, and was elected to local office several times. Bemis, a prominent citizen in the little Puritan town, and Old Knop, a notorious one, must have been well aware of each other, but there is no record of the two families intersecting, for Joseph's respectability and William's raffishness would have put some social distance between them. That intersection would come later.

After the settlement of Massachusetts Bay there came the "Great Reshuffling," in which settlers pulled up stakes and moved inland, over and over again, as they searched for new places to wrest a living from New England's rocky soil. One line of Bemises settled for several generations in the eastern part of Connecticut, and then, in the 1760s, pushed northward into southeastern Vermont's Windham County, which lies on the Connecticut River. Meanwhile, a line of Knapps was moving more directly that way, living successively in Newton, Worcester, and Petersham, Massachusetts, before settling in Vermont at about the same time as the Bemises, and only a few miles from them. Both families stayed and, over the generations, attained respectability in Windham County as farmers, storekeepers, and cattle merchants. Old Knop and his transgressions had long since been forgotten.

In 1929, nearly three centuries after they came separately to New England, the two family lines connected when Marion Alice Knapp, a direct descendent of notorious Old Knop, married Guy Henry Bemis, a direct descendent of respectable Joseph Bemis. It was a union for which I am profoundly grateful. Guy and Marion Knapp Bemis became prominent merchants and civic leaders, living long, active, and honored lives in Walpole, New Hampshire, just across the river from Vermont's Windham

County. They also had one child. Guy and Marion died in the 1990s, never having learned about Old Knop's checkered career. Joan Bemis—their daughter and my wife—just has.

The Voice

Sometimes, they say, you can hear it rolling through the Upper Valley like thunder, a giant's voice from up Hanover way that sweeps southward past Mount Ascutney, rumbles across the river terraces, and bounces off the steep face of Fall Mountain before fading away down around the Massachusetts line. All along the river farmers look up from their milking and chuckle. "There's Dan'l Webster," they say to themselves. "There ain't nobody to beat ol' Dan'l."

And, mostly, nobody did. Not even the Devil, who lost a famous contest to Daniel Webster that generations of schoolchildren have read about. But

somebody, somebody very close to home indeed, did beat Daniel Webster, keeping him from the victory he wanted most of all and eventually killing him. But that story comes later, because right now I want to tell you about one of Daniel's finer moments. It means a lot to the valley.

Daniel Webster was born in 1782 in Salisbury, a small town in the middle of New Hampshire. Later he lived on a saltwater farm in Marshfield, Massachusetts, but there isn't anybody who doesn't think of Daniel Webster as a New Hampshireman. Dark-complected, with coal-black hair, the boy was called Black Dan. He

"God-like" Daniel Webster, New Hampshire's mighty voice in the mountains

had no talent for farming, so when his father agreed to send him to Dartmouth at age fifteen, he cried for joy.

At Dartmouth, young Webster became a top scholar and a renowned debater, although his arrogance made him unpopular outside his own circle. Interested in history and literature, the young Dartmouth graduate reluctantly took up the study of law at his father's behest. Admitted to the bar in Boston in 1805, he returned to Salisbury and built a respectable country practice, despite his "haughty, cold and overbearing" ways. Then, moving to Portsmouth and allying himself with the merchants and ship owners, he built another thriving practice and developed a reputation as a stunning courtroom performer. A friend remarked, "There never was such an actor lost to the stage."

Webster worked constantly on improving his delivery. The courtroom taught him that a good speech, to be effective, had to be terse and to the point. Sentimental and emotive, he learned how to use dramatic phrasing and poetic skills, such as alliteration and repetition of words. One listener recalled, "He was a black, raven-haired fellow, with an eye as black as death, and as heavy as a lion's—and no lion in Africa ever had a voice like him. . . ."

A political conservative, at age thirty he was elected to Congress from New Hampshire on the Federalist ticket and was re-elected twice, serving from 1813 to 1817. In 1816 he moved his practice to Boston and was returned to Congress in 1823, where he served until 1827. In the intervals between congressional stints, he became a favored attorney for the city's businessmen and one of the most highly paid lawyers in the nation. Throughout his life he argued a number of major cases before the U.S. Supreme Court, but the one that mattered the most to the valley was the Dartmouth College case of 1818.

Dartmouth College had its roots in a charity school for Indians founded in Connecticut in 1754 by the Reverend Eleazar Wheelock. When New Hampshire's Upper Valley opened for settlement, he moved his school north and, in 1769, King George III approved its charter. Named for the earl of Dartmouth, a benefactor, the little school opened for business the next year in a forest of white pines in what is now Hanover. It had thirty students, only three of them Indians.

In 1779 Eleazar died and was succeeded in the presidency by his son, John, a man who was as autocratic as his father, while lacking his diplomatic skills. In 1815, the college trustees ran out of patience with Wheelock and fired him. He appealed to the New Hampshire legislature, which responded by passing legislation to turn the private college into a public university. The college's trustees refused to back down and for three years the state's "Dartmouth University" and the private Dartmouth College coexisted uncomfortably in Hanover. Fighting for their private college's survival, the trustees sued and so the case *Trustees of Dartmouth College v. Woodward* (Woodward was an official of the university) arrived at the U.S. Supreme Court in 1818.

Daniel Webster took the trustees' case. For three days in March 1818 he and his opponent argued before the Supreme Court in its cramped, temporary quarters in Washington. Webster spoke for nearly five hours, calmly and with precision. "It was hardly eloquence in any strict sense of the term," someone wrote; "it was pure reason," impressive for clarity and logic. Webster urged the justices to recognize the Constitution's "contract clause," a line of argument his predecessors in the case had developed and which Webster employed here with little change. He asserted that Dartmouth's charter of 1769 constituted a contract that, under the Constitution, states were prohibited from violating. As he drew to a conclusion, he became more emotional:

> Sir, you may destroy this institution; it is weak; it is in your hands! I know it is one of the lesser lights in the literary horizon of our country. You may put it out. But, if you do so, you must carry through your work! You must extinguish, one after another, all those greater lights of science which, for more than a century, have thrown their radiance over our land!
>
> It is, sir, as I have said, a small college. And yet there are those who love it—

Overcome, Webster paused. Tears filled the eyes of the chief justice and the audience sat transfixed. Then, with a few final words, Webster was finished. A "deathlike stillness" followed. Eleven months later the court delivered its opinion: it ruled in favor of the private Dartmouth College. A landmark decision, the Dartmouth College case has allowed American private education to grow without fear of government confiscation. At Dartmouth, the following words were later placed in bronze before Webster Hall: "Founded by Eleazar Wheelock, Refounded by Daniel Webster."

Webster's reputation soared and kept soaring as he took high-visibility cases and engaged in major debates in Congress. He became the prize speaker for a public holiday or the laying of a cornerstone, so thrilling audiences with his oratory and reasoning that he came to be referred to as "God-like Daniel." Professor George Ticknor of Harvard wrote, "I was never so excited by public speaking before in my life. Three or four times I thought my temples would burst with the gush of blood...."

The overwhelming Webster persona—what we would call charisma or command presence or the ability to fill a room—became so legendary that even today children know about it, thanks to a story published in 1937 by Pulitzer Prize–winning author Stephen Vincent Benét. "The Devil and Daniel Webster" tells of an unlucky New Hampshire farmer named Jabez Stone who sold his soul in desperation to a "dark-dressed stranger" who had a frightening smile. But when the Devil came to collect on his bargain, the frantic farmer turned for help to a fellow New Hampshireman, Daniel Webster, a "man with a mouth like a mastiff, a brow like a mountain and eyes like burning anthracite." With a voice that called "on the harps of the blessed," Webster won over a hostile jury. Before kicking Stone's vanquished tormentor out the door, however, the fictional Webster let the Devil tell his fortune. It was not quite the fortune Webster would have wanted.

For Webster was very, very ambitious. He could no more stay away from politics than a moth from the flame and the presidency was always on his mind. Webster served as U.S. senator from 1827 to 1841 and 1845 to 1850, and twice as U.S. secretary of state, but none of that was enough. A presidential trial balloon launched in 1831 attracted no support. In 1836 he was bitterly disappointed when he won only the Bay State's vote in the Whig presidential primary. A friend told Webster, "You will be king of this country if you simply let it be known that you are unalterably resolved never to be a candidate for the presidency." This Webster could not do. Once again, in 1840, he tried and failed to secure the Whig nomination.

His reputation as a staunch defender of the Constitution and a champion of the Union against all talk of secession brought him much support in the North but enmity in the South. But things changed when Congress debated what would become known as the Compromise of 1850. Rising once again to defend the Union, Webster took a position that won him applause from the South, where he had previously been an anathema. Speaking "not as a Massachusetts man, nor as a Northern man, but as an American," Webster condemned demands for abolition from the North as unnecessary and divisive. His Northern allies were horrified and abolition-ists were infuriated. Critics began calling him "Black Dan" again.

Webster's presidential support had never been widespread and now was eroded even further. At the 1852 Whig convention in Baltimore Webster was humiliated when the convention chose Winfield Scott as their nomi-nee for president. He had a more serious problem. In May, a few weeks before that convention, Webster had been thrown from his carriage and injured more seriously than first appeared. He consulted doctors, but to no avail. In August, as it did each year, the "summer catarrh" (hay fever) re-turned to plague Webster. By September he also was suffering from diar-rhea. A friend reported that he looked like a ghost. On October 10 he dictated the inscription for his tombstone.

On Sunday morning, October 24, 1852, the residents of Marshfield were awakened by the tolling of the church bell. At first, it rang violently, to warn townspeople of important news. Then, after a pause, it rang three times, the signal that a man had died. Then the bell began a long, slow tolling of the man's age. Seventy times it struck, and everyone knew who it was. They knew that, at long last, The Voice had fallen silent.

That voice, and his imposing head, had given Webster a giant's image. He was not a remarkably large man, except for a head which, as his hair receded, revealed a brow as imposing as one of New Hampshire's granite outcroppings. Artists were fascinated by it and phrenologists were sure it supported their "science." Indeed, Webster's hat size was bigger than the average man's and an autopsy revealed an unusually large brain (almost sixty-four ounces, compared to the average of fifty ounces).

What the phrenologists did not address was the curious imbalance of that brain's intellectual and moral sides. Throughout his life, Webster could overwhelm audiences with oratory that was a mighty trumpet for a stag-gering intelligence. And yet there was a coldness, a hauteur, an insensitivity to moral nuances and a detachment from the pain of others. This had troubled observers throughout Webster's life, but the Compromise of 1850 and his support for the Fugitive Slave Act (and, later, his aggressive en-forcement of it when he was secretary of state) shocked them most of all. The North's moral voices compared Webster to a fallen angel and one of the greatest men that "God ever let the devil buy." Ralph Waldo Emerson said the word *liberty* in Webster's mouth sounded like *love* in the mouth of a whore. Black Dan had vanquished the God-like Daniel.

And there was a certain shabbiness about the everyday affairs of Daniel

Webster. He built up huge debts and neglected to pay them. He used people. He seemed blind to the implications of letting wealthy men pay some of his debts. He was egotistical and egocentric. He was disrespectful of his opponents, branding abolitionists as fanatics and traitors. And he was a heavy drinker: his autopsy revealed a liver so badly diseased that it must have hastened his death.

And yet for many years Daniel Webster was our most eloquent defender of the Constitution, our fiercest supporter of the Union. His criticism of the abolitionists came from a conservative's sincere devotion to social and political stability. And he left his mark upon the Connecticut River Valley, where Dartmouth College to this day officially calls him "Dartmouth's Favorite Son."

Even now, the distant rumble of thunder in the valley makes you think of the great orator. But as you do, you wonder: *Who is that? God-like Daniel or Black Dan?*

Our Phineas

Phineas Gage has a secure position at Harvard, an international reputation, the acquaintance of a wide circle of professors of psychology, neurobiology, and anatomy, and an excellent set of teeth. He also has a hole in his head.

Phineas—or, rather, his skull—rests on a glass shelf in a display case in the Francis A. Countway Library of Medicine at Harvard University, on permanent display for medical students, professors, and the public. "He's our Mona Lisa, our premier attraction," Suzanne Fitz, collections manager, smilingly tells a visitor. How Phineas, a simple country fellow, came to his tenured position at Harvard never fails to impress visitors. Sometimes it also makes them want to throw up.

Phineas Gage probably came from old New England stock and may have been an eighth-generation descendent of John Gage, a Puritan who landed in Salem in 1630. Phineas himself was born around 1823 near Lebanon, New Hampshire. He must have had a starving-poor childhood. His teeth appear to be complete and free of cavities, but they are striated, suggesting that he was malnourished as a child.

Nothing in Phineas's early life suggested that he was headed for (as a biographer put it) "an odd kind of fame." Instead, he lived the sweaty anonymity of a nineteenth-century working man, a foreman on a railroad construction crew. It was hard, dangerous work, and if a man died now and then, well, that was just the cost of doing business in those days. But for the farm boys of northern New England who had watched their parents trying to scratch out bare livings in rocky hill country, working on the railroad and getting paid every week didn't look half bad.

In the 1840s a flurry of railroad building began in Vermont, with one of the lines, the Rutland and Burlington Railroad, being constructed diagonally through the Green Mountains, from Brattleboro in the southeast to Lake Champlain in the northwest. On September 13, 1848, Phineas Gage was supervising a gang of men building roadbed near Proctorsville, about thirteen miles northwest of Bellows Falls. They were making a "cut" through rock, breaking it apart with blasting powder tamped into drill holes.

Gage was a healthy young man, about twenty-five, rather short but very muscular. He was said to be a "shrewd business man," suggesting he may have been a subcontractor who employed the men he supervised. Blasting through rock required considerable know-how to get the job done without blowing anyone up. Gage was said to be of "temperate habits" and "a great favorite" of his men.

At about 4:30 p.m. on this cool September day, Gage was standing near a drill hole, holding a tamping iron which a blacksmith had made especially for him. The tamping iron was a rod weighing about thirteen and a quarter pounds, three feet and seven inches long, and about one and a quarter inches in diameter, except at one end, where it tapered to about a quarter inch. The drill hole had been filled with blasting powder and Gage had told a worker to pour in the usual safety barrier of sand before he began tamping everything down. Standing above the hole, with his head turned slightly away as he looked over his right shoulder, Gage let the tamping iron drop down the hole. Perhaps he assumed the sand had already been poured; it had not. Or perhaps he let the iron slip. In any case, it struck rock, caused a spark, and exploded the powder.

The explosion drove the heavy tamping iron out of the drill hole like a missile, ramming it through Gage's left cheek and out the top of his head before the iron landed twenty-two to twenty-eight yards behind him. Gage was thrown on his back, but after a few convulsive movements was able to speak. He walked to a nearby road, climbed into an oxcart, and was taken three-quarters of a mile to the tavern where he had been staying. He stood up by himself in the cart but allowed two men to help him to a chair on the piazza, where he sat while medical attention was summoned.

Edward H. Williams, M.D., of Proctorsville, arrived at the tavern about half an hour after the accident and Gage greeted him by saying, "Doctor, here is business enough for you." An hour later, John M. Harlow, the railroad's doctor, arrived and the two physicians accompanied Gage to his room, where they cleaned and dressed his injuries. Conscious and rational throughout the treatment, Gage insisted he would return to work in a day or so. He did not, of course. Dr. Harlow expected him to die and a local cabinetmaker measured Gage for a coffin (can you imagine what that must have been like?). Although Gage had periods of delirium over the coming days, he remained lucid for the most part . . . and very much alive.

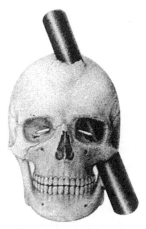

How an iron rod passed through Phineas Gage's head

The tamping iron had entered Gage's left cheek just above the jawbone and below the cheekbone, passing behind the left eye and through the frontal and middle left lobes of the brain ("disintegrating and pulpifying" the brain substance and "drawing out a considerable quantity of it," Harlow wrote). It exited just in front and to the left of the center of the top of the skull, punching a hole larger than a dollar coin.

Gage had suffered a serious loss of brain matter. The tamping rod was smeared with it and some additional brain material was found on the rocks in the vicinity. A considerable amount of blood, mixed with brain matter, also flowed into Gage's throat from the hole in the roof of his mouth and then went to his stomach, causing him to vomit. Dr. Harlow estimated that Gage's first vomiting brought up half a teacup of brain material. Probing the wound with his bare fingers, the physician removed several small fragments of bone and about an ounce of brain before he replaced some of the bone and drew the scalp wound together. By the next day, bleeding had stopped but other problems began: for nineteen days Gage suffered from infection severe enough to cause two short periods of delirium, and for about a week he was comatose. There were fetid discharges and growths of "fungi" from the wounds, but Dr. Harlow kept them as clean and disinfected as the medical science of the day allowed.

Twenty-two days after the accident, Gage started improving. After thirty-seven days, the head wound was closing rapidly, eventually healing over the entire hole. By late November, Gage was able to leave Cavendish to return to Lebanon. Early in January, Dr. Harlow visited him and found

Gage "walking about the house, riding out, improving both mentally and physically."

Before the accident, Gage was said to be a "shrewd, smart business man, very energetic and persistent in executing all his plans of operation." Gage's bosses considered him "the most efficient and capable foreman in their employ." Immediately after the accident, observers were impressed with how "rational" he seemed, with good memory and good "sensorial powers." However, within a few days there were ominous signs of "childishness" and "obstinacy." Dr. Harlow said Gage had become "a child in his intellectual capacities (with) the animal passions of a strong man." He was, the doctor said, "fitful, irreverent, indulging at times in the grossest profanity . . . manifesting but little deference to his fellows"—all new behaviors for him. He was so changed that his acquaintances said he was "no longer Gage." The railroad refused to rehire him.

At first Gage worked on the family farm, but then he and his tamping iron went on tour in New England. In August 1852, he traveled by ship to Valparaiso, Chile, where he cared for a stable of horses and often drove a team of six pulling a Concord coach, a job requiring considerable skill. In 1859, his health failing, Gage left for San Francisco, where his parents had moved. According to Dr. Harlow, Gage had "conceived a great fondness for pets and souvenirs, especially for children, horses and dogs—exceeded only by his attachment for his tamping iron, which was his constant companion during the remainder of his life."

Gage held a succession of jobs in California. Then he suffered a series of convulsions and died May 20, 1860, with "epilepsy" recorded as the cause of death. Not until 1866 was Dr. Harlow able to contact the family, for he had lost touch with Phineas in Chile. Ever the scientist, the doctor set to work persuading the Gage family to disinter the body and let him have the skull and tamping iron for study. In 1868 the skull and iron arrived in Boston and Dr. Harlow was able to make a presentation about the case to the annual meeting of the Massachusetts Medical Society. The lack of an autopsy has prevented our drawing specific conclusions about the relationship of parts of the brain to various behaviors, but the case did do this: it memorably drew attention to the likelihood of such connections.

Incredibly, Phineas Gage had lived for nearly twelve years after his injury. However, he was "no longer Gage," so his existence was disjointed and restless, a period of roaming discontent. His constant companion was his custom-made tamping iron, the object that had changed his life and that he clung to, as if it were a connection between his past and present lives. Dr. Harlow donated Gage's relics to the Warren Anatomical Museum, now at Harvard, and they are on display there today. Gage's wanderings are over and so is his disconnectedness: to educate students, he has been given an honored place, with his tamping iron beside him. And he has acquired a family of sorts: library and museum staff call him, not without fondness, "Our Phineas." After years of roaming, Phineas Gage has found a home, a job, and a family.

The Poor Woman

She could see it from her window when she got up in the morning, she could see it the moment she stepped out on her front porch, and even when she couldn't see it, Hetty Green knew it was there. It was about a third of a mile away, spread across the western horizon in both directions, more than three hundred feet high. Geologists said it was a drumlin, a leftover from the glacier that had passed this way thousands of years before, but folks in this part of the valley simply called it Fall Mountain. It was a heap of rock with a steep, ugly face, scorched by repeated brush and grass fires set off by sparks from the steam locomotives passing below.

Hetty Green, the richest woman in America, had chosen to spend some of her life in Bellows Falls, Vermont, on the west side of the Connecticut River. Fall Mountain was on the opposite side of the river, in North Walpole, New Hampshire. Nobody could quite fathom why Hetty, who could live anywhere and whose business was in New York anyway, chose to stay in the homely little industrial and railroad town of Bellows Falls as much as she did, but she and the mountain were certainly two of a kind: hard, dark, and forbidding, with nothing soft about either one of them.

Hetty had been born 120 miles away, in the old whaling town of New Bedford, Massachusetts. Her great grandfather, Isaac Howland, Jr., had been a crafty little man who had built a fortune in the whaling business. After Isaac died, his business partner, second cousin, and son-in-law, Gideon Howland, a widower, continued to live in Isaac's mansion, as did Gideon's two daughters, Abby and Sylvia, and his mother-in-law. Then, in 1833, an ambitious young Quaker from Rhode Island, Edward Mott Robinson, came to town, married Gideon's daughter Abby, and joined the firm.

In 1835, Edward and Abby had a daughter they named Henrietta Howland Robinson but called Hetty. Because of Abby's poor health, Hetty was sent at eighteen months to live with her sixty-six-year-old grandfather,

Gideon Howland, and maiden aunt, Sylvia Ann Howland. Known around town as "Uncle Gid," Gideon conducted his household with Quaker simplicity and frugality, although that didn't keep him from drinking or indulging in an occasional eccentricity. The only child in this wealthy household, Hetty was spoiled with attention, though certainly not with fine clothing or other luxuries scorned by the Quakers.

A precocious child, by age six Hetty Robinson was reading the business and financial news out loud to her grandfather, whose eyesight was failing. "In this way I came to know what stocks and bonds were, how the markets fluctuated, and the meaning of bulls and bears," she later recalled. "By the time I was fifteen, when I went to Boston to school, I knew more about these things than many a man that makes a living out of them." Hetty started accumulating wealth early, too. At age eight, on her own initiative, she took a store of coins she had hoarded to a New Bedford bank and got a passbook.

Little Hetty followed her grandfather when he toured the whalers in port and she acquired a sailor's vocabulary from what she overheard there and on streets crowded with merchants, farm boys, and cannibals from the South Seas. As an angry adult, Hetty would either use a sailor's language or she would cry. A Howland family retainer remembered that Hetty had been manipulative, willful, and crafty even as a child.

After Gideon died, Hetty returned to her father's tutelage. A ruthless slave driver and tightwad, Edward Robinson was not loved in New Bedford and was nicknamed "Blubber Robinson" and "Black Hawk." "My father," Hetty recalled, "taught me never to owe anyone anything, not even a kindness." Uncharacteristically, Robinson gave Hetty an expensive coming-out party when she was nineteen. By this time, the blue-eyed, buxom young heiress-apparent was attracting attention from males, but she dismissed them as fortune hunters. The day after her party she sold the unused portions of the candles. When her father gave her money to spend a well-dressed winter in New York, she returned home early, having invested most of the money in bonds.

With the whaling business in decline, Edward Robinson moved to New York, while daughter Hetty remained in the Howland ancestral home, badgering her Aunt Sylvia into bequeathing her fortune to her. That accomplished, she would periodically visit New York to attend balls and dance with the cream of society. Back in New Bedford, however, she continued to be such a nag to her aunt that she was banished from the house and had to take up residence in New York. There she launched a campaign to make sure she was her father's sole heir.

Now a third fortune came into view. Shortly after Hetty turned thirty, her father introduced her to forty-four-year-old Edward Henry Green, a tall, portly gentleman who was a shrewd investor and fond of the good things in life. Green, the son of a Bellows Falls merchant, had spent eighteen years in the Orient and had become a millionaire trading silks, tobacco, tea, and other merchandise. Edward and Hetty began keeping company.

Then, in little more than two weeks' time in 1865, both Black Hawk Robinson and Aunt Sylvia died. Hetty's father left her about a million dollars and several million more in trust, so she was now a rich woman in her own right. But what she heard at the reading of Sylvia's will stunned her. Sylvia had changed her will, giving half of her two-million-dollar fortune to charity, public works, needy people in the community, and various relatives and friends. From the other half of Sylvia's fortune Hetty would get only the income during her lifetime, following which it was to be divided among the descendents of Isaac Howland.

Hetty flew into a flurry of activity. She attempted, unsuccessfully, to bribe a probate judge. Advised by the increasingly devoted Green and by a lawyer suggestively named William W. Crapo, Hetty launched all-out war. She produced a document which supposedly stated her aunt's intention to leave everything to her, regardless of any other wills created before or after. Then followed a long court battle with charges and countercharges, expert witnesses and conflicting testimony, much of it centering on whether the key document produced by Hetty was authentic.

It turned out not to matter: in 1868 the court dismissed the case on a technicality, leaving Hetty no better off than before—which, of course, was very well off, indeed, but forever embittered against lawyers. By now, she had become Mrs. Edward Green, having married in 1867. Immediately after the wedding the couple went to Europe to live for several years, perhaps because Hetty feared she would be charged with forging the document she had produced in court. In a sign of the paranoia that would increasingly plague her, she also feared she would be murdered by relatives seeking her trust fund.

In London Hetty used her market smarts to trade in U.S. bonds, to her great profit. She also found time to give birth to a son, called Ned, in 1868, and a daughter, named Hetty Sylvia Ann, in 1871. After seven years abroad, however, the Green family returned to America, larger, markedly richer, and basking in Hetty's claims that she had consorted with aristocracy and been presented to Queen Victoria (none of which was true).

The Greens had come back to the States during the Panic of 1873, which was no panic for Hetty. Instead, she had plenty of cash to buy stocks and bonds offered at bargain prices by frightened sellers. "There is no great secret in fortune making," she said. "All you have to do is buy cheap and sell dear, act with thrift and shrewdness and be persistent." Hetty stuck to that principle, whether she was buying a million dollars' worth of railroad bonds or a basket of apples. "She had the best banking brain of anyone I knew," a finance man said.

The Greens chose to live part of each year in his hometown of Bellows Falls, where the locals, who had been expecting to meet American royalty, were sorely disappointed by Hetty's appearance and nickel-pinching ways. She wore cheap, unstylish clothing that was usually old and shabby, she looked for bargains at every turn, and she added no grace or grandeur whatsoever to the plain little town. Allegedly, some local merchants tried to overcharge her for products and services and Hetty, who was not only tightfisted but shrewder than the average merchant, developed many tricks to defeat them. She haggled over every purchase, sometimes washed her own clothes, and buttonholed doctors and lawyers on the street to cadge free advice. But one incident did more than any other to freeze Hetty's image as a skinflint. At fourteen, Ned dislocated his kneecap while sliding, causing him excruciating pain. Hetty delayed seeking medical attention, trying to save money by treating the boy herself with poultices and applications of hot sand. A full five years after the accident, the untreated leg had to be amputated, with the event becoming the symbol of Hetty's miserliness.

Some of Hetty's biographers believe she genuinely loved her children and husband, but that her compulsion to save money overwhelmed every other impulse. When her husband, on whose counsel she had relied for so long, made a series of disastrous investments, lost his fortune, and borrowed against hers, she refused to live with him. In 1885 they began living apart most of the time, leaving him in comfortable but not lavish circumstances even as her wealth multiplied. "My husband is of no use to me at all. I wish I did not have him. He is a burden to me," she said.

However, Hetty worked hard to bring young Ned along. She sent him to Fordham University, gave him an allowance, found him jobs, and set him up in business, first in mortgage lending in Chicago and then as president of a Texas railroad. Wherever Ned went, he attracted women with dollar signs in their eyes and Ned, who didn't mind the attention of a young lady, whether showgirl or strumpet, shooed no one away. He was the kind of guy whose eyes always dropped to chest level with women he met. Despite that, and his cork leg, he never lacked for arm candy. The good-natured Ned liked other things, too, and spent money lavishly: he had many hobbies, owned a fine yacht, took up flying, even ran for governor of Texas. Somewhere he picked up the honorary title of "colonel," and used it thereafter. As Hetty had ordered, the "Colonel" waited twenty years to marry, then wed a Chicago prostitute named Mabel. He had already named a railroad car after her, the "Mabel."

When she was not in Bellows Falls, which she considered her legal residence, Hetty lived in a succession of New York–area fleabag hotels and cheap boarding houses, moving constantly. She said that was because of her fear of being murdered by fortune-seeking relatives, but it also saved her from being taxed as a New York resident. To manage her affairs, she set up camp at the Chemical National Bank, where she had huge deposits. The bank let her store many of her belongings there,

Hetty Green

including her wardrobe. Sometimes she sat on the bank's floor to conduct business and could be seen recycling used envelopes as stationery. When she wasn't in the bank, she was in court, for she was constantly suing or being sued. Her face and hands were frequently smudged from lack of washing and she liked to chew an onion in the morning for health reasons, giving her a breath that could wilt a flower. In cold weather she insulated herself by inserting newspapers inside her clothing. On one occasion she startled several women by inviting them for a seven-course meal, only to take them to a boarding house that charged but twenty-five cents a person.

She had hatreds: all lawyers (although she employed them constantly), most doctors, and a long list of business opponents. And she had delusions. She came to believe that both her father and her Aunt Sylvia had been murdered. Ned's sledding accident became no accident at all in her mind, but the attempt of enemies to hurt her. Within two years of her husband's death she was saying that he, too, had been murdered. She began carrying a revolver ("To protect myself from the lawyers," she said with her typical sense of humor. "I'm not afraid of other kinds of burglars"). But Hetty may not have been quite as hardhearted as popularly believed. Although they lived apart most of the time, she returned to personally nurse her husband during a period of illness in 1894. Here and there she would perform a small kindness, such as finding a job for an old man who had been fired by her bank. She was said to like children and she kept a Skye terrier, called Cupid (or Cutey) Dewey, that she pampered and taught tricks. (To disguise her identity, she sometimes called herself "C. Dewey.") She lent money to the city of New York at lower interest than the banks (although this gave her useful influence at city hall).

In 1902, Hetty's husband died, fortune-less, in the Green family home in Bellows Falls. For the rest of her life Hetty would wear mourning clothes and her wraith-like appearance contributed to her image as the Witch of Wall Street.

Daughter Sylvia Green had cared for her father in his last years. In 1909, at age thirty-eight, she married fifty-seven-year-old Matthew Astor Wilks, a member of the famous Astor family. Hetty was not enthusiastic about the match but she agreed to it and even paid for a lavish trousseau for her daughter.

In 1910 Ned returned from Texas and went to work helping his mother, who tried to stay active but was slowing down. He proved an able manager, even planting two nurses in his mother's household in the guise of seam-stresses. (Hetty never would have agreed to spend the money needed for nurses.) She suffered strokes in April 1916, during a spat with a cook, and again in June, and died, age eighty-two, on July 3, 1916. Her body was trans-ported to Bellows Falls by chartered Pullman car (an extravagance she would have abhorred), where she was buried in the Green family plot beside her husband and (it is believed) the leg of her son. Her will made small gifts of cash to three acquaintances and her son-in-law, Wilks; the rest of the estate was divided equally between her son and daughter. There were no bequests to charity or the arts. She left behind no great collections, no businesses or industries—only money and real estate.

At her death, Hetty's estate probably was worth around a hundred million dollars and included seven to eight thousand parcels of real estate throughout the nation. She had started with a million dollars and in half a century was able to multiply it a hundred times, a remarkable achievement, especially for a woman in a man's society and a woman who was, at the very least, emotionally disturbed. She died America's richest woman, but there is no way of measuring the poverty in her soul. From her grave in the burial ground of Immanuel Episcopal Church in Bellows Falls you can see the scorched rock they call Fall Mountain.

Mind Your Head

Science tells us that the average brain fires its synapses several million times every hour. David Fairbanks Ford's brain probably fires its neural popguns at least four or five times as often, producing intracranial light shows to rival the aurora borealis or, at the very least, a Chinese salute to the Year of the Goat. Not to put too fine a point on it, Mr. Ford's brain is, well, different.

Ford is founder, president, curator, conservator, interpreter, fundraiser, business manager, publicist, maker of display cases, and floor sweeper for the Main Street Museum of Art, a cabinet of curiosities that could have been designed by P.T. Barnum if only he had been *really* creative. At last sighting, the MSM (as the cognoscenti call it) was more or less in Hartford, Vermont, but when and where fortune will take it next, God only knows, although Ford is hoping for another storefront in White River Junction. You won't find the MSM in the usual guidebooks, but in Vermont, at least, it has developed a certain reputation and even attracted some funding from the Vermont Council on the Arts and a few other daring sources. Ford happily admits that the MSM has been called "Vermont's Strangest Museum" and that he himself is often referred to as "quirky." However, he prefers to call the MSM "Vermont's most amiable museum."

Most of the MSM's collection is housed in an ancient back-road warehouse which also shelters Ford and three artist friends in genteel shabbiness. Some MSM items are on exhibit a mile away in a White River Junction café's corridor (which Ford has dubbed the Hall of Industrial Activities) and more can be seen on the World Wide Web at a handsome site that also features a virtual restroom. The warehouse collection is best of all, of course, but the warehouse is unmarked and can take some effort to find. For those who persist by making an appointment and getting directions, these are some of the rewards:

- Elvis Presley's gallstones (allegedly), floating in bleach in a glass canning jar and resembling fuzzy white squid.
- Pickled eggs in tar, a demonstration of preservation techniques that can result in sulfurous fumes.
- A small bottle that contained salve used to treat the horrific injuries of Phineas Gage (*q.v.*).
- A glass canning jar filled with shredded paper ("A translation of concept to physicality").
- The Virgisaurus: a Madonna figure with a dinosaur head. (If you find this more shocking than thought-provoking, it's probably time to leave. However, you'll miss the Miraculous Picture of the Virgin Mary, miraculous "because it survived the Flood of 1927.")
- Mink in a jar. Go figure.
- Twin bottles of almost identical blue fluid: one, wildberry drink; the other, windshield washer fluid. This may be a commentary on the chemical concoctions of the American food industry. Or something.
- Slides of brains from a mental hospital and a piece of brain coral, apparently an illustration of comparative morphology.
- A softball from a Dallas thrift shop, a substitute for the cannonball which the MSM collection lacks.
- Dried plants (and weeds) collected on a local woman's world tour in 1886; Napoleon's tomb, Shakespeare's house, and Henry VIII's Hampton Court are among sites represented.
- The Connecticut River Sea-Monster, a collection of bones fished from the river just below White River Junction's wastewater treatment plant and assembled with wax and fishing line into an eight-foot, five-inch specimen. (Biologists from Dartmouth College have studied this. I asked Ford what their professional opinion had been. With a face as innocent as a nun in a wimple, he told me, "They said they had never seen anything like it.")

There are more than two thousand other items, but you get the idea. Some, such as old phonograph records, were collected by Ford as a child. Some were inherited from Ford's grandmother. Some were contributed by the kind of artist friends who like to find meanings in strange objects. Others could only have come from a garage sale at Dr. Frankenstein's workshop.

Founded by Ford in 1992, the MSM has led a footloose and threadbare existence, but nonetheless has all the features of its better-known brethren: a board, a membership organization (you can join at the "Carbohydrate Level" for $4.95), volunteers, an insufficient budget, a newsletter ("The Electric Organ"), a "gift shoppe" with items at outrageous prices, and various contributions from various experts. The Sea-Monster, for example, was assembled for the MSM by a "crypto-zoologist," someone who may have emerged from the same gene pool as the oft-remarked-upon but never seen Prof. Josiah Carberry, professor of psychoceramics at Brown University.

The MSM also has special events, very special events, in fact, that have ranged from a photography show, "Big Fish & Good Looking Women" (featuring a live performance by transvestite comedian Cherie Tartt), to a minimalist cellist who played pieces that had only one or two notes. Bluegrass bands have provided entertainment on occasion and so have Elvis impersonators. All of this might lead you to think that Ford is just goofing off, but I think it goes deeper than that. Ford may be doing something important here.

All objects have meaning and many have stories, he says, but the meanings are only what we give them. It is my guess that Ford is a student of Symbolic Interaction Theory

David Fairbanks Ford and "Elvis Presley's gallstones"

from the perspective of the Chicago School of Sociology. SIT grew out of the pragmatism of philosophers William James and John Dewey, was elaborated in the "Mind, Self and Society" lectures of George Herbert Mead, and more recently has influenced and been influenced by European post-structuralism and post-modernism. It argues that meaning isn't inherent in an object but, rather, derives from our experience with it and especially our interaction with each other (i.e., a chair isn't a really a chair until we agree to ascribe qualities of "chairness" to it). While Kuhn and others at the University of Iowa insisted that concepts of symbolic interaction could be studied quantitatively, Mead and Herbert Blumler of the University of Chicago held that only case studies and histories offered such an avenue. Which may be why Ford is creating a museum of "objects with stories." He's creating a demonstration of epistemology, qualitatively derived.

On the other hand, he may just be pulling our chain.

My guess is that he's probably doing both and having a lot of fun. An MSM tour conducted by Ford proceeds with solemn explanations interrupted periodically by happy cackles. Ford, a genial man who was born in 1961 and is distantly related to the Fairbanks scale and museum people in St. Johnsbury, has as much suave as any high priest of the Met, the MFA, the Izzy, the Goog, or the Cork, including a mellifluous voice that could sell rocks to Vermont farmers. His career path has been rather squiggly, however: an art and art history major at Connecticut College, mural restoration work in New York City, five years driving a taxi in Boston. He makes no woulda-coulda-shoulda noises about all this, but instead seems to be having the time of his life being a "curator" (it pays better than being an artist, he says) and making ends meet by doing carpentry, painting restoration, and other work as it comes to hand. He came to northern New England, land of his ancestors, when he grew tired of the elitism of the urban art scene. "I like it here," he says. "Vermont is very welcoming to eccentrics."

Yes, indeed. And that's how the usual toughs might dismiss him if they can't understand what's going on here. Ford has even suffered indignities at the hands of fellow professionals. Recently he received a postcard—a mere postcard!—from the Metropolitan Museum of Art asking that it be taken off the MSM's mailing list. What the hoity-toities don't appreciate is that the MSM is trying to make you *think*. Which is why Ford would like you to lend him your head. Having collected your head, however, Ford will return it to you with its wiring slightly re-arranged. You may leave his museum highly amused. Or perhaps you will have re-thought your view of some of the things in your life: how, for example, the humblest of objects can be wrapped in stories and carry great meaning. ("I'd rather exhibit a brick than a Faberge egg," says Ford. "The brick comes with the human stories of everyone who's handled it, while the egg may not.") Or perhaps some memories will have been stirred. (The MSM's acquisition methods may seem more like dumpster diving than anything else, but they are akin to the heterodoxy of the typical little country museum of long ago, which could house everything from Aunt Fanny's paintings to a two-headed calf, all of it garlanded with memories. The MSM is very, very Old Vermont.) Or perhaps you will see things in a new way, whether from the underside or the other side. In any case, says Ford, you will have thought about the meaning of things a little differently, and then thought about what you thought.

"We provide a museum that people can get involved in directly, and it points out that objects in our everyday lives can have value," he explains. Providing open access to artists, artifact hunters, and the public is also important to Ford, who is committed to democratizing gallery space while satirizing stuffy art and museum elites. "The MSM proceeds as an *experiment* in curation," says Ford. "If we didn't do it, who would?"

Who would, indeed? So look for the Main Street Museum, wherever it is. Try a little chairness. But mind your head.

Fort Number 4 has been recreated as a living history museum in Charlestown, New Hampshire, and is open May through October each year (www.fortat4.com; 888-369-8284). Daniel Webster's home in Marshfield, Massachusetts, burned long ago, but the Daniel Webster Birthplace State Historic Site is open to the public in what is now Franklin, New Hampshire (www.nhparks.state.nh.us/parkops/parks/dwebster.html; 603-934-5057). You can pay a visit to Phineas Gage in the Warren Anatomical Museum at Harvard's Countway Library of Medicine, 10 Shattuck Street, Boston. For directions, see http://countweb.med.Harvard.edu/rarebooks/warren_museum/warren.html; 617-432-6196. The Green homestead in Bellows Falls, Vermont, was demolished long ago and, fittingly, a bank occupies part of the site. The rest is Green Park, at the corner of Church and School streets. Hetty is buried in the Immanuel Church graveyard, immediately behind the Bellows Falls Middle School on School Street. The grave is marked by a tall obelisk. The Bellows Falls Historical Society exhibits some artifacts from Hetty's household in its rooms at the Rockingham Free Library, open for limited hours only during the summer (802-463-4270). In New Bedford, Edie Nichols portrays Hetty for audiences and also maintains a small museum (52 Union St.; 888-55H-ETTY) as well as two web sites: www.hettygreen.org and www.hettygreen.com. The Main Street Museum in Hartford, Vermont, can be viewed virtually at www.mainstreetmuseum.org and telephoned at 802-295-7105.

CHAPTER THIRTEEN

WHERE THE RIVER BEGINS

The sky seems bigger in the valley's far north. The closer you get to the headwaters of the Connecticut, the smaller and farther apart the towns are. The roads are emptier, the landscape lonelier, the forest more in control. You can tell that life is different here by stopping for coffee and pie at any roadside diner. "Down below" these parts (as they say around here), diner talk is all about political shenanigans (there are ALWAYS political shenanigans Down Below), and the Sox, the Celtics, the Pats. Up here, the topics chewed along with the meatloaf special are timber and hunting and high school basketball.

Folks like to call the northern New Hampshire side of the river the Great North Woods. Properly speaking, this is New Hampshire's Coos (pronounced COH-os) County, an area of eighteen hundred square miles, the largest and northernmost of the state's ten counties. All by itself, Coos is bigger than the state of Rhode Island, but scarcely thirty-three thousand people live here. Large parts of Coos County are inhabited by little except moose, bears, coyotes, bobcats, and foxes, and maybe a cougar or two. It is here, in the very northern part of the county, that the 410-mile Connecticut River originates in the Fourth Connecticut Lake. Fourth Lake is really only an isolated pond, scarcely a stone's throw from the Canadian

The barrel-vaulted main hall of the Fairbanks Museum

border. From it a small stream heads south. It is hardly worthy of being called a river, but it is the Connecticut, nonetheless, building strength as it connects Fourth, Third, Second, and First lakes and, finally, Lake Francis. Then the Connecticut flows over a dam at the west end of Lake Francis and heads for Vermont, a real river now with real work to do. For the next two hundred miles or so it will form the visible boundary between New Hampshire and Vermont. It will rush over dams that supply much of the region's power and serve as the reason for being for three covered bridges as well as a host of less romantic ones.

On the west side of the Connecticut River, across from New Hampshire's Coos County, is the "Northeast Kingdom" of Vermont. The region was given its admiring nickname a long time ago by then senator George Aiken. It is still pristine. Composed of Caledonia, Essex, and Orleans counties, this land of lakes, mountains, and forest, hill farmers and loggers, covers more than a fifth of the state but has only a tenth of its people. The regally named Northeast Kingdom holds down Vermont's upper right corner and forms part of our border with Canada.

St. Johnsbury, unofficial capital of the Northeast Kingdom, is the last large settlement you'll see on the Vermont side if you're heading north. It's also the last place you think would be beguiling, for it is an old industrial town, very unlike the stereotypical Vermont place. It's crisscrossed by railroad tracks and small rivers and has its share of the shabby. But "Saint Jay" (population seventy-six hundred) is surprising. It has the piquant charm of the Victorian era, with lots of gingerbread, old red brick and sandstone, huge Queen Anne houses with porches and towers, and a downtown as unpretentious and comfortable as an old shoe. It seems to be stuck in time, for, as one resident put it, "It has that when-you-were-a-kid feeling." It does, indeed. Saint Jay is the kind of place that's retro without even knowing it. Walk down the street and you may hear, drifting from a window, the Bronxial keening of the *über* Ronette, Ronnie Bennett: *Pity me, I used to have it oll. . . .* A voice from the Sixties.

St. Johnsbury is largely the product of the Fairbanks family, who invented the platform scale. There is still a scale factory here (and a big maple syrup and candy plant, allowing locals to boast that their town is "the Maple Center of the World"). Thanks to the family's largess, St. Johnsbury also has the St. Johnsbury Athenaeum and the Fairbanks Museum & Planetarium, two institutions that are better than time machines for experiencing a bygone era. (Thousands of northern New Englanders know the Fairbanks Museum for its friendly, authoritative "Eye on the Sky" weather reports delivered over public radio stations.)

The museum was built of red sandstone in 1889 and contains a main gallery with an enormous barrel-vaulted ceiling of golden oak. The Fairbanks has an eye-popping collection of collections displayed in glass cases the old-fashioned way: thousands upon thousands of stuffed birds and animals, as well as toys, dolls, Civil War memorabilia, art, and the *pièce de résistance*, bug art, which is just what it sounds like: thousands of insects, mostly common flies and moths, arranged in "impressive scenes," such as George Washington, Abraham Lincoln, and the United States flag. Where else can you see anything like this?

A few doors away, on the opposite side of the street, is the Athenaeum, an almost perfectly preserved Victorian library and art gallery built in 1871. It is one of only a handful of libraries in the United States designated a National Historic Landmark. Its art gallery has been called the nation's "oldest unaltered art gallery still standing," and looks it. Marble busts in Victorian dress keep an eye on you as you crane your neck at the walls crowded with art, nineteenth-century style. Dominating the room is one of the nation's biggest paintings, Albert Bierstadt's *Domes of the Yosemite.*

But if you plan to go further north, start with the Fairbanks Museum. Bypass its enormous stuffed bears, who look ready to chew a piece out of you, and contemplate the Guardian of the Great North Woods in residence there, a bull moose in a large glass case. Meeting him is a very good way to begin your visit to the source of the Connecticut. You're in moose country now.

Big Al

Big Al is pretty much top dog in the Great North Woods. He goes where he wants and people get out of his way, especially when he has lovemaking on his mind. Homely as mud, big as a car, and tough as an old boot, he kills someone almost every year. And he is extremely horny.

Big Al—*Alces alces americanus*, the North American moose—is king of the hill in the Great North Woods. He is also the North Country's mascot, emblem, and drawing card, monitored and protected by state officialdom and never far from the public mind. He appears on T shirts, coffee mugs, stationery, and everywhere you drive there are yellow, diamond-shaped Moose Crossing signs. Those signs have spread as far south as Massachusetts, but especially in northern New Hampshire you'll see additional, larger ones: BRAKE FOR MOOSE, they warn. IT COULD SAVE YOUR LIFE. And the signs carry an ominous footnote: HUNDREDS OF COLLISIONS.

It's just another ecological reminder that moose and men have coexisted and interacted, for better or worse, for thousands of years. Like the eagle and the turkey and the bison, quintessentially American animals all, the moose seems one of us. So, although the moose is not, strictly speaking, an "unforgettable person," it nonetheless has an unforgettable *persona*. And that's not just because a cartoon moose named Bullwinkle can talk our language, making friendly noises that sound like English piped through a Boy Scout bugle.

North Country drivers should beware of the moose

Moose were advance scouts for humans in settling North America, getting here not long, relatively speaking, before people first crossed the Bering Strait ice or land bridge from Siberia to Alaska. As a source of food and hides, the moose helped the earliest tribes survive in a land still largely covered by glacial ice. As the ice receded, both moose and humans spread over the continent, and over the centuries moose continued to be an important resource for the Indians.

After Europeans arrived, however, deforestation and over-hunting shrank the North American moose population, which may have numbered more than a million at one time. By 1954, there were only twenty-five or thirty moose in all of New Hampshire. Now there are about six thousand in the Granite State (and once again a million on the continent), thanks to some lucky environmental breaks for the moose and some smart management.

It helps to have friends in high places, and the moose have them in New Hampshire. In 1985 the state legislature passed a law giving the state's Fish and Game Department the authority to manage the moose herd and teach people about life with *Alces alces* as a neighbor. You might make the sexist mistake of thinking that a man would be managing all those bull moose and their cows. Wrong. Since its beginning, the New Hampshire Moose Project has been led by Kristine Bontaites. A native of the state, Bontaites is a wildlife biologist with an infectious laugh, a fine singing voice, a fondness for hunting game birds, and a commitment to biodiversity and wildlife that is as solid as New Hampshire granite.

"It took me six years to land a job with Fish and Game in 1983," Bontaites recalls. At first "they told me they didn't hire women." Basically, her job now is to find ways for moose and people to live together. Using methods both high tech and low, the Moose Project team counts moose noses, surveys the public to gauge tolerance for moose, and then calibrates the number of hunting licenses issued for the annual season in late October. About twenty thousand applications are received for the lottery in which about five hundred licenses are granted. Bontaites, who loves moose meat (it's said to be "light," less gamey than deer meat, and lower in cholesterol than other meats), has been entering the lottery herself for more than a decade and half, and has never won a license.

Craggy, stubborn, and sturdy, *Alces alces* is a perfect poster animal for wildlife, born free and seemingly indomitable. Moose can be found in all ten counties in New Hampshire, but the largest number live up north. Moose trot down main streets and pop up in backyards in North Country towns. One bull stumbled into a children's swing set in Colebrook and carried it away on his horns. In early mornings and evenings, May through October, you can almost be sure to see gatherings of moose seeking road salt in

"Moose Alley" along U.S. 3 north of Pittsburg, New Hampshire. All by themselves, moose bring busloads and cars full of hopeful moose-peepers and
their cameras to the North Country, helping make tourism one of that
region's two biggest industries (timber is the other). A local newsman teases
visitors by telling them the moose are trained by Eastman Kodak.

What the gawkers have come to see is an animal that is lovable for its
homeliness and awesome for its size. The biggest member of the deer family, moose are second only to bison as the largest land animals in North
America. In New Hampshire, bull moose weigh nine to twelve hundred
pounds; cows, six to nine hundred. Both males and females stand about six
feet high at the shoulder and a bull with a full set of antlers seems to scrape
the sky. Those antlers can spread more than five feet across and have as
many as twenty-two points. Though weak-eyed, the moose has an extraordinary sense of smell and excellent hearing. And you can't outrun a moose:
an adult can attain a speed of forty miles per hour.

If a camel is a horse that was designed by a committee, the moose is
something that only a mad Soviet geneticist could have concocted: it looks
like a giraffe with a hat rack on top and a gigantic schnozzle up front. But
almost everything about the moose makes sense. Its big nose, for example,
is a complex device far more sensitive than ours and capable of letting the
moose graze, nose under the surface, in shallow water. Moose are good
swimmers, too, sometimes even diving for plant food growing on the bottom of ponds. Moose teeth are designed for feeding on twigs and leaves,
the animal's common name coming from an Indian word meaning bark or
twig eater. The moose's extraordinarily long legs (the front pair is longer
than the back) let it move quickly through deep snow. The huge, palmate
antlers, grown only by bulls, are used in struggles for dominance with other
bulls. About the only useless part of the moose is its ridiculously small tail,
which is only two to five inches long and has no known function. More
proof that Mother Nature has a sense of humor.

Those highway warning signs, which titillate first-time visitors, are no
joke. Every year in New Hampshire more than two hundred moose are
killed instantly in collisions with vehicles and probably as many more
wander off and die later from their injuries. Far fewer humans die in such
encounters, which approach five hundred a year, but in the seventeen years
Kristine Bontaites has been monitoring moose, there have been a dozen
human fatalities, many more injuries, and thousands of damaged vehicles.
With their dark coats, moose can be hard to see at night on an asphalt

highway. Unlike deer, they are not programmed to run when something approaches; they stand their ground. And, with their greater height and weight, they cause far more damage than deer: a vehicle striking a moose's long legs can cause a half-ton or more of animal to come crashing down from above.

Even law enforcement can't avoid close encounters of the moose kind. In July 2001, within a ten-day period, two New Hampshire State Police cruisers hit moose, with fatal consequences to the moose, severe damage to the cruisers, and minor injuries to one trooper. Earlier the same month, a Colebrook ambulance was hit and slightly damaged by a moose near Dixville Notch. The ambulance was able to continue on its way with no injuries to the occupants, the patient being transported giggling about the encounter.

The animal might make you giggle, but do NOT try to give a moose a muffin. It may look like a big, friendly galoot, kinda cute in its own homely way and appealingly ready to stand still and stare back at you. However, New Hampshire Fish and Game people warn that moose are "unafraid, not friendly." In "rutting" (mating) season, bulls are highly unpredictable and cows always are extremely protective of their young. Using sharp hooves, a moose may attack the careless observer with little or no warning. In one notorious case in Alaska a moose knocked down a man with its front legs, then stomped him to death with its rear feet.

In recent years, New Hampshire's only known moose attack with physical contact occurred when a state legislator was knocked to the ground, but otherwise unhurt, by a moose with whom she was trying to pose for a picture. Perhaps the legislator thought the moose owed her one because of the Moose Project. The point of the picture was supposed to be how friendly moose are, but the woman said afterwards, "Boy, that really opened my eyes." Because more and more people are coming to view New Hampshire's moose and because some of them are not cautious, Kristine Bontaites fears it is only a matter of time until someone gets hurt. "People do not use common sense at all," she said. "They treat these animals with less respect than you'd show your average Shetland pony." A Colebrook native says, "We go up to Moose Alley now, not to watch the moose, but to watch the idiots."

Even Kristine Bontaites had a close call. A bull that had been tranquilized for collaring with a radio transmitter unexpectedly came awake and charged her. "I'm running hell-bent for election and he's gaining on me with every step he takes," she recalls. Then a colleague yanked her to safety behind a tall stump and the moose roared by like an express train. She and her Fish and Game team left the woods shaken but unhurt.

Taking a leaf from Texas and adding their own spin, some Vermonters have bumper stickers that say, "Don't Mess With Vermont." New Hampshire people love their moose, but they also respect them, and suggest that you do, too. Right beside the Granite State's license plates proclaiming "Live Free or Die," there ought to be bumper stickers with this message: "Don't Mess With Our Moose"—for their sake and yours.

It's What We Do

On a clear, sunny Tuesday afternoon in August 1997, New Hampshire state trooper Scott Phillips was in his cruiser on U.S. 3 near the state's northern tip when he noticed a badly rusted pickup truck. Phillips turned on his blue lights and followed the truck into the parking lot of LaPerle's IGA store, just north of Colebrook. Phillips knew the driver, sixty-seven-year-old Carl C. Drega, and knew Drega's reputation as a gun-toting loner notorious for his explosive rages.

An intimidatingly big man who wore tinted glasses, Drega was a millwright and lived near the Connecticut River in the tiny town of Columbia, just south of Colebrook. Rabidly anti-government, he was known for making threats and using firearms to chase people off his land. A UPS man who regularly delivered mysterious packages to him was the only person allowed on the property. Drega had had clashes with state, county, and town officials and had become so menacing that one of them, a lawyer and part-time judge named Vickie Bunnell, took to carrying a gun in her purse.

Trooper Phillips may have wanted to check out Drega while also citing him for the large rust holes in his truck bed. He didn't have a chance to do either. The older man leaped from his truck and began firing a semiautomatic assault rifle that had been equipped with a large magazine. The trooper fired back as his cruiser was riddled with bullets and its glass shattered. Wounded in the hand and unable to quickly reload, he ran for cover in some tall grass.

Then another trooper, Leslie Lord, forty-five, drove up, unaware of what has happening. Drega shot Lord in his cruiser at a distance and again, closer up, killing him. With Lord dead, the killer returned to Phillips, pursuing him up an embankment and executing him with four pistol shots. The young trooper died less than two miles from his home in Colebrook, where he had been a familiar sight as he jogged while pushing his son's stroller.

Next, Drega took Phillips's cruiser and drove a mile and a half into Colebrook, parking near the low, one-story building on Bridge Street that housed both the town's weekly paper, the *News and Sentinel*, and Vickie Bunnell's law office. Spotting the bullet-riddled cruiser and its driver from her window, Bunnell ran through the building, shouting, "It's Carl! He's got a gun! Get out!" The time that took her to warn others probably cost the forty-five-year-old woman her life, for Drega was able to circle around the building and shoot her five times in the back as she fled across a parking lot. She fell dead on the asphalt. Then the *Sentinel*'s fifty-one-year-old co-editor, Dennis Joos, tackled Drega and pushed him against a car. Drega shook off the smaller man, snarling, "Mind your own (expletive) business!" and fatally wounded him with eight shots.

Drega got back in the stolen cruiser and headed south, first pausing outside Colebrook's police station. When no one appeared—all the officers had gone to the shooting scene at the market—he drove on. In Columbia, just south of Colebrook, he kicked in the door of a former Columbia selectman with whom he had clashed, but he left when he found no one home. Back in his own home, Drega changed his clothes and shaved his beard, set his house on fire, and crossed the Connecticut River, firing a shot that wounded a game warden he passed on the highway in Vermont. He parked the stolen cruiser on a logging road, turned up its radio so it could be heard from a distance, and, wearing Trooper Phillips's Stetson hat and a bulletproof vest, set up an ambush position on a wooded hillside about fifteen miles south of Colebrook.

By now, Vermont and New Hampshire state police, sheriff deputies, and border patrol officers were in pursuit, with other police coming from as far away as Massachusetts. When a police dog alerted officers to Drega's hiding place, the fugitive began shooting. Three officers were wounded during a long firefight before Drega himself was killed, shot through the mouth. His rampage, which had begun around 2:30 p.m., ended shortly before 7 that evening. Later, authorities would discover that Drega had created a bomb factory on his Columbia premises and built a huge stockpile of materials for it.

Two or three hours before the shootings, John Harrigan, publisher of the *Sentinel*, had left for business in Lancaster, about thirty-six miles south. When he heard the news over a police radio scanner, he raced back to Colebrook, arriving to find that most of his terrified staff had scattered after hiding in closets and beneath automobiles. Harrigan had known both of the dead troopers and had worked daily with Joos, but he had an even stronger relationship with Bunnell. She had been his girlfriend for seven years and although they no longer dated, they were still good friends. Bunnell, someone said, "was the girl everyone wanted to marry," although she had never wed.

While Bunnell's body lay for most of the evening in the *Sentinel* parking lot—police said the crime scene had to be preserved—Harrigan spent the evening racing up and down Bridge Street, commiserating with Vickie's parents at her brother's home nearby, and rounding up his newspaper crew. "I told them, 'Look, we have to put this paper out,'" Harrigan recalls. "I'm looking at people who are hysterical, some of them dirty and scratched from hiding under cars. "I said, 'I know this is hell, but this is where we are in history. When firemen go to a fire and find it's their own house, they do their job. Doctors who have to treat their own children at accidents do the same thing. Ambulance crews do, too. Now, it's our turn.'"

Police and outside media were swarming over the *Sentinel* building, but by 8 p.m. Harrigan was able to sequester himself for thirty minutes and write a long news story about the day's events. He visited the Bunnells again and returned to his office to write two editorials, one expressing sorrow at the tragedy the community had suffered, the other saying, "We'll do a better job with the loss and what this has all meant in next week's paper. Right now, it's just too much, and getting the paper out is all we can manage."

Harrigan needn't have apologized. The crown jewel of journalism awards is the Pulitzer Prize and for his work that night he not only was nominated for it, but also achieved the distinction of being first finalist—i.e., second place—in the "breaking news" category in 1998. The wonder of it was not that the Harrigan and the *Sentinel* had come so close to winning, but that the winner, the million-circulation *Los Angeles Times*, with its hundreds of staffers and deep pockets, had come so close to being overshadowed by a tiny North Country weekly that had a circulation of forty-seven hundred (in 1997) and only four news personnel performing under great duress.

On the morning of August 20, the day after the shootings, the black-bannered *Sentinel* was circulating throughout the North Country, right on schedule. A visiting journalist wonderingly asked Harrigan how the paper could have been produced under the circumstances. "We're a newspaper. It's what we do," he replied.

Journalists for larger papers sometimes scorn the so-called "community journalism" practiced by small-town dailies and weeklies, but Harrigan, a genial, fast-talking guy who seems to know everybody in the North Country, turns out to be just as serious a journalist as his big-city cousins. "We cover the news like a blanket," Harrigan says, asking, "If we didn't do it, who would? We're the clearing-house for the rumors. When anything happens, you're apt to get six different stories in five minutes, so we're charged with separating fact from fiction. And getting it right and getting it out and getting it straight." Which is why he insisted on publishing a paper in the face of the devastation that had been visited on the *Sentinel* that day. The best journalists are not in the business for fame or fortune or "to sell more newspapers." Instead, they believe a democracy is best served by good information. *Give light and the people will find their way,* goes an old newspaper motto.

The NEWS and SENTINEL

INDEPENDENT BUT NOT NEUTRAL

| Vol. CXXVI | No. 34 | 1 Bridge Street, Colebrook, N.H. — Wednesday, August 20, 1997 | Established 1870 | Sixty Cents |

Four Gunned Down In Colebrook; Editor, Lawyer, Two Officers Dead

Despite the carnage affecting it, the newspaper appeared on time

"Independent but not neutral" is the *Sentinel*'s own slogan, appearing every week at the top of page one. The editorial page lives up to the motto, dishing out opinions salted by attaboys or raps on the knuckles regarding North Country matters large and small. Hard news ("Colebrook Family Loses All in Saturday Night Fire"), police blotters and court reports, sports, obits, recipes, seniors meals, anniversaries, and, yes, "locals" ("Win Dalley is looking for a hole in the ice to drop his line . . .") fill the rest of the paper. The *Sentinel* has a territory of nearly three hundred thousand acres to cover, ninety-seven percent of it forested. "We have more moose, bear, and coyotes than people," according to its publisher, a man who is always ready with a quip. A *Sentinel* promotion boasts, "In a tribal place like the North Country, nothing beats the tom-tom . . . except the local paper . . . covering moose, Mud Season, black flies, bears at the dump, eight months of winter and everything else we love about this place." The *Sentinel*'s paid circulation of fifty-one hundred in 2002 included not only readers in New Hampshire's North Country, but also many in nearby Vermont, as well as some in western Maine and even in southern Quebec. "We're one of the nation's few international newspapers," says Harrigan with a grin. "It gives us delusions of grandeur."

Less than ten miles from the Canadian border, Colebrook is part of New Hampshire's True North, more like Alaska than New England. Winter temperatures of forty below zero are not uncommon and snow occasionally falls in May. ("It keeps the riff-raff out," Harrigan says.) A town of twenty-seven hundred, Colebrook has no traffic lights. This isn't like the rest of "Asphalt America," where all the stores belong to the same few monster chains. Instead, Colebrook businesses are locally owned, many by the third or fourth generation of a family. (Harrigan's daughter Karen is managing editor of the *Sentinel,* making her the third generation of Harrigans at the paper.) The nearest McDonald's is thirty-six miles south, the nearest movie theater fifty-four miles away.

Publisher John Harrigan prepares another issue

"After the shootings I had several meetings with myself," Harrigan recalls. "One of the things I came away with was that I was never again going to do anything I didn't want to do. Because time is short. You never know. My number should have been up that day. My office is the furthest from the back door, so I would have been right behind Dennis. I would have been on the ground, without a shadow of a doubt."

Harrigan gives more time to other things now. He had been married once before, but has re-married, acquiring three stepchildren. The publisher and his new, young family live on a farm on Colebrook's South Hill, where they burn wood for heat, harvest apples from almost three hundred trees, tap twenty-five or fifty maple trees each year, and care for a "menagerie" that includes an average of twenty chickens and ninety sheep. Harrigan calls the sheep operation the "largest north of the Notches," the Notches being those gaps in the White Mountains which separate the North Country from the rest of the state. The Harrigan family also has two or three malamutes for dogsledding, two Maremma sheepdogs and a llama to guard the flock, and a fleet of support vehicles, ranging from a 1973 Mercedes to a 2000 Ford diesel pickup, as well as two snowmobiles and three canoes. Harrigan, a man who is built for the woods, says his family eats wild game "whenever we can." They keep twenty guns in the house for hunting as well as for an occasional skeet shoot off a rooftop deck.

In the years since that bloody Tuesday in 1997, Colebrook people have tried to forget the horror of the day without forgetting the victims. A monument with the images of Phillips, Lord, Bunnell, and Joos stands near the *Sentinel* building, next to the parking lot and grass where two of the victims died. The lawyer's bronze plaque that carried Bunnell's name when she was alive remains on the front of the building. Dennis Joos's name is on the masthead of every issue of the *Sentinel*, with the dates he served as editor: *1990-1997*. A portion of U.S. 3 has been renamed in honor of Troopers Phillips and Lord.

And every day, when John Harrigan steps out on his front porch, he can see the 2,723-foot peak that used to known as Blue Mountain, but has been officially renamed Bunnell Mountain. Then, after tending to farm chores, he goes into town to help prepare another issue of the *Sentinel*. Each week for more than one hundred thirty years, the paper has circulated among the farmers, loggers, and shopkeepers of the North Country, reporting the region's endless cycle of birth, life, and death, triumph and tragedy. Nearly seven thousand issues have appeared so far, bringing news that is sometimes good and sometimes bad, but is always an effort to separate fact from rumor and enlighten the people.

We're a newspaper. It's what we do.

Getting Googly

Lourraine Clough will never hear a discouraging word from me. She is such a nice lady that I yearn to believe in her and her cause, though I was born a skeptic, raised on the scientific method, and employed for a while as a cynical observer (meaning I was a newspaper reporter).

I visited Mrs. Clough in her office in Danville in northern Vermont one day and came away impressed, if not converted. Danville is a rural town of about twenty-two hundred people, nicely outfitted with an old-fashioned bandstand and a covered bridge. Danville is in the Connecticut River Valley, near St. Johnsbury, but a few miles from the river itself. Even so, plenty of water can be found here.

That's because Danville is the headquarters of the American Society of Dowsers (ASD), the nation's premier organization of diviners, water witches, doodlebuggers, questers, and other seekers. It began in 1958 with a small, one-day meeting of dowsers that was part of a local foliage festival. So much interest was generated that the ASD was chartered in 1961. Today, Danville is to dowsing what Mecca is to Muslims, Graceland is to Presleyites, and the Starship Enterprise is to Trekkies. It is the center of the known universe. There, in a small white house, an efficient office has been equipped with computers, files, and clerks. Dowsing Central serves an international membership of forty-four hundred persons, arranges conventions for them, and manages (and also sells) an exploding body of literature.

Lourraine Clough is operations manager for this enterprise, which I visited one spring day on short notice, which seemed to bother her not at all. She is soft-spoken and so pleasant in a down-home way that you'd expect her to serve you a slice of apple pie if only she had one handy. She was glad to introduce me to the new, modern world of dowsing.

"Everybody has it," she said, meaning the ability to dowse. "Accepting it is the hard part. It's clearing your mind to ask one question. You have to leave behind all the other things—whether your checkbook is balanced or not, for example." A popular dowsing manual suggests, "Relax and use your intuition. Let the information flow through you. You should always dowse with a loving heart and for the best good for yourself and others." Mrs. Clough told me, "You can lose your ability if you use it for bad things."

The dictionary says to dowse is "to use a divining rod," which is "a forked rod believed to indicate the presence of water or minerals by dipping downward when held over a vein." As a country boy, I knew that dowsers had a mysterious gift for finding good places to dig wells, which is why they were sometimes called "water witches." The thoroughly modern ASD and Mrs. Clough take a much broader view. Not only does everyone have the potential to become a dowser, but also, the forked rod, though helpful, isn't even necessary. Besides, dowsing is about a lot more than finding water. Dowsers can look for minerals, missing persons, or buried treasure. They can attempt to forecast the weather and divine the future. They can help us contact our ancestors ("Of course," Mrs. Clough said with a twinkle, "they may not want to talk with you.") In fact, says ASD's brochure, dowsing is useful for all sorts of things because it "is the name given to *a quest for information.*"

Lourraine Clough explains the seven-path Cretan labyrinth

Which is exactly what the rest of us are doing when we go on the Internet and poke through that Everest of stuff called the World Wide Web. To point the way, we use specialized *browsers* (which the astute reader will note rhymes with *dowsers*). Right now, the most popular Web browser of all is one with the beguiling name of Google. Tell Google what you want and with jaw-dropping speed it will point you to rich veins of information.

It looks to me as if modern dowsers are people doing Googly things, but doing them without a computer. Like Internet browsers, dowsers are looking for useful information, whether it lies underground or elsewhere, but with one thought that Internet Googlers seldom have: by dowsing, dowsers believe they are tuning in to the energy of the universe. "Harmonize with all creation—dowse," was the slogan chosen for the 2002 annual convention of the ASD, a sentiment that reflects dowsing's urge to make connections to a larger reality. "Harmony" and "balance" are words that dowsers use a lot.

The society frankly admits science has yet to explain dowsing ("Much research remains to be done") and Mrs. Clough's first efforts to explain it were as daunting to me as an advanced course in nuclear physics. Mention was made of stone circles; star elementals; divas, angels, and fairies; tetra-hedrons; Egyptian symbols; shamans; radionics; the Kabbalah; labyrinths; crystals; feng shui (dowsers like to keep up to date); and chakras (which are "red, orange, yellow, green, blue, violet spinning things on your body").

But most of all, she talked about *energy*. Apparently, all things—even rocks—have "a readable energy that we can access." All people have the potential to sense the energy, although aptitudes differ. Some people have to study and practice to learn how to do it and do it well, which is why so many how-to books on dowsing are published. The ASD maintains a full-time bookstore in St. Johnsbury and issues a fat catalog. The 2002 ASD annual convention, which was scheduled for June at a nearby college campus, featured sixty to seventy speakers, nine schools (an example was "Map Dowsing," which permits dowsing at a distance), and seven work-shops (for instance, "Intermediate Level Integrated Energy Therapy" which promised that attendees could learn "to clear energy imprints resulting from past life Karma"). About a thousand persons were expected to attend the convention.

After a short demonstration of dowsing by using a small weight on a string to answer a few simple yes-or-no questions (it swung back and forth for Mrs. Clough but not for me), I was taken into the ASD's backyard, where a labyrinth had been built. It consisted of several concentric circles of rocks, each about the size of a five-pound bag of sugar, entirely surrounded by stumps. "It's a seven-path Cretan labyrinth," Mrs. Clough explained to me. "It does a lot of different things. It can be used for walking meditation. When you walk in one of these, it kind of balances the chakras. It's an align-ment machine."

Like cars or computers, labyrinths can be built to various levels of per-formance. "We redid the whole thing last year, to kind of crank it up," she said. "It was on beginner mode, so we've added a lot of heavier-duty stones. You can read the energy of a stone." Individual rocks, I was told, can be dowsed to determine their energy and their predilections. "Does this stone want to come to be in the labyrinth?" Mrs. Clough asked of a hypothetical river-dwelling rock. "It may not want to come – its energy may be needed to keep that river in balance." On the other hand, some rocks signal *yes*, "so then they get to come, so they can live here."

Dowsing has its detractors, of course, skeptics who unkindly argue that backyards are not the only places dowsers have rocks. These killjoys miss the point. In their own way, dowsers are trying to center themselves, screen out distractions, and get back to nature, something too many of us forget as we grind out our daily routines in building Asphalt America. While we are engaged in the pursuit of loneliness, dowsers are feeling a connectedness with the Cosmic All, a significance in not only being *in* this universe but also *undeniably of it,* eternally woven into the great fabric of being. As Lourraine Clough puts it, "It makes us more than a bug on the earth"— something that can be squashed or forgotten. Non-dowsers who wonkishly insist on hard data are like wallflowers sitting on the sidelines while the dowsers dance to the music of the spheres.

I don't believe in dowsing. But I believe in dowsers. They strike me as goodhearted people who are searching for the river that flows through us all. They want to feel a frisson of connection with the Great Mystery, that delicious shiver that comes from realizing how grandly eternal the universe is. It's the feeling that some of us get from a mountaintop view, or a starry night, or, most of all, witnessing the birth of new life.

I am reminded of nineteenth-century feminist and full-bore skeptic Margaret Fuller (who was not a dowser). On achieving some kind of philosophical breakthrough, she giddily wrote British historian and essayist Thomas Carlyle, "I accept the universe!" (At which Carlyle exclaimed, "By God! She'd better!") Dowsers accept the universe. And, by golly, we'd better.

Colebrook, New Hampshire, is bisected by an invisible line: the forty-fifth parallel, the half-way point between the Equator and the North Pole. It's great country for moose-watching, hunting, fishing, and, in winter, snowmobiling on its vast network of logging roads. The tourist claptrap that spoils some other places in New Hampshire is mostly absent here, too. To keep up on some of the news from the North Country, check John Harrigan's *News and Sentinel* web site: www.colbsent.com. (To get ALL the news, though, you're going to have to subscribe to his paper, because, he says, "We're cheap Yankees.") North Country guest accommodations range from motels with decor that take you back to the Fifties to The Balsams near Dixville Notch, a four-star resort in the "grand hotel" tradition. On the Vermont side, don't miss St. Johnsbury with its Fairbanks Museum & Planetarium, 1302 Main Street (802-748-2372 or www.fairbanksmuseum.org) and the St. Johnsbury Athenaeum, 1171 Main Street (802-748-8291; www.stjathenaeum.org). The headquarters of the American Society of Dowsers is on Brainard Street, just off U.S. 2, in nearby Danville (802-684-3417; www.dowsers.org).

The Great North Woods is rich in history, too. Pittsburg, New Hampshire's largest town in terms of area, occupies the extreme northern portion of Coos County. It was here that a group of independence-minded settlers set up the Indian Stream Republic, an effort to break away from the United States. That rough-and-tumble territory is brought to life in a novel by Jeffrey Lent, *Lost Nation*, while the definitive history is Daniel Doan's *Indian Stream Republic: Settling a New England Frontier, 1785-1842*. Another great story took place in the northern Connecticut River Valley late in 1759. "Rogers' Rangers" were the American Special Forces of the French and Indian War (and an ancestor of today's Army Rangers). They became famed for their daring raids on the enemy (and were vividly described in Kenneth Roberts's novel *Northwest Passage*, first published in 1936 and still in print). The Rangers' leader was Robert Rogers, a New Hampshireman and born soldier who, were he alive today, would love the smell of napalm. In September 1759, a "soldier of the king" named Lord Jeffery Amherst ordered Rogers and his Rangers to wipe out the Indian camp at St. Francis, Quebec. The Rangers did, looting the Roman Catholic chapel and, legend has it, bringing down a curse on themselves. Lugging their booty, small parties of Rangers made their escape eastward across Quebec and then south through Vermont, aiming for Fort Number Four in Charlestown, New Hampshire. Pursued by the enemy, plagued by famine and harsh, wintry weather, the exhausted Rangers struggled to reach Charlestown. Reduced to walking skeletons, some never did reach safety and crawled into caves to die. From time to time since then, various objects have been uncovered along their route: a pair of candlesticks, an incense vessel, and other things possibly taken from the chapel. However, a six-pound silver statue of Our Lady of Chartres has never been found and to this day the location of the "treasure of St. Francis" remains a mystery, but is thought to lie somewhere in the Northeast Kingdom or in the Connecticut River Valley. Sounds like a job for the dowsers.

No Degrees of Separation

Recently I rolled into my bank's drive-through to get some walking-around money and found that something had changed. The ATM apparently had been to charm school, for its screen greeted with me with a new kind of green-eyed enthusiasm, declaring after a certain amount of beeping and clicking, "We treat you like the unique individual you are!" I've always considered myself unique, so I liked that, but somehow it wasn't quite the same as the conversations we used to have with the tellers: *Sorry to hear your dog died. How are the grandkids? How about those Red Wings!* And, of course, the capper always was *Haveaniceday, Mr. Bissland!* a phrase that never grated on me the way it does some grumps. It is, after all, a little bouquet—trite as pansies, perhaps, or as déclassé as dandelions, but a bouquet nonetheless, a real person's stab at empathy in an increasingly robotized world.

I thought about that as I drove away, the ATM recycling itself in the background to flash *We treat you like the unique individual you are!* to each of the several hundred customers it would see that day. It was another example of how electronics are replacing human contact in our world: *Your call is important to us; please hold for the next available agent. . . . Press or say "One" for. . . . Scan the item and place it in the bag. . . . To serve you better, we are. . . .*

They always say it's "to serve you better," of course, and sometimes it really is. But it also signals yet another depersonalization of our daily discourse, another step in distancing *you* from *me*. It only adds to what Harvard professor Robert Putnam is talking about in his book *Bowling Alone*, in which he describes the decline of "civic engagement" in American life. Compared to a few years ago, we belong to fewer organizations, socialize less, know fewer of our neighbors. Fewer of us join bowling leagues, even though more of us bowl. We go bowling alone.

So it seems as if our degrees of separation are increasing, even as we contemplate a world that appears to be shrinking, a new age of instant contact by e-mail, fax, teleconferencing, 24/7 services, and your local television station's Eyewitness/Action/Instant News—*Our coiffures take you there!* And hovering over all of this, ironically, is social psychologist Stanley Milgram's "Small World Theory." You probably know it as "Six Degrees of Separation" or its parlor-game mutation, "Six Degrees of Kevin Bacon," the idea being that anyone on earth can be linked to anyone else by a chain of only six people, each connected to the next by personal acquaintance.

All of that is in the here and now, of course. What no one is looking at are *degrees of separation over time*. How far away are we from, say, Abraham Lincoln? Or George Washington? Or Napoleon or Cleopatra? Right away we assume we are X years or generations away from them and that those years form a tall stone barrier, with only a few cracks through which we can peek. "The past is another country," playwright Harold Pinter insisted.

I don't think so.

I would like a team of ambitious young academics to look into this. Instead of thinking of time as a wall and trying to figure out how to penetrate it, they should concentrate on all the connections that already exist between us and our ancestors, all the ways they shaped us, and all the things we carry with us, thanks to them. We may find that the huge disconnect we impose between ourselves and the past is unnecessary and that, in a certain sense, there are no impenetrable degrees of separation between the generations. I agree with William Faulkner, who said, "The past isn't dead. It isn't even past." (After a writing career spent exploring the mossy memories of Yoknapatawpha County, who would know better?)

With imagination, empathy, the help of artifacts, and the remembrance of all the things that connect us as human beings, not only through space but through time, we should be able to hear the murmur of distant voices on a summer night. As the stars wheel slowly in the night sky, the cicadas drone, and the odor of lilacs hangs in the air, we may even hear this: those voices are telling stories.

"Only connect!" E.M. Forster famously implored us. The Connecticut River Watershed Council, a citizen group dedicated to conserving and protecting the river, likes to say, "It's the river that connects us," starting with its very name: CONNECTicut. That's true, but I believe what connects us most of all to our past are the stories. A story rings true when it resonates deep inside you, making that shared experience a message from one person, the subject, to another, the listener. And even if the two parties are separated by hundreds or even thousands of years, there is still a communication there. A connection.

So gather those stories and keep telling them and you will begin to feel the existence of life in another time and place. Remember, the living and the dead need each other. Only connect!

Two rivers flow through the valley.

Remember us.

Confluence of Connecticut and Deerfield Rivers *by Orra White Hitchcock (1835)*

ACKNOWLEDGMENTS

New Englanders don't give strangers the hearty la-de-da they get in some other parts of the country. That's just good old Yankee horse sense. After all, the guy on the doorstep may be a serial killer or a politician, and there's no need to waste a howdy-do on the likes of them.

But that doesn't mean New Englanders can't be friendly and helpful, once you've established your bona fides. After they sized me up, folks in the Connecticut River Valley and elsewhere practically fell all over themselves to help me gather information for this book.

They left me with many happy memories. A lovely lunch *al fresco* with Polly Murray, who has done so much to fight Lyme disease. A police car ride-around in Holyoke with Chief Anthony Scott, while onlookers wondered if I was yet another perp collared by their hard-charging top cop. (To support The Chief, I did my best to look guilty.) An all-day truck tour of the Great North Woods, including a border crossing into Quebec, conducted by the genial press lord of Colebrook, New Hampshire, John Harrigan, a Pulitzer Prize–winner if there ever was one. Long hours of labor on my behalf by Rose and Bob Sokol, Thompsonville's angels to historians. The dedication to task by Peter Weis, the friendly, helpful guardian of Northfield Mount Hermon's institutional memory. And many others.

I wish I could say something about each and every one of my other sources, but they'll have to settle for the fact that I am thinking fondly of them, and can only list their names here: Martha Ackmann, Richard Archer, Betty Arnold, Bill Batty, Jim Bennett, Kristine Bontaites, Bowling Green State University Library, Brooks Memorial Library, David Bryan, Lorrie Byrom, Prof. Josiah Carberry, Jerry Carbone, Virginia Chamberlin ("Aunt Gin"), Lourraine Clough, Tina Cohen, Connecticut River Watershed Council, Lt. Marc Cournoyer, Cindy Dickinson, John H. Dryfhout, Robert Duncan, Suzanne Fitz, Suzanne L. Flynt, David Fairbanks Ford, the

Ghost of Thankful Arnold, Dorothy D. Gifford, Patricia L. Gimbel, Augusta Girard, Historical Society of Glastonbury, Kathleen L. Housley, Nora Howard, Marge Howe, Stephen and Gwen Huneck, Virginia Hunt, Stephen Jendrysik, Carrie Keser, Elizabeth H. Klekowski, Dennis Ladd, Carol Lebo, Melinda LeLacheur, Richard D. Little, Meg Lyons, Patty Mark, Joan Marr, Raymond L. Massucco, Esq., Archer Mayor, Jane M. McCarry, Frances Meigs, Memorial Hall Museum, Brenda Milkofsky, Tom Miner, Laura D. (Mimi) Morsman, Richard W. Mueller, Cynthia W. Nau, Edie Nichols, Richard Odman, Old Saybrook Historical Society, Brian and Judy Ramirez, Doris Ransford, Rockingham Free Public Library, Valerie Saint-Gaudens, Gregory C. Schwarz, Ethan Allen Hitchcock Sims, M.D., Elaine Staplins, Thomas St. John, Randy Stevens, Rev. Elizabeth Stookey, Jan Sweet, Vermont State Library, David K. and Pamela Tuttle, Craig Walley, Sue Ward, Kyp Wasiuk, Wethersfield Historical Society, and Lee Wicks (the cordial voice of DeeYay).

Who am I forgetting only at this moment, to be remembered just after the deadline passes? My apologies to you, whoever you are.

I cannot forget, even momentarily, the warm hospitality and helpfulness of Stuart Parnes, executive director, and Alison C. Guinness, curator, who skillfully pilot the Connecticut River Museum at Steamboat Dock, Essex, Connecticut.

And, of course, where would I be without the friendly professionals of Berkshire House—Jean J. Rousseau, Philip Rich, Carol Bosco Baumann, Sarah Novak, Jane McWhorter, and Leslie Ceanga—who seem to have a bottomless reservoir of patience with know-it-all authors. Speaking only for myself, of course.

Finally, the most important person of all, She Who Always Believes in Me—Joan. She is my fellow traveler along the valley's rivers, both of them, and when we are home, my babe in arms.

— Jim Bissland

PICTURE CREDITS AND PERMISSIONS

Front cover: Fruitlands Museums, Harvard, Massachusetts

Frontispiece: Maps.com

21, Old Saybrook (Connecticut) Historical Society

28, Bettmann/Corbis

35, Merriam-Webster, Incorporated, publishers of *Merriam-Webster's Collegiate Dictionary*

38, Historical Society of Glastonbury, Connecticut

42, Erik K. Johnson, Lyme, Connecticut

49, Connecticut River Museum, Essex, Connecticut

56, *Dictionary of American Portraits*, ed. Hayward and Blanche Cirker (New York: Dover, 1967)

60, Connecticut State Library, Hartford

73, The Mark Twain Memorial, Hartford

78, Huntington Library, San Marino, California

95, *Dictionary of American Portraits*

99, Corbis

109, Edward Bellamy Memorial Association, Chicopee, Massachusetts

141, The Dickinson Homestead, owned by Amherst College

148, Memorial Hall Museum, Old Deerfield, Massachusetts

152, Northfield Mount Hermon School, Northfield, Massachusetts

156, Northfield Mount Hermon School

161, Deerfield Academy, Deerfield, Massachusetts

175, Brooks Memorial Library, Brattleboro, Vermont

189, Ethan Allen Homestead, Burlington, Vermont

194, Brooks Memorial Library

200, Saint-Gaudens National Historic Site, Cornish, New Hampshire

201, (right) SGNHS

201, (left) Valerie Saint-Gaudens

208, Vermont State Library, Montpelier, Vermont

215, University of Vermont, Burlington

221, *Dictionary of American Portraits*

239, *Colebrook News and Sentinel*

274, Barbara Vogel

Pp. 4, 7, 13, 69, 87, 90, 104, 113, 132, 249: author's collection

Pp. 12, 16, 17, 53, 74, 117, 163, 170, 173, 179, 187, 225, 230, 232, 240, 243: by author

FOR FURTHER READING

Among the best travel guides ever published are the volumes in the American Guide Series. They were written state by state by the Federal Writers' Project as one of Franklin Delano Roosevelt's WPA projects to create work and fight the Great Depression of the 1930s. Produced before the age of interstate highways, SUVs, and fast-food chains, they not only evoke a sweet nostalgia, but also are so rich in historical detail that they qualify as armchair travel literature. Occasionally one is republished, but usually original copies of American Guide Series books can be found in libraries, used bookstores, or on Web book and auction sites. Each of the New England states has its own guide.

The Pioneer Valley Reader: Prose and Poetry from New England's Heartland, edited by James C. O'Connell (Stockbridge, Massachusetts: Berkshire House Publishers, 1995) is a cross section of three centuries of literary creativity in this fertile territory.

A handful of other books form my favorite reading about the Connecticut River region and its people: *Tidewaters of the Connecticut River: An Explorer's Guide to Hidden Coves and Marshes* by Thomas Maloney and others (Essex, Connecticut: River's End Press, 2001) concentrates on the natural features of the southern estuary. *Upstream: A Voyage on the Connecticut River* by Ben Bachman (Chester, Connecticut: Globe Pequot Press, 1988) relates one man's travels by canoe. *River Days: Exploring the Connecticut River from Source to Sea* by Michael Tougias (Boston: Appalachian Mountain Club, 2001), is an outdoorsman's view from the vantage point of canoe and kayak.

In *The Widening Circle: A Lyme Disease Pioneer Tells Her Story* (New York: St. Martin's Press, 1996), Polly Murray quietly recounts her dramatic story. The life and times of the Smith sisters of Glastonbury, as well as their parents, are thoroughly described by Kathleen L. Housley in *The Letter Kills But the Spirit Gives Life* (Glastonbury, Connecticut: Historical Society of Glastonbury, 1993). I found the story of the illicit romance between Emily Dickinson's brother and another woman recounted in *Austin and Mabel* by Polly Loomis Longsworth (New York: Farrar, Straus & Giroux, 1984) to be a historical page-turner. Martha Ackmann has written a useful review of Emily Dickinson's life and biographers in *The Emily Dickinson Handbook,* ed. Gudrun Grabher et al. (Amherst: University of Massachusetts Press, 1998).

Two other fascinating histories, both authoritative and thoroughly readable, were written by John Demos. *Entertaining Satan: Witchcraft and the Culture of Early New England* (New York: Oxford University Press, 1983) helps us understand the madness, while *The Unredeemed Captive: A Family Story from Early America* (New York: Vintage Books, 1995) is the gripping story of Eunice Williams's capture and then adoption by the Indians.

The life of Peter Rabbit's American creator is described in *My Grandfather, Thornton Burgess* by Frances B. Meigs (Boston: Commonwealth Editions, 1998).

In the North Country, favorites include *Hands on the Land: A History of the Vermont Landscape* by Jan Albers (Cambridge: The MIT Press, 2000), *Uncommon Clay,* Burke Wilkinson's life of Augustus Saint-Gaudens (New York: Harcourt Brace Jovanovich, 1985), *Tall Trees, Tough Men*, Robert E. Pike's lively account of loggers' life and work (New York: W.W. Norton, 1984), and every mystery ever written by Archer Mayor.

INDEX

ABOUT THE AUTHOR

Jim Bissland was born in the Connecticut River Valley and raised in New England. His ancestral roots reach back to Gerard Spencer, who came to Massachusetts Bay in the 1630s and later helped settle Haddam, Connecticut. His wife's go back further: she is descended from John ("Speak for yourself, John") Alden of Plymouth Plantation, and has no trouble speaking for herself. The author studied history, then worked as a newspaperman and in public relations in New England. Later, he moved to the Midwest, earned a Ph.D in mass communication, and became a professor of journalism. On some misty mornings he looks across the achingly flat Midwestern fields of corn and soybeans and thinks he can almost see the hills of home.